Bob Church's
Guide to the Champions'
Fly Patterns

FISHERMAN'S PRAYER:

GOD THAT I MAY CATCH A FISH

SO BIG THAT EVEN I

WHEN SPEAKING OK IT TO MY

MAY NEVER NEED TO LIE FRIENDS

ANON

Happy 60TH BIRTHDAY

SYLVIA & RONNIE

@ EMBSAY RESERVOIR

The Crowood Press

First published in 1998 by
The Crowood Press Ltd
Ramsbury, Marlborough
Wiltshire SN8 2HR

www.crowood.com

Paperback edition 2003

British Library Cataloguing-in-Publication Data
A catalogue record for this book is available from the British Library.

ISBN 1 86126 635 9

Acknowledgements
Thanks go to all my expert contributors for giving away their secret fly
patterns. To John Holden for his excellent photography of the flies.
Finally to my daughter Nicola for all her hard work in typing up the
manuscript.

Typeset by Phoenix Typesetting, Burley-in-Wharfedale

Printed and bound in China

Contents

Introduction

There is no doubt that books featuring trout flies and how to fish with them are of great interest to the serious fly fisherman. Back in 1987 I wrote for The Crowood Press *Bob Church's Guide to Trout Flies* and in doing so created a winning formula of presentation for such a book. This reference work sells well to this day and is a best seller.

Some years later in 1993 I produced another fly book with a similar easy-to-follow format called *Bob Church's Guide to New Fly Patterns* and had another best seller running. No fly pattern was repeated in either book as there are many thousands of named creations to choose from.

With some time now passed by, a third fly book was planned. I have kept to the same winning formula but this time involved my expert fly fishing friends and acquaintances – fly fishers and fly tyers who were known by reputation as some of the best around.

Many of the flies featured are new patterns, but others are variations that have improved on older existing designs. I am sure there is much to be learnt from this book, even for those of great experience. What better than to know the secret favourite patterns of all the experts? All you have to do then is select the right one for the day's fishing.

This book couldn't have happened without the cooperation of the many contributors. I thank them all for making this such an educational volume which all fly fishers and fly tyers will want to keep for reference.

Fishing's Love

Silver streams and bubbling brooks,
Delicate casts and well dressed hooks.
Cast out your hopes; and your dreams can come true,
The love of the sport is beckoning you.

From silver 'bows to each lady of the stream,
The tightly bent rod; and the reel's scream.
Gather the catch deep into your net,
And the love of your sport you will never forget.

The vast loughs of Eire with their picturesque views,
Stillwaters in England; which love will you choose?
All of them special with a style of their own
When you're in love with this sport you're never alone.

This love will last your whole life through,
It embeds in your heart; it will always be true.
Go to it often and cast away care,
The love of our sport will always be there.

Julie Emerson
December 1997.

Nymph Fishing

Nymph Fishing

Of the four styles of flies and fly fishing methods described in this book nymph fishing is currently the most popular on all UK stillwaters and, for that matter, many of the rivers too.

Nymphs is the name we use for all aquatic insects, this includes those that hatch like chironomids, olives, mayflies, and so on, and those that do not hatch such as snails, shrimps, etc. The latter are sometimes called 'bugs' as well.

Take any competent stillwater trout bank fisher and note how he fishes once the mad early season easy fishing has passed – as likely as not he will be a nymph fisher. Of course when nymph fishing, you are deceiving the fish to take your artificial rather than attracting them as you would perhaps with a lure. Becoming a good nymph fisher means you need to study the facts about underwater life. This you can do naturally by observation, and checking trouts' stomach contents. But there are many excellent books on the subject, so study these and take a short cut as to what is happening down under.

The general tyings of nymphs by the experts show some dramatic changes over the last few years. A far more experimental approach has crept in with hot spots in fluorescent materials quite common. Pearl lurex ribbing is now at least as popular as the normal silver or gold. Flashback thorax covers in coloured pearl spectraflash are very common and very effective at catching trout. It's an exciting time indeed for the nymph tyer/fisher.

After fishing against the Czechs in several World Fly Fishing Championships it soon became apparent to me that their team was made up of quite ordinary performers on stillwater lakes and reservoirs, but when it came to rivers, in particular grayling fishing, they were brilliant anglers.

Their method of fishing the rolled nymph was so simple yet so effective and all the other teams learnt a lot from watching them. Grayling fishing from October to December has become very much the sport to follow. The stillwater trout fisher has rediscovered this branch of our sport for suddenly he has realized how nice it is to fish a river. As for the grayling they are excellent fish to catch and these days you do not have to cull them as was the case on many rivers up until the mid-eighties. 'Czech nymphing' tactics mean you need to wade usually with chest waders. You can use one, two or even three weighted nymphs on the cast; this is judged to get your flies deep down according to the pace and depth of the river. Wade carefully and slowly, make a short cast upstream and then hold the rod high as the nymphs sink quickly and trundle back towards you. All the time you watch the bow of the line for a take. Strike indicators can be used where allowed, to give a more definite take indication. With practice you can get very good at this method.

During the 1996 season the team from Bewl Reservoir really did the business in the team events winning most of the major trout competitions. They became known as nymph experts, using the 'in' nymph pattern for reservoirs – the skinny superglue buzzer or epoxy heavily varnished buzzer. With a simple tying style using ordinary tying silk as the body and thorax, just add a pair of wing-cases and a rib, then cover all over with one of the above-mentioned substances – the result, a perfect hatching chironomid. Because these nymphs have no buoyant hairy bits in their construction they sink very quickly – almost as fast as a weighted nymph – but the latter would be outlawed under international competition rules. The method of fishing is to use a floating line and as long a leader as you can sensibly handle. A sight bob of fluorescent wool is ginked up to float high and give a good indication when a take comes. A sacrificial big dry fly or even a buoyant lure of deer hair or ethafoam can also be used as an alternative bite indicator. This method, though, does have its limitations if you need to use a very long leader as the fly stops at the tip ring and makes it difficult or impossible to land the trout properly. With the ginked fluorescent wool method you can attach this so it will slide back and forth through the rings while playing a lively fish.

The secret of success when fishing this method is to have great patience after casting out, allowing the nymphs to sink correctly, then doing very little in the way of retrieval. These buzzers look so realistic lots of takes come in clear water when the nymphs are completely static – although little slow twitches often induce a trout to take as the artificial rises.

Where the small clearwater fisheries are concerned some kind of leaded nymph is by far the most popular approach. Because bigger stock rainbows are often the target fish, usually a size 10 or 8 strong quality hook is used to tie the artificial on. On the gin-clear waters of the south of England like Chalk Springs, Avington and Dever, the stalking approach is used. In other words, select your fish by observation with polarized glasses then carefully present your weighted nymph to the trout and watch the reaction carefully. A newly stocked fish usually takes first time, but some fish get hooked and lost

and then they become difficult to tempt again.

It is when faced with this situation that the imaginative fly tyer/fisher scores. A particular fish lives in my mind – an 8lb 6oz golden rainbow trout from Chalk Springs. Being a highly visible 'goldie' it had been fished for by other anglers for about an hour before they gave up and I took over. I had tried for this particular fish for as long as half an hour, continually bombarding it with different nymphs until after the sixth fly change the trout suddenly took as though it was my first offering. The complete ignoring of the first five patterns to taking the sixth without hesitation was fascinating fishing giving me, the fly tyer, a great deal of satisfaction.

The later Oliver Kite was a great character and excellent nymph fisherman. Oliver was a great believer in the induced take which, he explained often, succeeds when the expected voluntary take has failed to materialize. One example is to cast a nymph upstream of the trout's lie and allow it to sink to the fish's level and then trundle back with the current. To induce the trout to take, lift the rod tip sufficiently to make the artificial rise just before the nymph reaches the fish. If the timing is right, the trout cannot resist the action and will take without hesitation. Oliver believed in using very simple nymphs for his river fishing. I am sure we have better imitative patterns these days, but even so when you are river fishing for a difficult trout remember the induced take technique.

John White

John is a security manager for American Express, a high-powered occupation. Luckily he lives just ten minutes drive from Bewl Water where he is a season ticket holder. John has been trout fly fishing for 38 years so he is very experienced. He is a member of the successful Weald of Kent Team.

He started competition trout fishing in 1987 and since then has qualified to fish for England four times, winning three team golds on the way. Also in the Benson & Hedges he won four medals, one gold, two silver and a bronze. Finally he has won silver in the European Grand Slam. These show his very consistent skills.

John is a regular visitor to Ireland's Western loughs and is also a keen saltwater and pike angler when time allows. His preferred method of fly fishing is with these anorexic nymphs, on a floating fly line and a long 30 feet fluorocarbon leader. Most of the fishing is static or a painfully slow retrieve. Great tips from a master.

1 White's Holographic Oliver (Superglue Buzzer)

COMMENT

John designed this life-like looking buzzer nymph for bright days and in clearwater conditions. This slim-line style of nymph has been popularized by a group of top-class fly fishing friends who fish Bewl regularly. To say they are just good would be an understatement – results have been nothing short of outstanding, as evidenced by the Bewl club in 1996. Fish on a long leader, fine fluorocarbon, fish near static or static and concentrate on watching your line sail away.

DRESSING

Hook: Heavy grub size 8–14.
Tying silk: Olive.
Butt: Orange fluorescent silk.
Body: Olive silk.
Thorax: Build-up of olive silk.
Wing buds: Gold or silver holographic tinsel.
Whole fly: Covered in one even coat of superglue.

2 White's Holographic Claret (Superglue Buzzer)

COMMENT

A tip from John, obviously take great care when applying the superglue. If it goes milky just after the glue dries, apply a coat of clear cellire varnish. This buzzer was also designed for deep fishing on bright days and in clear water. Some fly fishers use sight indicators to detect sensitive takes; these take the form of fluorescent tow wool ginked up. The beauty of this set-up is that they can be designed to go through the rings when playing a trout.

DRESSING

Hook: Heavy grub size 8–14.
Tying silk: Claret.
Butt: Fluorescent red silk.
Body: Claret silk.
Thorax: Build-up of claret silk.
Wing buds: Gold holographic tinsel tied under shank and brought up over the build-up.
Whole fly: Covered in one even coat of superglue.

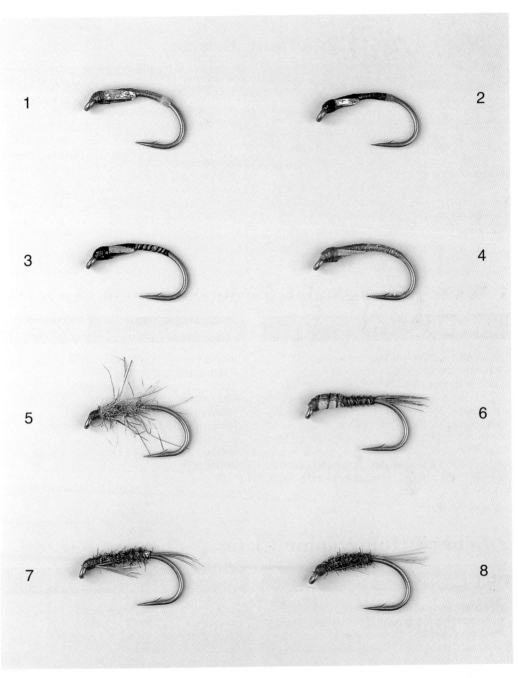

1 White's Holographic Oliver (Superglue Buzzer)   2 White's Holographic Claret (Superglue Buzzer)   3 White's Pearl (Superglue Buzzer)   4 White's Olive (Superglue Buzzer)
5 Barden's Hare's Ear   6 Orange Pheasant Tail   7 White's Diawl Bach
8 Anorexic Diawl Bach

3 White's Pearl (Superglue Buzzer)

COMMENT

Again, this nymph looks really life-like. If you are not convinced, try spooning out the stomach contents of any reservoir trout. Put the contents in a white plastic bowl so as to study them closely. As likely as not there will be several of these artificial 'look alikes' there. This is why so many trout are fooled by this realistic pattern. Remember, in such clear water the fish have plenty of time to inspect and reject patterns that don't look quite right.

DRESSING

Hook: Heavy or light grub size 8–16.
Tying silk: Black.
Body: Pearl flashabou strand.
Rib: Black tying silk.
Thorax: Black silk built up.
Wing buds: Four strands of luminous orange flashabou tied under shank and spread out and tied on top of thorax.
Whole fly: Evenly coated in superglue.

4 White's Olive (Superglue Buzzer)

COMMENT

Just editing John's eight nymphs has impressed me very much and I cannot wait to give them a try myself. It occurred to me that if I can get carried away like this, the book is undoubtedly doing the job I hoped it would. As John mentioned about this pattern, the permutations are endless because it looks so good. Fish as with the other superglue buzzer patterns – you can use them three at a time if you like.

DRESSING

Hook: Heavy or light grub size 8–16.
Tying silk: Olive.
Body: Pearl lurex over olive silk.
Rib: Olive silk.
Thorax: Olive silk built up.
Wing buds: Orange luminous flashabou, four strands for large hooks, two for small hooks.
Whole fly: Evenly coated in superglue.

5 Barden's Hare's Ear

COMMENT

Rob Barden is John's regular boat partner at Bewl and he is the other half of the think tank. Rob was responsible for the original anorexic sparse nymphs which were making an impact prior to the superglue designs. John rates Rob as one of the best, certainly some of his designs of nymph have been revolutionary. Fish this one static or do a slow figure-of-eight retrieve on the same leader set-up.

DRESSING

Hook: Drennan B160 size 8 or B175 size 10–14.
Tying silk: Red.
Body: Hare's ear fibres scruffy but sparse.
Rib: Medium pearlabou, i.e. pearl lurex.
Head: Clear varnish.

6 Orange Pheasant Tail

COMMENT

John likes to use this nymph as a favoured middle dropper which as you know is usually the least effective position on the cast. Although John favours a floating line where possible, this pattern also performs well on intermediates, Wet Cel IIs and even fast-sinking fly lines. After casting out when using a sinker, figure-of-eight the slack line and allow the nymphs to drop naturally through the water before slowly retrieving.

DRESSING

Hook: Kamasan B160 size 8–10.
Tying silk: Red.
Tail: Pheasant tail fibres (natural).
Body: Pheasant tail fibres (natural).
Rib: Copper wire.
Thorax: Orange luminous flashabou.
Head: Clear varnish.

7 White's Diawl Bach

COMMENT

This is John's choice of a dropper pattern on bright days when fishing the slow deep method. Diawl Bachs in various guises have been used with great success for many years at Chew Valley Lake near Bristol. They can imitate various aquatic insects but are particularly effective when buzzers or caddis are active. Fish very slowly on floating or slow-sinking fly lines.

DRESSING

Hook: Heavy grub size 8–12.
Tying silk: Red.
Tail: Red game or white cock fibres.
Body: Gold holographic tinsel with open spirals of bronze peacock over.
Beard hackle: Red game or white cock fibres.
Head: Clear varnish.

8 Anorexic Diawl Bach

COMMENT

A very slimmed-down version of the Diawl Bach. This is in keeping with the very sparse dressed anorexic patterns of the mid-1990s. They have been hugely successful and once the fly fisher becomes confident and competent in using them he will never look back. It is true to say that this type of nymph tempts the better residential trout – so if you want to dodge the recent stockies follow this style.

DRESSING

Hook: Heavy grub size 8–14.
Tying silk: Red.
Tail: Red game cock fibres.
Body: One bronze peacock herl clipped short.
Rib: Fine copper wire.
Beard hackle: Red game cock.
Head: Clear varnish.

Russell Owen

I have watched this fine young Welsh fly fisherman come up through the ranks of the International stage. I first came across him at Llandegfedd Reservoir during a Youth International. That day he captained Wales and they won the event. Since then he has appeared in the Senior Welsh Team many times, both in the Home Country Internationals and in the World Championships. It is in the World event that he really came into full recognition by winning the individual title of World Champion in 1994 when it was held at Kamloops in Canada.

Russell is well known on the UK competition fishing scene where his fly-tying skills play a big part in his continued success. He regularly contributes articles to *Stillwater Trout Magazine* where he has built up a good reputation for knowing his stuff.

1 Black CDC Shuttlecock Emerger

COMMENT

I seem to be always telling fellow anglers about the good qualities of CDC patterns and this one has caught hundreds of fish for me. It is particularly effective on my home water Llyn Clywedog in mid-Wales. From midsummer onwards in calm conditions, watch the fish a couple of times to get an idea of their direction, put this pattern in the right spot and I would be very surprised if they ignored it. So I rate this as one of my top fish takers and looking back in my diary it seems to be confirmed every year recently.

DRESSING

Hook: Kamasan B100 size 10–16.
Silk: Black.
Body: Black tying silk.
Rib: Fine silver wire.
Wing: 3–5 Cul de Canard feathers.
Head: Clear varnish.

2 Hot Spot Buzzer

COMMENT

If you have fished in the middle of a heavy buzzer hatch, which you probably have, but had difficulty in catching many fish then take a serious look at this pattern. By incorporating a fluorescent orange butt it makes this pattern stand out from the wave after wave of natural pupae, but not too much as to put the trout off. Having a 'Hot Spot' in a pattern does focus the trout's attention onto the fly. There are many ways of fishing this pattern from a floater and a long leader to an intermediate and a team of flies, ideally suited to clearwater fisheries.

DRESSING

Hook: Kamasan B170 size 10–14.
Silk: Black.
Tag: Globrite floss no. 5.
Body: 2 strands sparse peacock herl.
Rib: Fine silver wire.
Cheeks: Orange goose biots.
Breather: White antron wool.
Head: Clear varnish.

1 Black CDC Shuttlecock Emerger **2** Hot Spot Buzzer **3** Montana Variant Nymph
4 J C Pinfry **5** Russell's Black Hopper **6** Russell Owen's Hare's Ear Emerger
7 Chew Special **8** Pearly Soldier Palmer

3 Montana Variant Nymph

COMMENT

Another pattern that came to me via Rutland. I was sharing a boat with England and Bath Team member Chris Timothy in the Bob Church Classic. We found some fish at Yellowstone but they were a bit shell shocked from other boats by the time we got there and were just plucking at the flies. Chris started to pick up fish regularly. After a bit of hint dropping on my part Chris asked if I would like one of his flies; I gratefully accepted his kind offer. We went on to catch ten fish each which gave us both a top 10 place.

DRESSING

Hook: Drennan Traditional Wet size 8.
Silk: Black.
Tail: Black cock hackle fibres.
Body: Black seal's fur.
Rib: Copper wire.
Wing-cases: Black floss.
Thorax: Globrite floss no. 10.
Hackle: Black cock.
Head: Clear varnish.

4 J C Pinfry

COMMENT

A fly that has proven very successful for me at Llandegfedd during early summer when there are literally millions of 'jelly fry' all over the lake. Normally when pin fry are around it tells anglers to use something totally different, such as an orange lure, as using imitations is like a needle in a haystack affair, but there are times when you do need to use such things and this one certainly works. Looking at the fly in detail it has all the characteristics of a pin fry, the Lite Brite head giving it a scaly look and the jungle cock its natural fluorescent little flash.

DRESSING

Hook: Kamasan B175 10–12.
Tail: Pinch of white marabou.
Body: Hare's ear.
Rib: Fine silver wire.
Cheeks: 2 jungle cock feathers.
Thorax: Pearl Lite Brite.
Head: Clear varnish.

5 Russell's Black Hopper

COMMENT

I just had to include this pattern in my selection of eight. Again like a lot of my patterns I've tried to improve on a standard pattern, in this case a black hopper – I think it's an improvement! I've incorporated a red butt and pearly rib; I've tried to think of a reason why I've done this but I can't apart from the fact that it looks the business. I've had most success with this pattern on Llyn Brenig in north Wales, one of the best dry fly waters from June onwards. It can be fished dry or wet.

DRESSING

Hook: Kamasan B400 size 10–14.
Silk: Black.
Tag: Globrite floss no. 5.
Body: Black seal's fur.
Rib: Medium pearl tinsel.
Legs: 6 black pheasant tail fibres (knotted).
Hackles: Black cock.
Head: Clear varnish.

6 Russell Owen's Hare's Ear Emerger

COMMENT

I first set upon this pattern during a practice session for a match on Rutland. There was a lot of fish moving in the centre of the South Arm off Yellowstone and having tried all the standard flies such as dries, shipmans, nymphs, etc., all without any real success, I struck upon this and I boated the next four fish that I covered. The fish were taking small buzzers from just under the surface; this pattern represents the buzzer just leaving its shuck, with the pearl flashabou representing the shuck. Needless to say I have caught an awful lot of fish on this.

DRESSING

Hook: Kamasan B160 size 12–14.
Silk: Black or brown.
Tail: 6–7 fibres of pearl flashabou.
Body: Hare's ear mix (brushed).
Rib: Fine silver tinsel.
Head: Clear varnish.

7 Chew Special

COMMENT

I won a Benson's sweater at Chew Valley Lake in 1996 with this little pattern. I'm sure anyone who fished the reservoir that year will remember it as the year of the nymph. A little nymph that does really well in clear water is this pattern. I know you might say that Chew is a water that is affected by algae. However, in early May it was extremely clear with about 8–10ft visibility. The pattern's little hot head attracts quite a bit of attention amongst the early season stock fish. It is best fished in conjunction with a clear intermediate line.

DRESSING

Hook: Kamasan B175 size 12.
Silk: Brown.
Tail: Pinch of white hare's ear fibres.
Body: Hare's ear mix.
Rib: Fine silver wire.
Wing case: Pearl tinsel.
Thorax: Hare's ear mix.
Head: Globrite floss no. 5 then apply clear varnish.

8 Pearly Soldier Palmer

COMMENT

Definitely an end of summer pattern when fish are up in the water. This usually occurs on windy overcast days when fish are more inclined to rise to the surface to enjoy the oxygen-rich water. This pattern is a cross between a pearly wickham's and a soldier palmer. Use on either a floater or intermediate on the top dropper with a retrieve of a steady strip (about 2 feet) or 'roly poly' (hand over hand). A little tip is: half way through the retrieve, stop and change to a figure-of-eight retrieve; this will often induce the take.

DRESSING

Hook: Kamasan B175 size 10–12.
Silk: Brown.
Tail: Globrite floss no. 7.
Body: Medium pearl tinsel.
Rib: Fine silver wire.
Hackle: Brown cock tied palmered.
Head: Globrite floss no. 7 then apply clear varnish.

Paul Miller

Paul is one of the most consistent fly fishermen I know. It all began for Paul when Rutland opened in the mid-1970s. Each year he would leave his local reservoir for a week's fishing on the River Deveron in Scotland. He still holds the record for the largest sea trout caught off that beat, a 14½-pounder which took a Black Pennell fly.

He started competition boat fishing in earnest in 1988, when he fished for the Peterborough Cormorants who won the team event of the Benson & Hedges that year. In the following ten years he qualified for England on six occasions being made Captain in 1994 on the Lake of Mentieth.

In 1993 he fished in England's World Team at Kamloops in Canada and won team gold. There have been many other competition successes in the last decade that include the Wychwood, Bob Church Classic and the Benson & Hedges.

All this success means keeping abreast of all the fashions in flies that come and go. In this selection Paul has included some of his old stalwart favourite patterns.

1 Bill's Damsel

COMMENT

This is a fly that I use as an anchor fly teamed up with two buzzers on a floating line. I fish it mainly with a figure-of-eight retrieve. It can also be very effective on a single hook fished on various sinking lines. It is a fly that will catch right through the season, but the best time of year to use it is when the damsels are just starting to hatch in late June. This fly was first given to me by Bill McHarg of Leicester when practising at Rutland Water for a Benson & Hedges heat a few years ago.

DRESSING

Hook: Kamasan B270 size 10 Double.
Tying silk: Green.
Tail: Olive marabou topped with a few strands of pearl crystal.
Body: Olive seal's fur or substitute.
Rib: Medium gold oval.
Hackle: Olive cock.
Head: Clear varnish.

2 Hot Spot Pheasant Tail

COMMENT

This fly can be used all year round. I fish it mainly on a Hi-Di line early season. The dressing can be varied by using dyed pheasant tail fibres and changing the colour of the thorax. Main variants are black and claret pheasant tail, and orange and silver thorax. The silver thorax version works well when the pin fry have just hatched. The retrieve can be varied as sometimes the trout like it pulled fast and other times very slow.

DRESSING

Hook: Kamasan B170 size 10–16.
Tying silk: Black.
Tail: Natural pheasant tail.
Body: Natural pheasant tail.
Rib: Copper wire.
Thorax: Globrite no. 12.
Shell back: Natural pheasant tail fibres.
Head: Clear varnish.

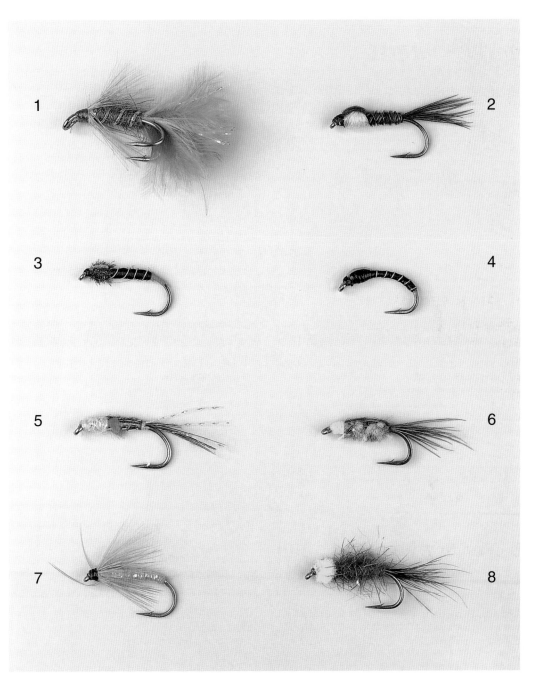

1 Bill's Damsel 2 Hot Spot Pheasant Tail 3 Phil's Buzzer 4 Superglue Buzzer
5 Pin Fry Nymph 6 Green & Orange Pheasant Tail 7 Orange Pearly 8 Minky Nymph

3 Phil's Buzzer

COMMENT

This buzzer was first introduced to me at Rutland Water in an Anglian Water match by Phil Thomas, an RAF team member, on a day when the trout were feeding heavily on buzzers and most of Phil's double limit were caught on this fly. It is best fished on a floating line as the point fly; the weight of hook can be varied depending on the depth you require the fly to fish. With the advent of fluorocarbon lines they can be fished at great depths when there is little or no wind.

DRESSING

Hook: B405 size 10–14.
Tying silk: Black.
Tag: Globrite no. 5.
Body: Black tying silk with a pearl flash back.
Rib: Silver wire.
Thorax: Peacock herl.
Wing case: Globrite floss no. 7.
Head: Clear varnish.

4 Superglue Buzzer

COMMENT

This very simple buzzer is one of my favourites because it is so simple to tie and the colour combinations are never ending. I fish it in two different ways, on a floater with a very long leader from the boat and bank, and on various density sinking lines from just the boat. It is good fished as the middle fly of a team of three when fishing the 'hang' method, watching the top dropper as the fish take the buzzer beneath. When tying this fly the final operation is to coat the whole fly with superglue, hence its name.

DRESSING

Hook: B110 size 10–16 or B100 10–16.
Tying silk: Black.
Body: Black tying silk.
Rib: Silver fine wire.
Thorax: Black tying silk.
Wing-case: Globrite floss no 12.
Head: Clear varnish.

5 Pin Fry Nymph

COMMENT

This fly, as its name implies, is best used when the pin fry are about flin to 1in in size. I use it mainly on a floating line or occasionally on an intermediate. The retrieve needs to be jerky to represent a darting pin fry. I mainly fish it as a point fly with a couple of palmers on the droppers, something like a Pearly Wickham's or a Silver Invicta which can also be taken as a pin fry. The best places to fish these flies are around the margins and near weed beds and other places that hold a lot of fry.

DRESSING

Hook: B175 size 10.
Tying silk: White.
Tail: Natural pheasant tail topped with pearl crystal.
Body: Silver tinsel.
Rib: Red wire.
Cheeks: Fluorescent red wool.
Head: Pearl tinsel and clear varnish.

6 Green & Orange Pheasant Tail

COMMENT

A lot of my flies have a touch of fluorescence in them; this nymph is no exception as the head is tied of no. 11 Globrite floss. The body is a variegated fine chenille that I purchased many years ago. The idea of the fly was based on an Iven's Green & Brown Nymph body. I find it fishes best early season from the bank on a floating line with a long leader and as the point fly. It is fished in a similar way to a long shank Pheasant Tail Nymph.

DRESSING

Hook: Kamasan B175 size 10–14.
Tying silk: Green.
Tail: Natural pheasant tail.
Body: Fine green and orange chenille (variegated).
Shell back: Pheasant tail.
Head: Globrite floss no. 11 and clear varnish.

7 Orange Pearly

COMMENT

This simple fly was devised for using on a Hi-Di line early season when the weather was very bright. I fish it on the middle dropper in a team of three flies. The top dropper is usually a lure of some description. When the retrieve is nearly finished and the top dropper is in the surface film, the retrieve is stopped and 'hung' for a few seconds. Most of the takes on the Orange Pearly come to the 'hang'. The colour of the fly can be changed to any variant; the two colours I use are orange or lime green, sometimes one of each colour behind a lure on the top bob.

DRESSING

Hook: Kamasan B400 size 10–14.
Tying silk: Black.
Body: Orange floss covered with stretched pearly tinsel.
Hackle: Soft orange cock.
Head: Clear varnish.

8 Minky Nymph

COMMENT

This nymph, as its name suggests, is made from mainly natural brown mink. The fur I use was obtained one evening in winter while out wildfowling on our local wash. I fish the Minky Nymph in two ways: on a floating line as a point fly from the bank with an underbody of lead for extra weight to get it round with the wind, using a figure-of-eight retrieve; or when fishing from a boat as a middle dropper or a point fly, the retrieve can be a figure-of-eight or a slow strip.

DRESSING

Hook: Kamasan B170 size 10–12.
Tying silk: Black.
Tail: Mink guard hairs.
Body: Dubbed mink fur.
Rib: Fine gold wire.
Thorax: Globrite fine chenille no. 11.
Head: Clear varnish.

Clive Collier

Clive is known as 'GB' by the match regulars at Bewl Water. I'm sure the enlightened can figure out what it means – it has something to do with a 6lb 15oz rainbow in a very difficult England qualifier event. He has been fishing since he was three years old and has fished all over the world catching from bleak to marlin. Clive started fly fishing and tying in 1989 and then entered the competition scene in 1991. The reason for the competitions was purely to learn how to loch style from people such as Ray Burt, Chris Howitt, John White, Bob Barden, and so on. However,

competitions have become a passion for him.

His first major success came when he qualified to fish for England at the English National at Kielder Reservoir finishing ninth out of 100 anglers. He fished at Lough Owel in the Spring International in Ireland, keeping his place to fish for the following international in the autumn by finishing fifth overall and second in the English team. Again he finished second in the team and fifth overall in the Autumn International in Wales on Traws' – a very consistent angler.

1 McKay

COMMENT

I firmly believe that there is nothing new in fly designs, therefore it goes without saying that someone somewhere has already designed the flies I use. Some of these patterns are my creations and some are modifications. So I would like to credit Bill Goodale for the McKay. Bill ties his version on long shank hooks and with a long tail, more like a lure. I have instead reduced the fly down to International competition size or smaller. This fly is a brilliant point fly, especially when the fish are hard on buzzers.

DRESSING

Tying silk: Drennan Traditional Wet size 8–14.
Thread: Dark brown.
Tail: Black marabou plus orange twinkle or crystal hair.
Body: Hare's ear.
Rib: Flat gold medium tinsel plus gold wire.
Thorax: Hare's ear.
Thorax cover: Canada goose or other grey feather fibre.
Rear cheeks: Orange Globrite floss.
Front cheeks: White Globrite floss or similar.

2 Hairy Montana

COMMENT

The Hairy Montana is an American lure/nymph publicized by Taff Price. Again I've reduced its size. To emphasize my first point, Jeremy Herrmann has a fly called a Monty which is similar, but where or how he came to the pattern I do not know. This is a classic green and black fly. When fish get turned off by lures or when takes dry up on the old Viva, use this fly. Basically it is a point fly, however in the smaller sizes it works well on the middle dropper. Like a lot of anglers, I like to fish with floating lines with flies on or in the water.

DRESSING

Hook: Drennan Traditional Wet size 8–14.
Thread: Black.
Tail: Black marabou.
Body: Black seal's fur spun in a dubbing loop, touching turns for body and open turns on thorax. Trim to nymph shape.
Thorax: Fluorescent lime-green wool or floss.

1 McKay **2** Hairy Montana **3** Half Bach **4** Yet Another Damsel
5 American Hare's Ear **6** Grey Boy Buzzer Nymph **7** Claret Pulling Buzzer
8 Light Hare's Ear

3 Half Bach

COMMENT

The Half Bach is a creation based on the Diawl Bach. It is tied on a heavy short shank hook and does not have the usual long beard hackle, hence the name. This fly was designed to be fished on the point and to be fished static or slowly pulled. Why this fly works I really do not know, however fish take it with confidence and like all the flies in this section has passed the Richard Walker test (over 60 trout on the fly). The Diawl Bach was extremely successful on the match circuit last year, but this little fly outfished the normal dressing many times.

DRESSING

Hook: Drennan Traditional Wet size 12–14.
Thread: Brown.
Tail: Ginger cock feather fibres.
Body: Bronze peacock herl.
Beard: Globrite scarlet floss.

4 Yet Another Damsel

COMMENT

It is well known by my colleagues that I have a surprising number of Damsel patterns, the reason for this is the huge variations in colour and size of the natural nymph. I have colours ranging from light olive to purple and brown and in different sizes and styles. So when I created this pattern, the comment was 'Yet another Damsel?' – hence the name. This pattern is a general representation that works well on any water. If I had to pick just one pattern this would be the one; again this is a point fly. If the day is bright, it works well.

DRESSING

Hook: Drennan Traditional Wet size 8–10.
Thread: Dark green.
Tail: Medium olive marabou (small pinch – i.e., 15 fibres).
Body: Medium olive seal's fur.
Rib: Medium gold wire.
Thorax: Dark olive seal's fur.
Back: Wide pearl tinsel on body and thorax.
Hackle: Dark olive cock (one turn basal fibres and one turn normal fibres).

5 American Hare's Ear

COMMENT

The American Hare's Ear is a standard pattern from the US. However, I use pearl lurex rather than gold tinsel for the rib. I would never want to be without this fly when the trout are on black buzzers or olive nymphs. This can be fished in any position on the leader. In calm conditions, I will throw a long line allowing the flies to sink to my desired depth and then start a slow retrieve (figure of eight). On my sinkers I have markers at 10ft and 20ft from the end of the fly line; on reaching the 20ft marker I will pause and hang the flies for as long as I can.

DRESSING

Hook: Drennan Wet Fly Supreme size 12–16.
Thread: Black.
Tail: Hare's body fibres.
Body: Hare's ear fur (dark brown).
Rib: Stretched pearl lurex tinsel.
Thorax: Hare's ear fur (dark brown).
Thorax cover: Black pheasant tail or any black feather fibres.

6 Grey Boy Buzzer Nymph

COMMENT

The Grey Boy Buzzer was inspired by a slide show showing natural nymphs at a Fly Dressers' Guild meeting. This buzzer is distinctive because of the wide silvery bands on its abdomen. Somewhere I had heard that very old dressings used an orange body, however on tying a pattern it did not look right, so I decided to dress the pattern with such a light dubbing that the black thread contrasted with the seal's fur. In the water this combination looks very much like the original. On a trip to Farmoor I caught a lot with this on a difficult day.

DRESSING

Hook: Drennan Wet Fly Supreme size 14.
Thread: Black.
Body: Light orange seal's fur very lightly dubbed.
Rib: Flat silver tinsel medium/fine.
Thorax: Natural mole fur.
Breathers: White baby wool.
Head: Clear varnish.

7 Claret Pulling Buzzer

COMMENT

The Claret Pulling Buzzer is for those occasions when due to weather conditions you need to pull the flies hard. Most buzzer patterns do not seem to work well in these conditions, so I designed this fly to have the buzzer trigger points: white tail, bright collar and orange cheeks. The fly is not tied round the bend but more as a classic nymph shape and is bigger than the actual nymph. This is taken by trout not just as a buzzer but as various nymphs. This can be tied in various colours, green and black being the best alternative versions.

DRESSING

Hook: Kamasan B175 size 10–12.
Thread: Black.
Tail: White cock feather fibres.
Body: Light claret seal's fur.
Rib: Stretched pearl lurex tinsel.
Thorax: Dark claret seal's fur.
Collar: Scarlet/red floss or wool.
Cheeks: Jungle cock.
Head: Clear varnish.

8 Light Hare's Ear

COMMENT

The Light Hare's Ear is designed to imitate a nymph that is about to hatch or is hatching. During the summer there are many light-coloured flies on the water, hence the colour. This does not represent a specific nymph but is just a general representation. It does however catch a lot of trout and if fished on a Hi-Di line it also catches large numbers of coarse fish. Once at Grafham my boat partner and I caught bream after bream up to 7lb on this fly. This is usually fished on the top or middle dropper. Try fishing the hang method.

DRESSING

Hook: Drennan Wet Fly Supreme size 12–16.
Thread: Orangy brown.
Tail: Pheasant tippets.
Body: Hare's ear fur (very light brown).
Rib: Fine oval gold tinsel.
Thorax: Hare's ear fur (medium brown).
Hackle: Ginger cock.

Iain Barr

Iain is aged 24 years and works as a computer systems engineer. He lives at Market Deeping. His ambition is to fish in the World Cup for the England team. Iain says 'I was introduced to fly fishing by my Dad when I was 6 years old. I used to roam the banks of Rutland and Grafham whilst my Dad used to fish. Occasionally I played a fish which my Dad had hooked, and at this point I was also hooked!'

Iain uses a Bob Church 10½ft Alaskan IM8 rod for all sunk line fishing and a Wychwood Lightline rod for floating and intermediate lines. His favourite fly lines are Airflo Di6 and 7, Wet Cel II, Air Cel intermediates and various others.

Some of his favourite flies are Viva, Cat's Whisker and Orange Lures, Hare's Ear type nymphs and Suspender type dries. Iain has come a long way quite quickly and I feel his ambition will soon be realized; all he has to do is keep up the competition form. His achievements already include fishing for the England Youth team and fishing for the England Rivers team in 1997, and he has qualified to fish for the England Senior Loch Style team for 1998.

1 Beavus

COMMENT

This is probably the most successful of my Hare's Ear patterns. I first used this fly at Chew Reservoir after seeing the large red and orange buzzers hatching off. Nine fish surrendered to it weighing over 20lb. It can be used on all fly lines but I have had more success on floaters and slow sinkers. This is also a fly that I find works on lure-bashed fish, as the orange is a good attractor. A slow figure of eight seems to be most successful, but be careful of the hard aggressive takes.

DRESSING

Hook: Heavy weight nymph size 10–12.
Tying silk: Red or orange.
Butt: Red or orange tying silk.
Body: Natural rabbit.
Rib: Gold wire.
Head: Red or orange thread and clear varnish.

2 Sussie Lug

COMMENT

Another favourite of mine when the fish are up and moving well. We all know of the microscopic green midges that cover our waters in the summer; this pattern for me does as well as any other. I fish this fly on its own on a floating line on a 10ft leader. This is for accurate casting, vital when the fish are moving in the surface film. I aim the fly about 2yd in front of the fish and pull it sharply to attract attention, then leave it static, just waiting for the fish to take it.

DRESSING

Hook: Kamasan B100 size 14.
Tying silk: Brown.
Tag: Green floss.
Body: Natural rabbit.
Rib: Pearl lurex.
Head: Black plastazote or white ethafoam.

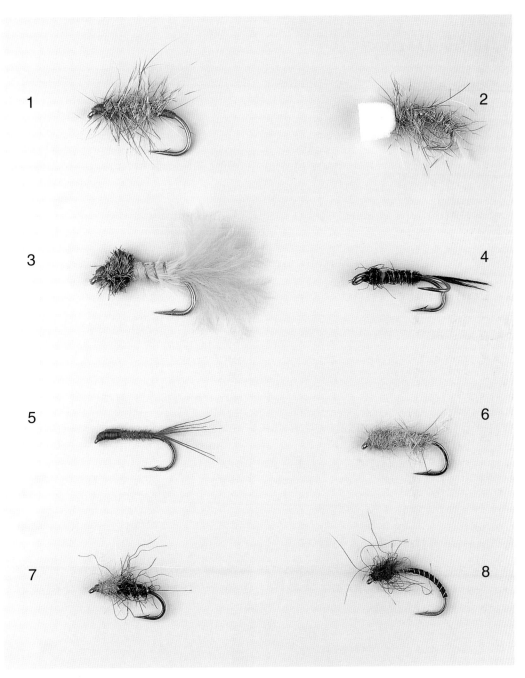

1 Beavus   2 Sussie Lug   3 Iain's Damsel   4 Foolish Nymph
5 Iain's Bloodworm Variant   6 Iain's Hare's Ear   7 Grey Head Buzzer
8 Iain's Buzzer Variant

3 Iain's Damsel

COMMENT

Having spooned fish last year on Rutland I discovered these very lime-green damsels so I tied some up. I caught plenty of plump rainbows on this pattern that for me outfished the darker olive patterns. It was very versatile as it caught on all lines at various speeds, the most successful being an intermediate or Wet Cel II with short, jerky, six-inch pulls. My most noticeable bag of fish that, apart from two, came to this fly was on a calm bright day on Rutland using a Wet Cel II – six fish for 21lb. It can also be tied on a double hook.

DRESSING

Hook: Ashima Heavy-weight nymph.
Tying silk: Olive.
Tail: Lime-green marabou.
Body: Lime-green marabou.
Back: Gold lace.
Rib: Copper wire.
Head: Peacock herl.

4 Foolish Nymph

COMMENT

A new pattern for my armoury that I find catches me the hard lure-bashed shy fish. Fish soon become timid towards lures stripped past them at incredible speeds. When this happens I will put this fly on the point, putting another nymph on the middle and keeping an attractor lure on the bob. I use this fly mostly on the sinkers, including the faster sinking lines, and have had some very successful victories in competitions with it. I continue to pull this fly with long steady retrieves not only fooling the trout but also fooling other competitors.

DRESSING

Hook: Double size 12.
Tying silk: Black.
Tail: Dyed black pheasant tail.
Body: Dyed black pheasant tail.
Rib: Fine silver wire.
Thorax: Globrite floss no. 5.
Head: Black seal's fur.

5 Iain's Bloodworm Variant

COMMENT

No surprises what I use this pattern for! It is very simple but deadly when the fish are feeding on the bloodworm early in the season. It can be used on any line but I have most success inching it back in fairly shallow water, 4–8ft, on an intermediate line. Try long steady pulls as I've also caught fish this way. I often fish two of these on my cast, separated by some other nymph, usually a buzzer.

DRESSING

Hook: Ashima Heavy-weight nymph size 12.
Tying silk: Red.
Tail: Dyed pink pheasant tail fibres.
Body: Dyed pink pheasant tail fibres.
Shell back: Dyed pink pheasant tail fibres.
Head: Red tying silk, apply clear varnish.

6 Iain's Hare's Ear

COMMENT

I came up with this pattern a few years ago and it has brought me great success. It is also the reason for my best rainbow at Rutland of 5lb 1oz. I am a great believer that the key to success in most flies is confidence, and I have immense confidence in this fly. Any sign of fish moving or any indications of the fish feeding just sub-surface will have me reaching for this pattern, especially buzzer feeding fish. I always fish this as a point fly on a floating line and will fish it with a slow figure of eight with the occasional slow pull across a fish's path.

DRESSING

Hook: Ashima Heavy-weight nymph size 12.
Tying silk: Red.
Body: Natural rabbit fur.
Rib: Fine pearl.
Thorax: Grey base of natural rabbit.
Head: Clear varnish.

7 Grey Head Buzzer

COMMENT

Another one of many buzzer patterns, similar to one of my hare's ear patterns and just as successful. Tied on a light hook to fish near the surface, this fly is a deadly pattern for me when the fish are feeding high in the water. Fished on a floater with a slow figure of eight proves most productive when the fish are feeding on black buzzers. I took 7 out of 10 fish on this fly when I first fished it on the top dropper (the bob) so this is now where I tend to keep it. These fish helped me to gain second place in a pairs match.

DRESSING

Hook: Kamasan B170 size 12–14.
Tying silk: Red.
Rib: Fine pearl.
Body: Black seal's fur.
Thorax: Grey base of rabbit fur.
Head: Clear varnish.

8 Iain's Buzzer Variant

COMMENT

When the fish are feeding on buzzers sub-surface this fly is extremely successful. There are many existing buzzer variant patterns, but I believe the bright orange wing case attracts more fish to the fly. It is best fished in calmer conditions on a floating line, preferably statically. I normally use this as a dropper fly due to its light weight. I have caught many quality fish on this fly when other patterns have proved fruitless. This is one of my favourite buzzer patterns at Rutland Water.

DRESSING

Hook: Curved emerger size 12–14.
Tying silk: Black.
Body: Black thread.
Rib: Fine silver wire.
Wing-case: Globrite orange floss no. 5.
Thorax: Claret seal's fur.
Head: Clear varnish.

Peter Dobbs

Peter, a life-long friend, is a very experienced fly tyer and fly fisherman. A founder member of the Pioneer Fly Tying Club, he ties some excellent trout catching flies. I know because I have tried plenty out over the years.

Peter and his fishing pal Chad have got together for this selection; their combined effort is quite impressive with some new ideas. Both are also members of the Mid-Northants Fly Fishers where they have come under the tying influence of 'Godfather' Cyril Lineham – Peter says 'I have learnt so much from Cyril'. Both anglers spend most of their time trout fishing at the reservoirs: Pitsford, Draycote, Grafham, Ravensthorpe and Rutland. During the winter months they take advantage of trips to some of the small fisheries that stay open for rainbows all year.

1 Damerham Damsel

COMMENT

When our group of friends fished at Damerham a few times we found it needed a true-to-life damsel pattern to tempt the wary fish of the lake's clear water. It takes a long time to tie this fly compared to more normal patterns, particularly cutting the V-shaped wing cases. Used as a single fly on a 20ft leader, it is retrieved very, very slowly. In other words let the trout have a good look at it, and they will then take it confidently. It has now proved itself on all gin-clear lakes when fishing to particular targeted fish.

DRESSING

Hook: Size 6–8 long shank.
Tying silk: Black.
Tail: Pheasant tail fibres.
Body: Light green scouring pad, varnished; when dry, back marked with dark green Pentel pen.
Thorax: Olive green antron.
Wing-cases: Translucent green plastic.
Legs: Stripped olive hen hackle stalks.
Eyes: Black nylon burnt ends.
Head: Clear varnish.

2 Steeple Langford Damsel

COMMENT

On its very first outing, at Steeple Langford fishery, this fly gave Peter two 4fi-pounders while his companions could do no better than ones and twos. Best fished slowly on a slow-sinking fly line.

DRESSING

Hook: Size 8 long shank.
Tying silk: Black.
Tail: Pheasant tail feather fibres.
Body: Two sections – rear dark olive, front orange antron.
Shell back: Two shell backs over the two bodies, also turn down to form legs at middle and throat.
Head: Clear varnish.

1 Damerham Damsel   2 Steeple Langford Damsel   3 Black Schwartza Nymph
4 Ribbed Olive Nymph   5 Greenwell's Variant   6 Sedge Shuck
7 Brown Shuck Variant   8 Parachute Emerging Buzzer

3 Black Schwartza Nymph

COMMENT

This nymph was devised by Chad. It can be fished with great success in the early season. Use on a floater and a long 15–20ft leader. Keep to a single fly and fish where there is a side wind. After casting allow to drift round with the wind. Even the famed Hector took a pasting on this fly. Now having adopted it for a few seasons he gives it the accolade of appearing in 'his' top ten.

DRESSING

Hook: No. 9143 size 6–8 lead underbody.
Tying silk: Black.
Tail: Three strands black heron.
Body: Black seal's fur.
Rib: Lead wire.
Thorax: Black seal's fur.
Wing-case: Black raffia.
Hackle: Black hen under wing case.
Head: Clear varnish.

4 Ribbed Olive Nymph

COMMENT

This is a superb segmented-body light olive nymph which works very well on all types of waters. Naturally, when the pond olives begin to hatch in May is a good time to try this one; from then to September it can be relied on. Works marvellously on the days when very difficult conditions prevail – flat mirror-calm surface, gin-clear water and bright sunlight. Because this nymph looks so realistic trout take it with confidence. Fish on a floater with a slow figure-of-eight retrieve.

DRESSING

Hook: Size 12 grub hook.
Tying silk: Light olive.
Body: Yellow multi thread.
Thorax: Yellow multi thread.
Shell back: Dark green multi thread.
Rib: Olive tying silk.
Hackle: Dark brown hen.
Head: Lime-green fluorescent silk, apply clear varnish.

5 Greenwell's Variant

COMMENT

Best fished when pond olives are on the water or known to be active. Fish on a light outfit rod and line, enabling you to use a very light leader. At Pitsford, Chad went seven up on Peter. He took pity on him and gave him the same fly. He waited for Peter to catch his eight fish limit before completing his. This is a nymph really for those special occasions when olives abound.

DRESSING

Hook: Size 12 fine wire.
Tying silk: Dark olive.
Body: Light olive antron.
Rib: Dark olive tying silk.
Shell back: Pale grey duck wing feather fibre.
Hackle: One turn of light ginger or olive.
Head: Clear varnish.

6 Sedge Shuck

COMMENT

Fished on a floating fly line it is quite deadly when sedge are on the water, usually during the evenings. It seems to attract the better browns to make a mistake at such times. Can also be very effective when snails begin to migrate. Fish either singly or with a smaller nymph on a dropper. The shuck cases come in several drab colours and are the brainchild of that genius tyer inventor Cyril Lineham – small purchases may be made from Cyril, Tel: 01604 403176.

DRESSING

Hook: Size 10–14.
Tying silk: Black.
Body: Cyril's amber floating shuck body.
Antenna horns: Two brown hackle stalks.
Hackle: Light brown cock, two turns.
Head: Clear varnish.

7 Brown Shuck Variant

COMMENT

These remarkable style flies have not reached their true potential yet. Both Peter and Chad recommend this to be fished in a flat calm evening rise. It can be used as a point fly indicator holding up two, often small, nymphs on droppers. Don't be surprised how many times the indicator will be taken; this pattern looks so much like sedge larvae (that live on the bottom). So a booby style approach can be fished – that is, fast sink line and short 2ft leader. The nymph floats up just off the bottom and takes are confident.

DRESSING

Hook: Size 8–10.
Tying silk: Black.
Body: Cyril's brown shuck case.
Thorax: Grey antron or mole fur.
Shell back: Pheasant tail feather fibre.
Legs: Pheasant tail fibres.
Head: Clear varnish.

8 Parachute Emerging Buzzer

COMMENT

The finished fly gives the perfect silhouette for the trout's view looking up – it imitates the emerging buzzer nymph almost exactly. Best fished in a light breeze or flat calm. If rising trout are moving, so much the better, but this is not essential. This nymph is perfect on all major trout reservoirs and gravel pits, from late April through to September.

DRESSING

Hook: Size 12 grub hook.
Tying silk: Black.
Body: Black tying silk.
Rib: Single strand pearl lurex.
Thorax: Peacock strand.
Parachute hackle: Grizzle cock. Tied on Cyril's idea of burnt end single strand of black 20lb nylon, in a pin vice. Tie in the nylon before the thorax; after both jobs are done, ensure that the right amount of nylon is there to receive the hackle.

Cyril Lineham

Cyril from Northampton is indeed a father figure to all fly tyers who belong to the large club of the Mid-Northants Fly Fishers. He also does much good work teaching younger beginners, improvers and experts alike at the local Fly Dressers Guild. Some of Cyril's techniques and styles of fly are completely revolutionary and, as you will see, his tyings are very neat and delicate. Cyril, a keen fly fisherman, started at Ravensthorpe way back when Tom Ivens was just learning his art. Now well into his seventies he still has so much to offer. In my opinion, Cyril is one of the very top fly dressers I have ever come across.

His recent heart by-pass operation has given him a new lease of life and I am sure that many more new patterns are about to grace the magazine pages.

1 Cyril's Black Buzzer Variant

COMMENT

This fly should be used as a point fly with leaders of about 3lb or 4lb breaking strain. Its weight allows it to sink at a reasonable speed and it should be fished over active midge beds (shallow hatching areas). Retrieves can be varied from a medium figure of eight or short pulls of 6–9in. A floating fly line is recommended and the best depths to fish over are about 8ft upwards. The chironomid insects or, as we commonly know them, the buzzers, are the trout's most common food so it follows that good imitations like this take plenty of trout.

DRESSING

Hook: Gold size 10–12.
Silk: Black floss.
Body: Black floss.
Rib: Fine gold.
Thorax: Salmon-coloured floss.
Wing-case: Fawn syntho (carpet material).
Eyes: White beads black mono pupils.
Apply a coat of clear varnish to the whole fly, let dry and apply a second coat.

2 Cyril's Syntho Nymph

COMMENT

This fly can be used with my Black Buzzer Variant about 4–5ft apart. It is an attractor fly and should be fished sub-surface in the same manner as the Black Buzzer Variant. If it is used while boat fishing the distance between the flies may be increased. It is sometimes worth trying two or three of the Syntho nymphs on the same leader. If you do this, cast further and try retrieving much faster – this method attracts rainbows' aggressive instincts.

DRESSING

Hook: Size 10–14.
Silk: Fawn tying thread.
Tail: Syntho fibres.
Body: Black floss.
Rib: Fine gold.
Thorax: Orange syntho dub.
Hackle/wing-case: Fawn syntho (carpet material).
Head: Clear varnish.

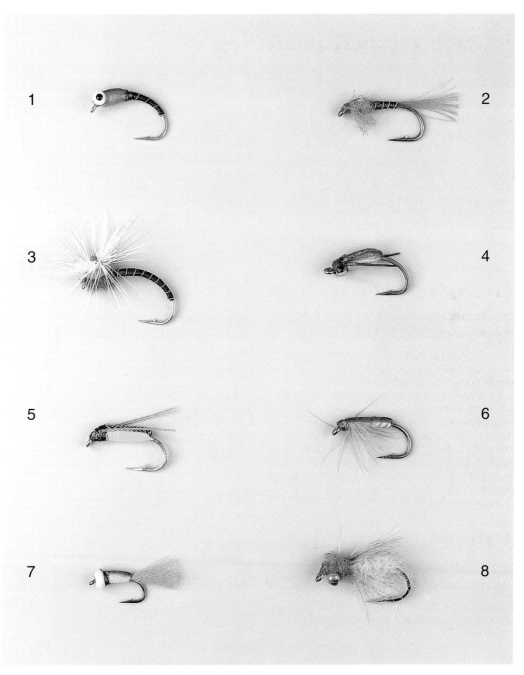

1 Cyril's Black Buzzer Variant   2 Cyril's Syntho Nymph   3 Cyril's Hatching Buzzer
4 Cyril's Eyed Corixa   5 Cyril's Speckled Back Corixa   6 Cyril's Chomper
7 Cyril's White Bead Head   8 Cyril's Updated Limeade Sedge Pupa

3 Cyril's Hatching Buzzer

COMMENT

This fly is for surface fishing and should be used when the hatch is active. It is designed to hang in the surface with the body submerged, the small orange foam ring helping the fly to rise and fall with the ripple or wave action. It is recommended to fish a single fly or two at most, keeping a distance of about 3ft between flies. Works well at all major reservoirs and gravel pit trout fisheries. The hatching buzzer pupa is the stage of the insect found most in trouts' stomach contents.

DRESSING

Hook: Size 10–12.
Tying silk: Black floss.
Body: Black floss.
Rib: Fine gold.
Thorax: Natural ostrich (or white ostrich).
Hackle: White cock (parachute).
Head: With small orange foam plastic ring between hook and hackle.

4 Cyril's Eyed Corixa

COMMENT

It is important when tying this nymph that the hook has a reasonable gape as the body is rather bulky. The green back material is tied in after the eyes are fixed in. Note that the eyes are set a small way from the eye of the hook – this is to allow the back material to pass between the eyes. Tie down with two firm turns of thread to form a bold head; the surplus is then clipped off. Fish on a floating line in shallow areas where the corixa insect is prolific. This is a very realistic pattern.

DRESSING

Hook: Size 10–12.
Tying silk: Silvery white flat floss.
Body: As tying silk.
Back: Olive Syntho (carpet material).
Head: Pair small silver beads joined with black monofilament.
Paddles: Cock centre tail fibres.

5 Cyril's Speckled Back Corixa

COMMENT

The corixa's natural movement is to dart up and down continuously from the bottom. This movement can be made artificially by using a floating line and not too long a leader, as you will only be fishing in shallow water up to 8ft deep. A fast rise and fall of the artificial can be achieved by retrieving with a fast 1yd strip, followed by a 10-second pause before repeating the action. When trout go on a feeding binge on corixa, their stomach contents can be filled with 100 to 200 of the naturals.

DRESSING

Hook: Gold size 10–12.
Tying silk: Black.
Body: Lime-green floss.
Back: Speckled black and silver ribbon.
Paddles: Cock centre tail fibres.
Head: Clear varnish.

6 Cyril's Chomper

Fished in teams of three or four on certain reservoirs, positioned about 3ft apart. Retrieve in a standard figure of eight unless the elements help you to do nothing but cast and allow a side wind to drift your floating line round in a semi-circle. Takes cannot be missed as your line begins to straighten after the trout has mouthed the fly and turned. Chomper bugs were originally popularized by the late Dick Walker, but I think Dick would have approved of this new design.

Hook: Size 12.
Tying silk: Black.
Body: Pearl strip over black tying thread.
Rib: Fine gold wire.
Shell back: Olive green syntho.
Hackle: Olive hen.
Head: Clear varnish.

7 Cyril's White Bead Head

Fished on a floating line with reasonably fine leaders it makes a nice plopping attractor nymph. It can be used in teams of three and fished fairly fast. Takes will be vicious so use a softish rod to avoid breakages. Another method is to use it as just the point fly of the team of three but this time try one of the clear slime fly lines. Now a slower normal nymph-like retrieve can be made with great effect.

Hook: Size 12–14.
Tying silk: Lime floss.
Tail: Vivid range floss.
Body: Lime floss.
Back: Olive syntho.
Head: White bead.

8 Cyril's Updated Limeade Sedge Pupa

This pattern has been updated only by the addition of the eyes and the quality of modern synthetics. The body should be loosely dubbed so as to hold as much air as possible. This forms into small bubbles as the nymph sinks and into one large air bubble when retrieved as slowly as possible. This is primarily a sedge pupa imitation and works well for both browns and rainbows in the period late June to September. A great evening pattern on all reservoirs and lochs of Scotland or loughs of Ireland.

Hook: Gold size 10–8.
Tying silk: Lime.
Body: Dubbed synthetic.
Rib: Gold wire.
Thorax: Fawn dub synthetic.
Hackle: Hen fawn small black centre.
Head: Pair orange bead eyes.

Mick Stevens

Mick Stevens has been very fortunate during his trout fishing years to have been associated with a great number of the top anglers during the competition days. During that time he qualified four times for the England team and was captain in 1989. It was a very proud day indeed for Mick. Fishing in the Benson & Hedges International was also an experience in itself over the three-day event. Over the past ten years Mick has been associated with the England Youth Fly Fishing Association: Mick has had the pleasure of being on the committee and assisting with the team coaching to begin with, and then going on to manage the Youth Team for the past seven years.

As the years have passed, it is now time to move over from competitive fishing because he is seeing ex-youth team members' names coming up regularly in the news.

He is now doing what all good grandads should do and that is passing on his knowledge to his grandson.

1 Crisp and Goose

COMMENT

This nymph was one I tied about two years ago and has been very successful throughout the season from April to October. It has been fished on a variety of lines from a floater down the range to a Wet Cel II. One of the most effective methods during bright calm days is to fish it on a slow-sinking line with a very, very slow figure-of-eight retrieve. Also good at anchor – when all other methods have failed this has worked well. It performs best of all fished on a long leader of about 16–24ft with a single fly.

DRESSING

Hook: Short shank sproat size 8–14.
Tying silk: Black.
Body: Grey goose wing feather fibre tied Cove style.
Rib: Silver fine wire.
Thorax: Black silk.
Cheeks: Yellow crisp packet.
Head: Clear varnish.

2 Orange and Goose Nymph

COMMENT

I've used this brighter colour of orange in this type of nymph for some years, especially when there have been algae in the water and daphnia-feeding fish. The depth to fish depends on the depth of algae and weather conditions – whether dull or bright – as the daphnia move up and down in the water. The most effective way I have found is to fish it very slowly in coloured water and a fast figure-of-eight or slow pull for daphnia feeders. The orange should be changed for fluorescent green for clear-water conditions.

DRESSING

Hook: Bob Church Nymph size 8–12.
Tying silk: Black.
Tag: Orange fluorescent floss.
Body: Black goose wing feather fibre.
Rib: Gold fine wire.
Thorax: Fluorescent orange floss.
Head: Black varnish.

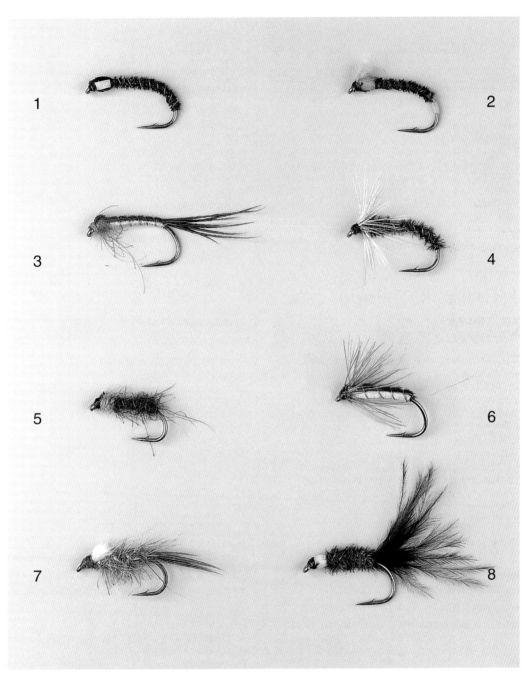

1 Crisp and Goose **2** Orange and Goose Nymph
3 Pheasant Tail Nymph Variant Orange **4** Peacock Nymph **5** Seal's Fur Nymph
6 Pitsford Nymph **7** River Keeper **8** Green Pea Nymph

3 Pheasant Tail Nymph Variant Orange

COMMENT

A pheasant tail nymph with a difference. This style of nymph has been a favourite of mine for many years now. I was shown this style of tying by a well-known fly dresser in Northampton, Cyril Lineham. The nymph can be tied with different coloured bodies: seal's fur, orange, green carper or even rabbit. I have found it to be most effective in the smaller sizes. It works well on most of the Midlands reservoirs. There is one important thing to remember when fishing these small nymphs, the naturals only move very small distances.

DRESSING

Hook: Bob Church Nymph size 8–16.
Tying silk: Gold.
Tail: Cock pheasant tail natural.
Body: Gold tying silk.
Rib: Gold fine wire.
Wing-case & back: Pheasant tail natural fibres.
Thorax: Orange seal's fur.
Head: Gold tying silk, apply clear varnish.

4 Peacock Nymph

COMMENT

The Peacock Nymph was tied for early- to mid-season use, when the bright-coloured nymphs are not so effective. I have found that this particular pattern does work very well on the day because of its presentation. It sits in the water vertically, the cock hackle acting like a parachute as it drops naturally through the depths of the water. This style of nymph can be fished at almost any depth. The best I have found is a floating line in light wind and an intermediate line in rough wind conditions.

DRESSING

Hook: Sedge hook size 8–14.
Tying silk: Black fine.
Body: Black base, one bronze peacock strand.
Rib: Fine silver wire.
Thorax: Peacock.
Hackle: White cock.
Head: Clear varnish.

5 Seal's Fur Nymph

COMMENT

Many of my nymphs using seal's fur or substitute are dubbed in this way. First dress the hook in the normal way to the bend, form a loop about 3in long, still at the bend of the hook, tie over itself to lock the loop, then take a few quick turns back towards the eye. Wax the loop with beeswax, then place the seal's fur between the two strands forming the loop and pull them together and spin them to form a rope. When formed, wind around the shank of the hook in even turns to just before the eye.

DRESSING

Hook: Kamasan B170 size 10–14.
Tying silk: Fine black.
Body: Claret seal's fur or substitute.
Rib: Fine gold wire.
Thorax: Yellow seal's fur or substitute.
Head: Clear varnish.

6 Pitsford Nymph

COMMENT

I devised this nymph many years ago when we were allowed to fish all of the small side of the reservoir at Pitsford. I have found a proportion of the aquatic life in the water possess a very bright green in them, from beetles to nymphs. This fly is a favourite of mine that has fished extremely well in the shallows and margins throughout the year on the floating line. Once again, use a single fly and a long leader. As I've mentioned before, this has proved very good on corixa feeding fish if fishing traditional style over the front of the boat.

DRESSING

Hook: Bob Church Nymph size 8–14.
Tying silk: Black (fine).
Body: Fluorescent green floss.
Rib: Fine red copper wire.
Back: Pheasant tail natural fibres.
Hackle: Light brown cock hackle.
Head: Fine black tying silk finished with a spot of superglue.

7 River Keeper

COMMENT

The Hare's Ear Nymph has been one of the most popular and successful nymphs of all time but has many variants. I would like to introduce to you just one more very good and successful pattern. I'm sure that someone somewhere has tied a similar one, but I have found that this tying has been the downfall of many a fish in my area. Again it requires to be in different sizes depending on the water's aquatic life size. This fly was introduced to me by two very good friends of mine, Bill Kingston and Gordon Groome (Old Father Time).

DRESSING

Hook: Kamasan B200 size 8–14.
Tying silk: Red.
Tail: Brown cock or natural pheasant tail fibres.
Body: Hare's fur left scruffy.
Rib: Oval gold.
Breathers: White marabou trimmed tight.
Head: Red tying silk finished with superglue.

8 Green Pea Nymph

COMMENT

This nymph has been excellent for me for a very long time now. It evolved from the Green Pea which I devised some thirty years ago. The original 'Pea' was tied on size 10 sproat with a black marabou tail, 4 turns of black chenille and two turns of bright green for the head, and three turns of fine lead wire for weight; for International rules obviously use no weight. The nymph was devised from the original pea when the fish became a bit more selective and not moving to the pulled fly. A really good nymph that can be fished at all depths.

DRESSING

Hook: Bob Church Nymph size 8–14.
Tying silk: Fine black.
Tail: Black marabou.
Body: Bronze peacock.
Rib: Fine copper wire.
Thorax: Fluorescent green floss.
Head: Fine black tying silk, spot of superglue.

Julian Hubbard

When Rutland opened, Julian met up with Fred Wagstaffe, a legend in specimen hunting especially for brown trout catches. He took Julian under his wing teaching him how to catch big trout on Rutland with lead lines and big lures. When Fred gave up fishing because of back problems Julian went on inventing the gold and silver tube flies that are now common knowledge. They catch many trout at Rutland, but Julian was using his invention years before anybody else. He has had three double-figure brown trout from Rutland and one from Grafham, as well as many browns close to double figures.

When rudder fishermen found out how he was catching these trout he gave up. Julian wanted a new challenge so he decided to go into competitions. He fished for the 1997 England team and that was the highest honour he has ever had in fishing. He also finished second in the Wychwood Team event. Julian's fly-tying skills help him no end to achieve his good results.

1 Hubbard's Invincible

COMMENT

This pattern is dynamite on a floating line from bank and boat when the fish are moving on the top. The trout take this fly very hard because it is so slim and natural. This is my best pattern for fishing on a floating line – I fish it with a long leader and two on the cast. I caught a brown trout at Rutland of 9lb 3oz and have had very big rainbows on this fly at Draycote. It works well on the anchor with a figure-of-eight retrieve. I always use this fly in the summer months.

DRESSING

Hook: Kamasan B160 size 10.
Tying silk: Red.
Body: Winter rabbit fur.
Wing: Fine lite gold lurex.
Head: Red with clear varnish.

2 Pheasant Tail Special

COMMENT

This pattern catches fish on every water I have fished from bank and boat. It is best fished on a floating line from the bank on the point or middle dropper on an intermediate line. The trout take this fly either as a small fry or a nymph. Use constant retrieves which seem to work best. A good back-end pattern at Eyebrook when the trout are on fry. This fly is successful at Rutland tied on a bigger hook with some weight added. I've had many limits at Eyebrook and Rutland especially from the bank on the Pheasant Tail Special.

DRESSING

Hook: Drennan B160 size 8.
Tying silk: Red or black.
Tail: Brown hen hackle fibres.
Body: Brown pheasant tail.
Rib: Bronze electrical wire.
Thorax: Winter rabbit.
Thorax cover: Pearl lurex.
Head: Clear varnish.

1 Hubbard's Invincible 2 Pheasant Tail Special 3 The Sorter 4 Julian's Damsel
5 The Impressor 6 Tadpole Nymph 7 Green Pearl Head Nymph 8 Cheeky Bugger

3 The Sorter

COMMENT

Called The Sorter because it really sorts out the trout at the start of the season. It has caught so many fish for me at Rutland. It is best fished on an intermediate line from the bank on a slow figure-of-eight retrieve. It can also be leaded, when it is best fished on a floating line. It works very well because it's so slim and long with a small hook. This is my favourite pattern at the start of the season. You don't have to fish a large Dog Nobbler – this is just as good and I've caught hundreds of limits on this pattern.

DRESSING

Hook: Drennan B175 size 8.
Tying silk: Black.
Tail: Light olive marabou.
Body: Medium olive seal's fur.
Thorax: Winter rabbit.
Thorax cover: Pearl lurex.
Head: Clear varnish.

4 Julian's Damsel

COMMENT

Always have one in your fly box. It is my favourite pattern and catches everywhere from reservoirs to small waters. It is best fished on an intermediate fly line and a long leader on the point. It should be fished very slow which is how it works best. This pattern has won me so many competitions and caught a lot of trout. It works best at Draycote and Rutland from a boat in light winds. The best result seen on this fly was at Bewl in 1995, which was five fish on a very hard day. This gave me top rod on a Benson & Hedges event, winning a jumper.

DRESSING

Hook: Drennan B160 size 8.
Tying silk: Red.
Tail: Light olive marabou.
Body: Winter rabbit fur.
Back cover: Pearl lurex.
Head: Clear varnish.

5 The Impressor

COMMENT

This is called the Impressor because it impresses me so much. A brilliant fly from bank or boat all year round because it's taken as any nymph or buzzer. Add lead to the front of the fly if you use it on a floating line from the bank. This pattern works well at Bewl, Grafham and Hanningfield from a boat. This pattern got me into the 1997 England team fishing two on the same cast on a fast glass intermediate fly line. I caught seven trout on a very hard day at Bewl. It also gave me twelfth place in the Hanningfield Masters out of a hundred anglers.

DRESSING

Hook: Drennan B160 size 8.
Tying silk: Black.
Tail: Black marabou.
Body: Dark green spike hair and black rabbit.
Thorax: Winter rabbit fur.
Thorax cover: Medium pearl lurex.
Head: Clear varnish.

6 Tadpole Nymph

COMMENT

I use this fly a lot at Grafham on a fast sink fly line and a slow retrieve. It also works well from the bank if you add lead to the front. I always use it on the top dropper from the boat on a sinking line which I've found is the best method. It's also good on the hang. This pattern seems to get me fish on hard sunny days. I use this fly a lot from the bank at Rutland on a floating line. It is a killer at the start of the season. Use a slow retrieve off the bank.

DRESSING

Hook: Drennan Traditional Wet size 8.
Tying silk: Black.
Tail: Black marabou.
Body: Black rabbit fur.
Rib: Bronze wire.
Thorax: Lime-green Fritz.
Head: Clear varnish.

7 Green Pearl Head Nymph

COMMENT

This fly is best used in shallow water on a floating or slow sink fly line and a long leader. It's a pattern that I use at Draycote and Rutland especially when the trout are on damsels or green nymphs. This pattern came about because so many anglers were catching fish on goldheads, so I made this fly to come inside competition rules without any lead at the head. It got me into the England final with twelve fish coming fourth, and second place in the Wychwood final.

DRESSING

Hook: Kamasan B160 size 8.
Tying silk: Red.
Tail: Light olive marabou.
Body: Light and medium olive seal's fur.
Thorax: Pearl mylar.
Thorax cover: Pheasant tail fibres.
Head: Red, apply clear varnish.

8 Cheeky Bugger

COMMENT

July is the best time for this fly at Draycote where very light green buzzers hatch. I always fish this pattern on a floating line just keeping in touch with the fly. I put one on the point and one on the top dropper. I tie this pattern very skinny as it works best like this. This is my favourite fly at Draycote in the summer when the fish are just under the surface.

DRESSING

Hook: Kamasan B160 size 8.
Tying silk: Red.
Body: Olive seal's fur.
Rib: Bronze wire.
Thorax cheeks: Jungle cock.
Head: Red, apply clear varnish.

Richard Sandford

Richard Sandford started competitive fly fishing at the age of 12 whilst living in Sussex, competing on small lakes. That was over 16 years ago. In 1991 he moved up to the Scottish borders and bought a fishing tackle and outdoor pursuits shop. He now competes on a regular basis on Rutland in a team called the Northumbrian Ospreys. In 1996 he fished for England twice, getting one team gold and one team bronze in Wales in the autumn. For most of the patterns Richard says he cannot take all the credit as part of this must go to his regular boat partner Kevin Glenn. It must be said that they are both fanatical about the sport. Richard has also started to tie competition flies to sell through his shop this year. His selection is a cross between nymphs and wets.

1 Richard's Pheasant Tail Buzzer

COMMENT

Prior to the evening rise this pattern can be fished just sub-surface either pulled or static. I put on the Globrite for peaty waters such as Kielder, but it worked just as well on the clearwater lakes of the Midlands. So it was kept on, making the older pattern redundant after fish catches improved with the addition of the orange. Can be made into a very good dry fly with the addition of a CDC shuttlecock wing.

DRESSING

Hook: Kamasan B170 size 14.
Tying silk: Claret uni-thread 6/0.
Tail: Pheasant tail fibres.
Body: Pheasant tail fibres.
Rib: Clear nylon.
Thorax: Three turns of Globrite no. 8 floss (rear), red seal's fur brushed with velcro.
Head: Clear varnish.

2 Root Beer Kate

COMMENT

This is another pattern that has been taken from an original pattern that always worked well, but now works better. It possesses a sparkle that was not available at the time it was invented. It works equally well on any line, but has been very good as a middle pattern for 'hanging' at Rutland. If you fish it with confidence this pattern really does work.

DRESSING

Hook: Kamasan B170 size 12.
Tying silk: Brown uni-thread 6/0.
Tail: A few strands of crystal hair – root beer colour.
Body: Pearl lurex.
Body hackle: Palmered Metz chocolate dun.
Head hackle: Metz brown neck.
Head: Clear varnish.

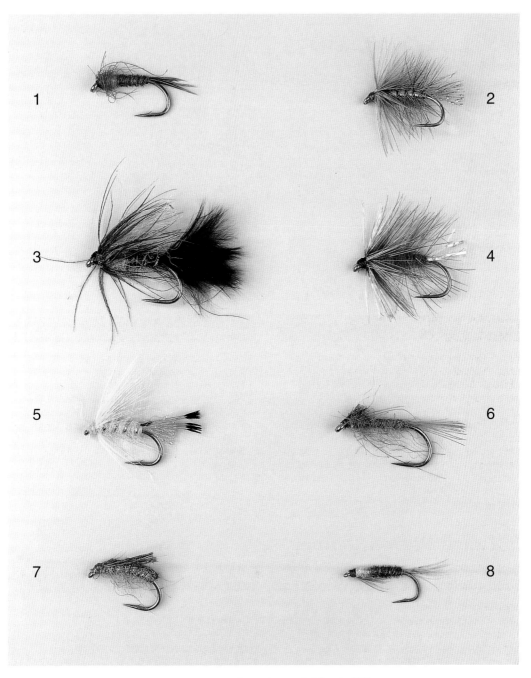

1 Richard's Pheasant Tail Buzzer   **2** Root Beer Kate   **3** Vive-la-Difference
4 Shadow Soldier   **5** Peach Poison Pennel   **6** Skinny Seal's Fur Damsel
7 R.S. Corixa   **8** The Nice One

3 Vive-la-Difference

COMMENT

This fly was an attempt to breach the gap between puller and nymph. It has been for myself and other fishing partners a worthwhile fly to tie. It has caught on all lines but really does excel on the Scientific Anglers Clear Stillwater line. Best catch so far has been a 9lb brown and a 7lb rainbow at Sweethorpe in Northumbria on consecutive casts. Also in 1996 my fly-fishing team qualified for the Benson & Hedges National Final. I used this pattern for best bag during the qualifiers at Rutland during May.

DRESSING

Hook: Kamasan B175 size 10–14.
Tying silk: Black uni-thread 6/0.
Tail: Black marabou.
Body: Black seal's fur.
Rib: Silver fine oval.
Thorax: Fluorescent green seal's fur.
Wing: 8–10 strands of mobile teased apart.
Hackle: Soft medium-length black hen.
Head: Clear varnish.

4 Shadow Soldier

COMMENT

The Shadow Soldier does well on Kielder. In 1995 it secured me a place on the English Fly Fishing team at the National Final in September. But the pattern has worked wherever there have been sedges coming off, be it Mentieth or Chew. Ideally fished as a top dropper and greased up on a floating line, then just simply pulled. Although it has had some marked success when fished dry on Chew, it excels in a big wave during the summer where it does seem to sort out the better fish.

DRESSING

Hook: Kamasan B170 size 10 or Partridge grey shadow wet.
Tying silk: Black 6/0 uni-thread.
Tail: 3 strands of pearl flashabou.
Body: Dark red seal's fur – palmered with Metz brown neck hackle.
Hackle: Badger.
Head: Three turns of Globrite no. 4 (optional) for peaty water, and clear varnish.

5 Peach Poison Pennel

COMMENT

Ideally fished in conjunction with other daphnia flies. This pattern has been most consistent 'on the hang'. The name came about whilst fishing in northern Scotland. After catching a respectable brown, an old gentleman popped up out of nowhere and asked me how I was doing. I showed him the fish and then the fly. He reeled backwards in shock and told me that I had poisoned a respectable Scottish pattern with a bag weight of 11lb – which was unheard of from that loch.

DRESSING

Hook: Kamasan B175 size 12.
Tying silk: Orange uni-thread 6/0.
Tail: Few strands of orange mobile under golden pheasant tippet.
Body: Peach seal's fur.
Rib: Fine oval gold.
Hackle: Peach hackle to match body.
Head: Three turns of Globrite no. 8.

6 Skinny Seal's Fur Damsel

COMMENT

This pattern, although designed to be fished at Rutland, Grafham and Bewl, has caught fish all over the country. Ideally it is most effective when teamed up in a three-fly cast with a buzzer above it and a corixa above that, then fished slowly whilst drifting along over weed beds. This fly accounted for personal catches of over forty fish at Rutland in 1996.

DRESSING

Hook: Kamasan B175 size 10.
Tying silk: Claret uni-thread 6/0.
Tail: Lightly marked furnace hackle fibres.
Body: Medium olive seal's fur with a pearl lurex shell back.
Rib: Gold wire.
Thorax: Medium olive seal's fur – brushed with velcro.
Thorax cover: Peacock herl, three strands.
Head: Clear varnish.

7 R.S. Corixa

COMMENT

This pattern has been for myself and my regular fishing partner Kevin Glenn a revelation. When the fish were feeding avidly on corixa this was a pattern that could not go wrong. We had tried for a long time to get that bubble look and silver Lite Brite did just that. This has accounted for browns up to 7lb and rainbows up to 8lb. Fished near weed beds you can't go wrong.

DRESSING

Hook: Kamasan B110 size 10–12.
Tying silk: Red uni-thread 6/0.
Body: Silver and golden olive Lite Brite mixed together 50/50 then brushed with velcro.
Shell back: Pheasant tail fibres, five strands.
Rib: Very fine gold wire.
Paddles: Pheasant tail – one either side with feather weld on them to make them stronger.
Head: Red varnish.

8 The Nice One

COMMENT

This slim profile fly has been known to work in a multiplicity of situations including when pin fry are about, when olives are hatching, or when olive buzzers are coming off. The pattern got its name after a session fishing at Weirwood in Sussex in 1986. Everybody on the lake was having a tough time except my father who had somehow extracted this fly from my box without me noticing. Whenever I asked what fly he was catching the fish on he just kept saying 'the Nice One'.

DRESSING

Hook: Drennan size 16–14 Nymph or Kamasan B200.
Tying silk: Claret uni-thread.
Tail: Summer duck or substitute.
Body: Dyed olive pheasant tail, three strands.
Rib: Gold wire.
Thorax: Pearl unstretched lurex.
Throat hackle: Summer duck or substitute.
Cheeks: Jungle cock eyes (optional).
Head: Clear varnish.

Jeremy Clarke

Jeremy has had the distinction of fishing for England in the Home Internationals on five occasions. In spring of 1997 at Bewl Water he was chosen as captain, at which time the team convincingly won gold.

Jeremy is from Bristol and the majority of his fishing takes place on Chew Valley Lake and Blagdon. These have been the training grounds for many top English fly fishers over the years. Jeremy is secretary of the well-known Bath & District Fly Fishers, a team which has done very well in recent years in major competitions. A keen and expert fly tyer, Jeremy has written a column in *Trout & Salmon* magazine for the past two years.

1 Jeremy Clarke's Black Nymph

COMMENT

Best described as a cross between a lure and a nymph, I find this pattern performs at its best during the early season. It combines a drab nymphy profile with the flash and colour of the Globrite and jungle cock. This fly is particularly useful once the initial opening day stockie bash is over, and the fish are no longer falling for the lures. I find that, presented on a floater or intermediate and retrieved slowly, this fly will continue to catch. In the smaller sizes it will also catch during the sparse buzzer hatches that can occur at this time of year.

DRESSING

Hook: Scorpion Competition Heavy weight size 10–14.
Tying silk: Black.
Tail: Single strand Globrite no. 11 and black hen hackle fibres.
Body: Black dyed hare's body guard hair, overlaid with broad pearl tinsel.
Rib: Fine silver wire.
Thorax: As for body.
Cheeks: Jungle cock.
Hackle: Black hen.
Head: Clear varnish.

2 Jeremy Clarke's Damsel Variant

COMMENT

An excellent high and late summer pattern, imitating the damsel, so prolific during the summer months. This pattern is also a great standby for use at any time of the year. The nymphs themselves are very agile and capable of great speed, although I have found this fly to be a killer with almost every speed of retrieve. This is another pattern that will be equally effective whatever line it is fished on, and will also take on any size stillwater. This pattern incorporates a wing-case of spectraflash to provide a bit of eye-catching sparkle.

DRESSING

Hook: Drennan wet fly size 10–14.
Tying silk: Claret.
Tail: Pinch of olive marabou.
Body: Olive seal's fur.
Rib: Olive copper wire.
Thorax: One turn of claret seal's fur followed by olive seal's fur.
Wing-case: Brown spectraflash.
Hackle: Pinches of olive dyed partridge hackle.
Eyes: Small clear beads.
Head: Clear varnish.

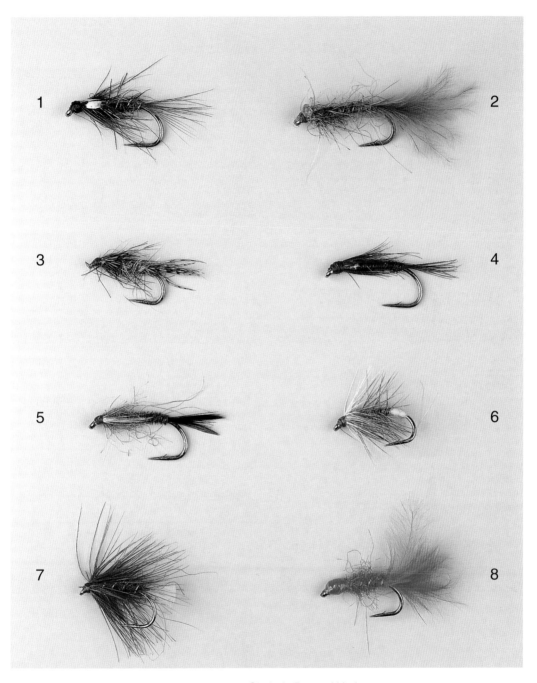

1 Jeremy Clarke's Black Nymph   2 Jeremy Clarke's Damsel Variant
3 Jeremy Clarke's Hare's Ear Variant   4 Claret Diawl Bach   5 Jeremy Clarke's Killer
6 Green Palmer Nymph   7 Brown Palmer   8 Jeremy Clarke's Orange Nymph/Lure

3 Jeremy Clarke's Hare's Ear Variant

COMMENT

A great fly for those days when there is nothing obvious hatching. In all respects this is a suggestive rather than imitative pattern. I have enjoyed success with this pattern right the way through the season, and again at a variety of depths. I also find this pattern deadly in the smaller sizes when tackling smutting fish. If necessary, with the application of a little floatant, this pattern will sit nicely in the surface film, though the use of lighter hooks will assist this. Being a nymph pattern this fly is best fished on a slow figure of eight.

DRESSING

Hook: Scorpion Competition Heavy weight size 10–14.
Silk: Wine/claret.
Tail: Brown partridge fibres.
Body: Hare's body guard hairs.
Rib: Fine flat gold.
Thorax: Claret seal's fur.
Wing-case: Cock pheasant tail fibres.
Hackle: Pinches of brown partridge hackle fibres.
Head: Clear varnish.

4 Claret Diawl Bach

COMMENT

This pattern can prove deadly at all depths, and as such is my candidate for the best all-rounder. When I first started using this version it was while nymphing on a floater, where in the smaller sizes of around 14s and 16s, it proved an instant success. Since then it has proved its worth on almost every reservoir I have fished and consequently almost always occupies a place on my cast. It has proved equally successful when fishing nymphs on the sinker, at any level, and is an ideal choice during the early season.

DRESSING

Hook: Scorpion Competition Heavy weight size 10–14.
Tying silk: Wine/claret.
Tail: Dark chocolate hackle fibres.
Body: Claret/bronze dyed peacock herl.
Rib: Fine red copper wire.
Thorax: Couple of turns of medium pearly tinsel.
Hackle: Dark chocolate hackle fibres tied as a beard hackle.
Head: Clear varnish.

5 Jeremy Clarke's Killer

COMMENT

A good general nymph and standby pattern, this variation is particularly useful during the summer, and latter months of the season. The pattern is derived from the Bewl Killer, and has produced the goods on Chew, Blagdon, Bewl and Rutland. I have had most success fishing this fly on the point on an intermediate or slow-sinking line when boat fishing, although it can be equally effective on a floater, and is one of my first choices when bank fishing in September.

DRESSING

Hook: Scorpion Competition Heavy weight size 8–12.
Tying silk: Wine/claret.
Tail: Olive cock hackle tips.
Body: Dark olive seal's fur.
Rib: Red copper wire.
Hackle: Pinches of white cock hackle fibres tied as cheeks.
Head: Clear varnish.

6 Green Palmer Nymph

COMMENT

A variation on a green palmer, this pattern has been very useful during hatches of green midge at Chew and Bewl. Again, it has pulled fish on floaters and intermediates and tends to be more effective at dawn and during daylight hours, rather than later in the day. It works well as part of a team of nymphs and would normally occupy the top dropper position. In the smaller sizes this fly has also been deadly fished to move fish during high summer under flat calm conditions, particularly when the tiny green midges are hatching.

DRESSING

Hook: Scorpion Competition Heavy weight size 10–14.
Tying silk: Olive.
Butt: Few turns of Globrite phosphor yellow no. 11.
Body: Light olive seal's fur.
Rib: Fine gold wire.
Body hackle: Medium olive cock hackle.
Hackle: Couple of turns of white cock hackle.
Head: Clear varnish.

7 Brown Palmer

COMMENT

This pattern excels as an attractor, being especially effective against stockies; however, it has also caused the downfall of some better fish, particularly at Rutland and Chew. Depending upon conditions, this fly fishes best with a fast figure-of-eight retrieve interspersed with a variety of twitches and pauses. As with other killing flies this pattern is equally effective on any line, although it is particularly useful when fishing a medium or fast sink, in the top dropper position, on a cast carrying a couple of 'nymphy' or more suggestive patterns.

DRESSING

Hook: Scorpion Short Shank Special size 10–14.
Tying silk: Brown.
Tail: Globrite fluoro orange floss no. 8.
Body: Dark brown seal's fur loosely dubbed.
Rib: Flat gold medium.
Body hackle: Dark chocolate hen.
Hackle: Dark chocolate hen.
Head: Clear varnish.

8 Jeremy Clarke's Orange Nymph/Lure

COMMENT

An excellent two-in-one pulling fly and really a mini lure or attractor nymph that, under the right conditions, works well for more resident and stock fish alike. Especially effective for those times when the stockies become a little shy. It also tends to excel under clearwater conditions, where lures will be effective but are too garish in the larger sizes. When tying this pattern go for the brighter more fluorescent oranges available. The fly can be tied with fluoro orange silk and then a prominent head built up that can then be covered in epoxy.

DRESSING

Hook: Scorpion Competition Heavy weight size 10–12.
Tying silk: Hot orange.
Tail: Fluorescent orange marabou.
Body: Hot orange seal's fur.
Rib: Medium gold wire.
Head: Globrite no. 5 built up to form prominent blob and then covered in epoxy.

Mick Broadgate

Mick is from Staffordshire and regularly fishes the Midlands reservoirs. He is a very adaptable angler, although he prefers to fish in the upper layers of the water when possible. A former England International team member he has been in the winning frame of the recent Hanningfield Masters. Mick is also a member of the Rutland Kingfishers. He has taken many good catches from both Rutland and Grafham including an 11lb 14oz brown trout in a Mixed Pairs competition in 1996 at Grafham. This was the largest brown trout ever caught in a competition to International Rules.

1 Pitsford Nymph

COMMENT

Back in the early 1990s Pitsford Reservoir was renowned for its nymph fishing and, as the name of this fly suggests, it was a killing pattern on Pitsford. It is fished just below the surface on a floating fly line and a long leader as a point fly. A very successful fly when the induced technique is used. The trout take the fly for any dark nymphs that may be swimming around. Not surprisingly this fly has been very successful on Rutland and Grafham and is a good standby pattern on any water.

DRESSING

Hook: Kamasan B175 size 10.
Tying silk: Black.
Tail: Bunch of white cock fibres.
Body/Thorax: Dark hare's ear.
Rib: Copper wire.
Wing-case: Pheasant tail fibres laid over thorax.
Head: Clear varnish.

2 Mick's Pheasant Tail Variant

COMMENT

The Pheasant Tail Nymph was originally developed by Frank Sawyer for the English chalk streams. The pheasant tail is a fine match for any dark nymph and this fly may be fished deep or just below the surface. The black and orange combination suggests the emerging nymph changing its coloration as so often happens. A very good fly throughout the season that is not often off my cast of three nymphs during a day's fishing. A good fly on all English reservoirs.

DRESSING

Hook: Drennan Specimen Crystal size 10.
Tying silk: Black.
Tail: Bunch of black pheasant tail fibres.
Body: Black pheasant tail fibres.
Rib: Oval silver tinsel.
Thorax: Burnt orange seal's fur.
Head: Globrite no. 5 and a coat of clear varnish.

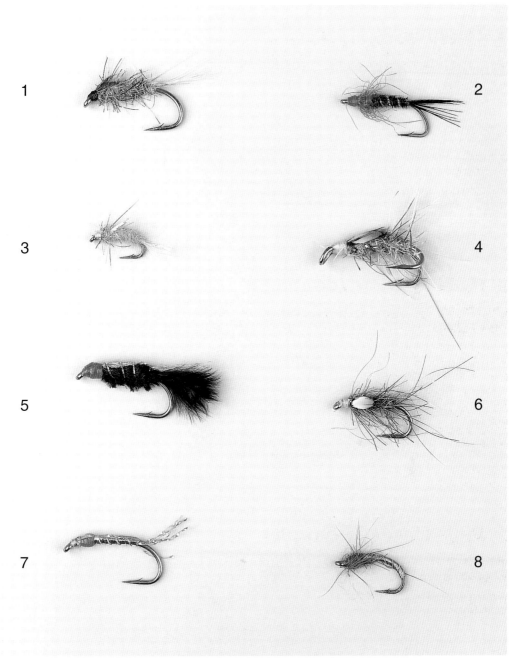

1 Pitsford Nymph   2 Mick's Pheasant Tail Variant   3 Daphnia
4 JC Hare's Ear (double)   5 Pink-Headed Nymph   6 JC Scruffy
7 Mick's Fry Nymph   8 Green Midge

3 Daphnia

COMMENT

Daphnia, are so small that individually they are impossible to imitate, although as so often happens they congregate to form vast blooms. Orange seems to trigger the trout into taking mode when gorging themselves on them. This nymph will work on such occasions and has taken many trout for me and my fishing friends in the past. It took the biggest fish award in the Bob Church Classic in 1996 for Margaret Godwin, weighing 4lb 3oz.

DRESSING

Hook: Kamasan B175 size 16.
Tying silk: Light Cahill.
Tail: Two strands of flashabou.
Body: Two-thirds orange, one-third seal's fur substitute.
Head: Clear varnish.

4 JC Hare's Ear (double)

COMMENT

The Hare's Ear originated long before the last century. It's an excellent medium or dark olive copy and as a general nymph probably has no match. This fly of mine is tied on a double hook so as to fish at a greater depth but may be tied on a single hook if required. This is a fly that is fished as a point fly below the surface on a floating fly line with a long leader and a nice slow figure-of-eight retrieve. Confidence is a must when fishing this fly.

DRESSING

Hook: Kamasan B270 size 10–12.
Tying silk: Light Cahill.
Body: Coarse natural seal's fur.
Rib: Copper oval tinsel.
Cheeks: Jungle cock on either side.
Head: Clear varnish.

5 Pink-Headed Nymph

COMMENT

A good early-season nymph fished on a cast of three flies, using sinking fly lines. I usually fish this fly in the 'bob' position which I have found to be the best on the cast. It has accounted for many fish from Rutland and Grafham. It can also be tied using green twinkle overlaid with a Globrite no. 12 head, varnished. This fly is very adaptable and is used as a point fly later on in the season. Try it on a floating line. For a slimmer body I sometimes use black marabou for the body which gives the fly a more scruffy look. This is a good all-rounder.

DRESSING

Hook: Kamasan B175 size 10.
Tying silk: Black.
Tail: Black marabou and pink twinkle.
Body: Black chenille and overlaid pink twinkle.
Rib: Silver oval tinsel.
Head: Globrite no. 1 coated with clear varnish.

6 JC Scruffy

COMMENT

This was originally based on the famous Gold-Ribbed Hare's Ear, which is likely to be the most popular nymph used. This fly is very easy to tie and, as is often the case, the good nymphs are often the simplest. By choosing the dark material from the grey squirrel tail, this nymph has more scope than its predecessor and represents the nymphs of the large and small dark olives. It's a great killer of trout on the reservoirs I fish.

DRESSING

Hook: Kamasan B175 size 12–14.
Tying silk: Brown.
Body: Grey squirrel tail (chopped up).
Rib: Copper flat tinsel.
Cheeks: Jungle cock on either side.
Head: Clear varnish.

7 Mick's Fry Nymph

COMMENT

As the name of this fly suggests it is a fry pattern. The combination of the blue to silver overbody and body give the fly a bluish hue as in a roach fry. It should be fished on the point of the leader near to reed beds. This fly seems to work best of all when the fry have just gone past the opaque pin fry stage and works on any large water where trout feed avidly on the fry. Fish just as you would an insect nymph pattern – slowly.

DRESSING

Hook: Kamasan B175 size 10 or Drennan Traditional Wet Fly size 8.
Tying silk: Any light colour.
Body: Flat silver tinsel.
Rib: Silver wire varnished clear.
Overbody: Blue twinkle.
Tail: Blue twinkle.
Head: Globrite no. 5 and blue twinkle, apply clear varnish.

8 Green Midge

COMMENT

The larvae from midge (Chironomidae) are commonly called bloodworms and whilst most people know the red variety as bloodworms or jokers they also come in other colours such as brown, green and shades thereof. They are thin and worm-like and move through the water freely. This pattern is the green midge common on most waters, in particular Rutland Water. I find that these patterns fish better on a sinking or sink tip fly line. This fly has caught me many trout from Rutland during 1997.

DRESSING

Hook: Kamasan B110 size 14.
Tying silk: Olive.
Body: Olive tying silk.
Rib: Fine silver wire.
Thorax: Olive seal's fur substitute.
Head: Olive, apply clear varnish.

Ray Burt

Ray Burt has been fly fishing for trout for twenty-five years. He started competitive fly fishing in 1987 and by 1989 was fishing his first International at Loch Leven where he won the Brown Bowl as top individual angler.

In 1990 he gained a Benson & Hedges gold medal with the Weald of Kent team, and a silver medal followed in 1991 in the same event. That same year he was in the World Championship team that was placed third in New Zealand. The following year he won the Wilcon Small Stillwater competition at Ringstead Grange and in 1993 was runner-up in the European Championship held in France. In recent years he has fished the small clearwater fisheries and has taken many double-figure rainbows up to over 15 lb and a brown over 10 lb.

He has now turned his attention to river fishing and has qualified for the River National for the last three years in an effort to try for the one thing that has so far eluded him – a place in the England Rivers team.

His collection of nymphs cover both bank and boat fishing as well as small stillwaters and rivers.

1 Tangler Nymph

COMMENT

This was a fly that I read about in one of the magazines for trout fishing many years ago when I first started nymph fishing. In its first year of use for bank fishing at Bewl Water it caught me more than a hundred trout. For some reason, though, it never produced such spectacular results from a boat. It got relegated to the 'has been' box until recently when the well-known fly dresser Peter Deane gave a talk to our fishing club and said it was a fly that was very effective on rivers. I now have some leaded versions tied up ready for such work.

DRESSING

Hook: Kamasan B175 size 12–14.
Tying silk: Olive.
Body: Rear half: Claret seal's fur.
Front half: Olive seal's fur.
Rib: Silver wire over both sections.
Head: Clear varnish.

2 Peacock Stickfly

COMMENT

This was a nymph that I tied for early-season bank fishing on long-shank leaded hooks. This one, however, has proved its worth when scaled down to International rules size. On its first wetting it caught me ten of the fourteen trout that I landed in a Benson and Hedges heat at Bewl Water and since then has picked up vital fish at several reservoirs around the country, especially in difficult conditions of wind and bright sunlight. It seems to fish best to the slowest of figure-of-eight retrieves in the middle dropper position of a three-fly cast.

DRESSING

Hook: Kamasan B175 size 10.
Tying silk: Brown.
Body: Peacock herl ribbed with tying silk for strength
Thorax: Lime yellow wool.
Hackle: Honey hen.
Head: Clear varnish.

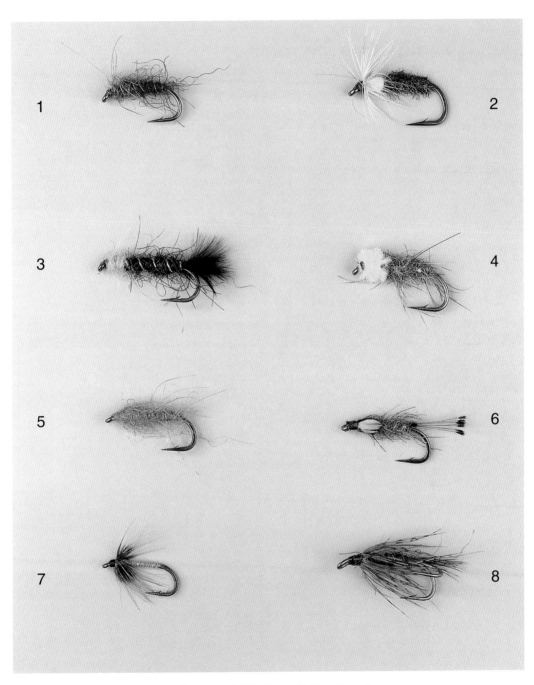

1 Tangler Nymph   2 Peacock Stickfly   3 Black and Yellow Nymph
4 Lime Head Nymph   5 Orange Nymph   6 Jungle Hare's Ear   7 Green Nymph
8 Sooty Olive Nymph

3 Black and Yellow Nymph

COMMENT

This fly is my version of the hugely popular Montana Nymph. As well as being a really good early-season bank fishing nymph it has also caught many fish for me during the years I fished in Belgium, France and Luxembourg in European events. The morning sessions in these matches invariably produce a lot of fish to various coloured tadpoles but during the afternoon sessions, when a lot of fish have by then been caught and returned, they have become very wary.

DRESSING

Hook: Kamasan B830 size 12 (leaded).
Tying silk: Black.
Tail: Short tuft of black marabou.
Body: Black seal's fur ribbed with silver oval tinsel.
Thorax: Yellow rabbit fur.
Head: Clear varnish.

4 Lime Head Nymph

COMMENT

This is a fly that I quite frequently use on the small clearwater fisheries, such as Chalk Springs at Arundel, where it has taken many rainbows for me in the 8–12lb bracket. It seems to work on large fish that have been stalked, by either fishing it on the drop in front of the fish or by casting across the line of vision of the fish and twitching it past its nose. The pattern can also be dressed with two turns of orange chenille at the head as an alternative and it was this pattern that took my largest rainbow of 15lb 1oz from Dever Springs.

DRESSING

Hook: Kamasan B175 size 10–12 (leaded).
Tying silk: Brown.
Body: Hare fur.
Rib: Silver wire.
Thorax: Two turns of lime-green chenille.
Head: Clear varnish.

5 Orange Nymph

COMMENT

This was a fly that caught fish for top Belgian angler Paul Vekemans when I went out for a day's practice with him before the 1993 European event at Grafham Water. I tied several up for use the next day and on a day of bright sun they helped me to win the match. It is useful as an attractor on the top dropper to draw fish on to other nymphs fished behind, but also catches its own share of fish. It seems to work when fished with the slowest of retrieves in light winds or when pulled quite quickly when the wind is stronger.

DRESSING

Hook: Drennan Wet Fly Supreme size 12.
Tying silk: Fluorescent orange.
Body: Orange seal's fur, thicker at the thorax.
Rib: Gold wire.
Wing-case: Hen pheasant fibres.
Head: Clear varnish.

6 Jungle Hare's Ear

COMMENT

I doubt whether there is any fly that has had more variations tied over the years than the good old Hare's Ear nymph. This is a variation that I tied that proved its worth at Rutland Water in August 1995 when I was fishing for the England team in preparation for a forthcoming International event in a triangular match with teams from the Men's Senior, England Ladies and the Royal Air Force. The majority of the fish were located down near the dam and I took my eight fish limit all on this fly by just after 12 o'clock in hot sunny conditions for top slot.

DRESSING

Hook: Drennan Wet Fly Supreme size 12.
Tying silk: Brown.
Tail: Golden pheasant tippet fibres.
Body: Hare fur.
Rib: Flat pearl tinsel.
Cheeks: Jungle cock.
Head: Clear varnish.

7 Green Nymph

COMMENT

This is a nymph that Jeremy Lucas showed me when we both fished for the Weald of Kent team. He used it mainly for the 'strip and hang' method but I have found it very effective when fish are taking small midge at the surface in calm conditions. It scored particularly well for me at the Autumn International on the Lake of Mentieth in Scotland in 1995. I started off the day with one in the middle dropper position and so successful was it that I ended the day with three identical flies on my cast. It took all of my eleven fish to make me top English rod.

DRESSING

Hook: Drennan Wet Fly Supreme size 14.
Tying silk: Black.
Body: Two layers of flat pearl tinsel giving a bright green effect.
Hackle: Two turns of Greenwell hen.
Head: Clear varnish.

8 Sooty Olive Nymph

COMMENT

A pattern that I dressed for the Spring International on Lough Owel in Ireland in 1996. It worked for me very well in practice on a Wet Cel II line and several team members tied some up and used them in the match. The most successful was Edward Foster who I believe took five of his seven fish on this fly to become top rod for England. Regretfully it didn't catch for me in the match, but this was down to my wrong choice of area for once. The fly proved its worth again at Rutland Water later on.

DRESSING

Hook: Kamasan B270 Double size 12.
Tying silk: Olive.
Tail: Dyed olive partridge hackle fibres.
Body: Sooty olive seal's fur.
Rib: Silver wire.
Hackle: Dyed olive partridge.
Head: Clear varnish.

Martin Introna

I have known and watched Martin's trout fishing career these last ten years. There is no one who is more dedicated to the cause, which has resulted in regular successful performances in big competitions. Martin, from Worksop, began to make a name for himself with a little fly fishing club from that town. With his success, his ambitions to do even better began to show.

A good team organizer and motivator, he formed his own squad of fly fishers called the Rutland Kingfishers. The idea was to compete in all major events and so continue the learning curve and enjoy it at the same time. Needless to say the Kingfishers have been very successful – even their B team holds its own with the best.

Martin has won many individual competitions but I know there is one thing that has eluded him so far in realizing his ambitions – that is to qualify for the England team, but this is only a matter of time.

1 Doodlebug

COMMENT

Fish were on black buzzers at Rutland one year; they were also full of bloodworm and green buzzers. Information told me of numbers of trout taking Montana Nymphs on the Hi-Di line. I set about tying Montana Nymphs ready for my next visit. While doing so I incorporated some red biots in the tail and in the wings. Predominant chironomid colours – red (wing and tail), green thorax and black body seem to trigger the feeding instincts of the trout. Fish on a fast sink line, which is excellent when all else fails.

DRESSING

Hook: Short shank size 10.
Tying silk: Black.
Body: Black chenille.
Rib: Silver wire.
Thorax: Fluorescent green micro-chenille.
Tail + Wings: Red goose biots.
Head: Clear varnish.

2 Close Copy Damsel

COMMENT

Rutland 1996 was the year of the Damsel – to omit one of these in your box was to put yourself at a serious disadvantage! Whilst on a practice I decided to look a little closer at the real insect. I saw bright green, dull green and brown nymphs with predominant eyes. I tied a pattern which when used caught for me a great deal of fish when I would like to think that the trout had seen their fair share of imposters and were difficult to tempt. Fished from June until late September and later, I found it works on all reservoirs.

DRESSING

Hook: Drennan Traditional Wet size 8 or Double size 12–14.
Tying silk: Olive.
Tail: Olive marabou.
Body: Olive marabou.
Rib: Green body wrap or thread.
Legs: Partridge hackle.
Thorax: Hare's ear and claret seal's fur, two turns of each.
Eyes: Fluorescent green chenille tied in figure of eight.
Head: Clear varnish.

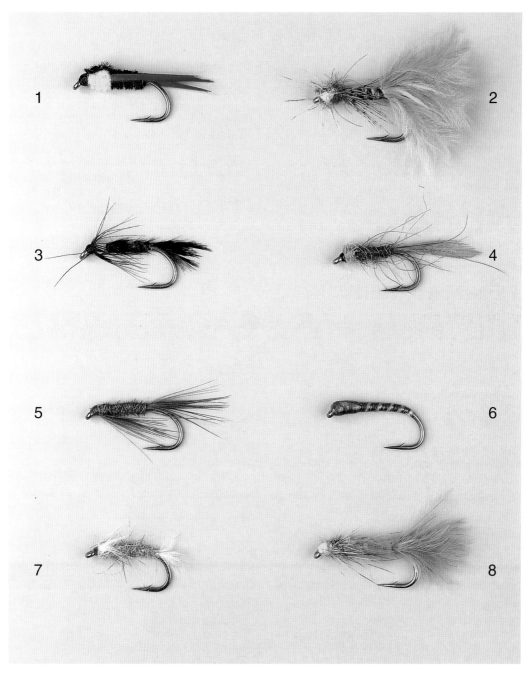

1 Doodlebug **2** Close Copy Damsel **3** Black Nymph **4** Flashback Killer
5 Diawl Bach Flashback **6** Green Varnished Buzzer
7 Brian's Pearly Ribbed Hare's Ear **8** Flashback Damsel

3 Black Nymph

COMMENT

As the season progresses the more resident trout are becoming choosier in their diet. As with the Doodlebug the predominant colours are always black, green and red. Here we have a more sombre pattern: black ostrich herl, green floss and pearl rib with red wire. This is another excellent pattern to fish on any line just when perhaps the trout have 'switched off'. As with most nymph patterns retrieve very slowly with slow pulls and twitches or figure of eight.

DRESSING

Hook: Kamasan B175 size 10–12.
Tying silk: Black.
Tail: Black ostrich herl.
Body: Black ostrich herl.
Rib: Red wire over pearl lurex.
Thorax: Fluorescent green floss.
Hackle: Black hen.
Head: Clear varnish.

4 Flashback Killer

COMMENT

The killer nymph! First tied by Robert Barden this is a fly that every angler should have in his/her fly box in all shapes and forms. Here is my pattern that I use sometimes fished with Rob's original on any line from the end of May right through the season. The Lite Brite head sometimes proves to be the trigger as proved by Paul Davison and me. During the season lots of olive-coloured flies hatch in all waters.

DRESSING

Hook: Size 10–12.
Tying silk: Olive.
Tail: Olive hen hackle tips.
Body: Olive seal's fur or substitute.
Rib: Copper wire.
Thorax: Green Lite Brite.
Back: Pearl lurex.
Head: Clear varnish.

5 Diawl Bach Flashback

COMMENT

Every season the same flies keep on 'popping up' when catching the fish from Bewl water to Loch Leven and one of these seems to be the faithful Diawl Bach. Now arguably the most consistent of all nymph patterns in its various guises. 'A something and nothing pattern' Chris Ogborne once said. Well this is 'something and everything!' This is a pattern that I am reluctant to pass on as it is absolutely brilliant at catching trout. Patterns such as this one in particular can give you that vital edge when the chips are down and no one else is catching.

DRESSING

Hook: Size 10–14.
Tying silk: Brown.
Tail: Red game hackle.
Body: Pheasant tail fibres.
Beard hackle: Red game.
Wing-case: Pearl lurex.
Head: Clear varnish.

6 Green Varnished Buzzer

COMMENT

Forget the superglue or epoxy resin, I find ordinary quick-drying clear varnish covers the finished nymph equally well and in a quarter of the time. If you are fussy, you can always apply two coats. There is a whole range of these skinny life-like buzzer nymphs and I advise you to tie up various colour combinations, black, red, orange, and so on. The nymphs can be fished three to a cast, where they will sink quite quickly. Use on a floating line and just mend the slack line for a retrieve. Watch carefully for takes – some use a sight indicator.

DRESSING

Hook: Kamasan size 10–12.
Tying silk: Green.
Body: Green tying silk.
Rib: White thread.
Wing buds: Orange floss.
Apply clear varnish to whole fly twice.

7 Brian's Pearly Ribbed Hare's Ear

COMMENT

This pattern was given to me by ex-world fly fishing champion Brian Leadbetter when fishing together at Grafham Water. There was a gentle breeze and we fished in about 12ft of water with the fish just a few feet down. Brian made it look easy as he caught trout after trout using this nymph on a sink-tip line. This is a fly line that is often neglected by the majority of fly fishers – yet for Brian to give it so much importance I too was converted. This line should be part of all serious fly fishers' armoury.

DRESSING

Hook: Kamasan size 12–14.
Tying silk: Olive.
Tail: Snips of white marabou.
Body: Dubbed hare's ear fur.
Rib: Pearly fine wire.
Breathers: Snips of white marabou.
Head: Clear varnish.

8 Flashback Damsel

COMMENT

The massive Rutland Water has been where I have tried and tested many of my new fly creations. If they work there you can bet they will work elsewhere too. So it was Rutland again where this pattern was first tried. I know every fly tyer has their own variations of the damsel nymph and I am no different. This pattern was so good in the summer of 1996 that it was rarely off my cast. You can fish with any line to suit the conditions of the day. It produced fish to pulling reasonably quickly as well as the more usual figure-of-eight retrieves.

DRESSING

Hook: Long or medium shank size 10–8.
Tying silk: Olive.
Tail: Olive marabou.
Body: Olive marabou.
Rib: Silver wire.
Thorax: Hare's ear.
Flashback: Medium pearl lurex.
Head: Fluorescent green floss no. 11, apply clear varnish.

Frank Cutler

Frank Cutler is 78 years old and I have known him as a trout fisherman for 35 years. Frank started trout fishing from a strong coarse fishing background, and won five championships and the first place gold medal when the Northampton Nene Angling Club won the National Championship in 1963. During this period he was also trout fishing.

Frank has also fished for salmon and sea trout regularly, catching a number of double-figure sea trout from the Welsh Conway and Dovey while fly fishing at night. His best sea trout weighed 12lb 3oz. Big salmon have also come his way and he has landed fish of over 20lb from the Hampshire Avon (three in one day), the Tweed, the Findhorn and the Morrum in Sweden – one of 30lb from the latter.

Frank has specialized in catching big brown trout from the reservoirs. He has landed an 8-pounder from Chew Valley, one of 8½lb from Grafham and 8lb 7oz from Rutland. On top of all this he has fished for England four times.

I asked him to recall some of his old secret favourites along with the modern nymphs he likes for his selection.

1 Dark Brown Nymph

COMMENT

Best fished on a long leader (18ft) on a floating line with a very slow figure-of-eight retrieve and does very well if brown trout are predominant. It has caught a lot of fish over the years when nymph fishing was in its infancy. After dressing, pick the dark brown wool out slightly with a needle. This was a nymph I used to great effect when I fished with the late Cyril Inwood in the 1950s and 60s. It still works well to this day.

DRESSING

Hook: Long shank size 12–14.
Tying silk: Black.
Tail: Pheasant tail fibre.
Body: Dark brown wool.
Thorax: Yellow seal's fur.
Rib: Fine gold tinsel.
Wing-case: Pheasant tail fibre.
Hackle: Pale yellow.
Head: Clear varnish.

2 Black Quill Back

COMMENT

This fly fishes well from the bank or near any weed beds and can be taken for a corixa. It is a fly that was fished by my late friend Cyril Inwood, a well-known fisherman in his day. It has that caddis look about it and I now realize that when it was catching lots of trout all those years ago, fish were taking it as a buzzer nymph. So you could say it is a good all-rounder.

DRESSING

Hook: Nymph hook size 12.
Tying silk: Black.
Body: Pale yellow wool or substitute.
Wing: Black quill tapered.
Rib: Silver wire.
Hackle: Very small black hackle.
Head: Clear varnish.

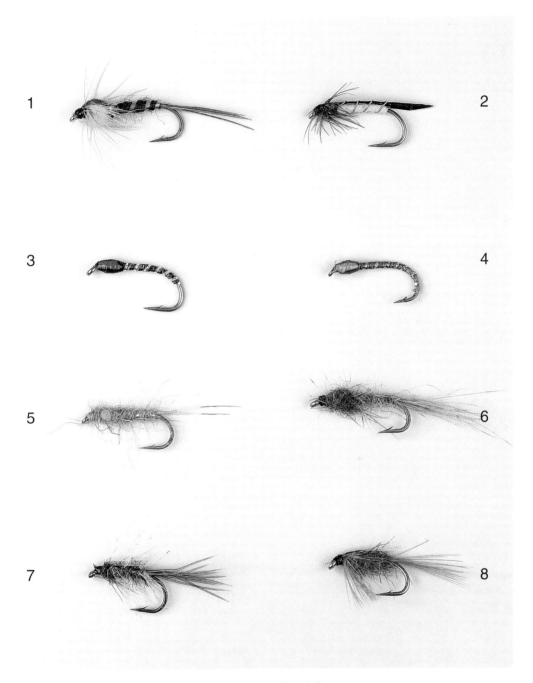

1 Dark Brown Nymph   **2** Black Quill Back   **3** Red Cheek Buzzer
4 Slimline Green Buzzer   **5** Orangehead Hare's Ear   **6** Hare's Fur Flashback
7 Hatching Midge   **8** Dilkes Hatching Nymph

3 Red Cheek Buzzer

COMMENT

This nymph is fished slowly, normally on a floating line and will catch fish all the year round from the bank. It will also catch on intermediate lines fished from boats. It is normally fished as the point fly in a team. The secret of this tiny nymph is that it looks so much like the real thing that trout take with confidence even in very clear water, normally difficult conditions.

DRESSING

Hook: Size 12–14.
Tying silk: Black.
Body: Black silk, tied to form the thorax as well.
Rib: Fine silver lurex.
Head: Formed as thorax, apply two coats of varnish and let dry before painting the red cheeks on.

4 Slimline Green Buzzer

COMMENT

When tying, keep body very slim. This colour buzzer comes into its own mid-season, fishing a team of three – black, green and claret. Change if trout are taking one colour to the point fly for a better result. It's surprising when fishing with a floating line, long leader, and three of these nymphs, how deep you can get and quite quickly. Because the nymphs are varnished and smooth they sink at speeds almost similar to a leaded fly.

DRESSING

Hook: Size 12–14.
Tying silk: Light green.
Body: Green silk, shaped with slim body and formed thorax.
Rib: Fine gold flat lurex.
Head: Green silk, shaped, apply two coats of varnish, allow to dry before painting on cheeks.

5 Orangehead Hare's Ear

COMMENT

Once again the secret of this nymph is to keep it slim. A good middle dropper when you are not sure what to put on and also a good exchange fly fished in conjunction with buzzers. It fishes best on most stillwaters from late April through to September. A very good general pattern and of course a variation of what has gone before.

DRESSING

Hook: Nymph hook size 12.
Tying silk: Black.
Tail: A few strands (long) pale hare's fur.
Body: Dubbed hare's fur; keep slim.
Rib: Fine flat tinsel.
Thorax: Dubbed hare's fur with a small orange thorax slightly back from head.
Hackle: Clear varnish.

6 Hare's Fur Flashback

COMMENT

When tying this fly, tie the pearl tinsel in at the tail, build a slim body and dub a bold dark thorax, then pull the tinsel over the back and tie in at the eye. Fished on a floater and long leader with a slow figure-of-eight retrieve. Will catch all year round. What can one say about a favourite tried and trusted nymph, another variation on the same killing theme. Mixes well on the three-fly cast with the slim varnished buzzers.

DRESSING

Hook: Nymph hook size 12.
Tying silk: Black.
Tail: A few fibres of long hare's fur.
Body: Pale hare's fur.
Thorax: Dark hare's fur.
Shell back: A strip of pearl tinsel to form back.
Rib: Fine gold wire.
Hackle: Just prick out dark fur to leave scruffy.
Head: Clear varnish.

7 Hatching Midge

COMMENT

Fished on a floating line it will take fish that are cruising on the edge of a ripple. It needs to be fished high up in the surface film hence the size 14 hook often kills best – this is very important. Only fish the larger size 12 hook in bigger wave conditions. On its day an absolutely deadly fly.

DRESSING

Hook: Size 12–14.
Tying silk: Black.
Tail: Pheasant tail fibres.
Body: Bronze peacock herl.
Rib: Silver wire.
Hackle: Badger palmered, keep small.
Head: Clear varnish.

8 Dilkes Hatching Nymph

COMMENT

This chironomid (buzzer) hatches out best in flat calms or very light ripples. It sits very upright and shows an orange speck when hatching hence size 14 to fish in surface. This is a fly that caught at Eyebrook and is favoured by John Dilkes, an old friend.

DRESSING

Hook: Size 14.
Tying silk: Black.
Tail: Orange hackle fibres.
Body: Hare's fur.
Rib: Fine gold wire.
Shell back: Pheasant tail fibres tied over to form casing.
Hackle: Small orange hen.
Head: Clear varnish.

Bob Church

Nymph fishing has grown in popularity at the same time as wet fly fishing is declining (in England). Usually the big reservoir bank fisherman is a nymph man with occasional binges on lures or dries. Nymph fishing gives you the option of fishing deep yet imitatively and this seems to be an important approach for success. The now popular varnished or superglued skinny buzzer nymphs allow for this style of fishing to be carried out. Southern reservoir specialists have developed a technique that involves 'sight indicators' and their more recent one, known as the

moustache, has caused some controversy, but only with international rules. The section on nymph fishing is larger than that of dries, lures and wets due to its current popularity. While weather and cormorant problems continue I cannot see this altering in the near future. The other point to consider is, that as the season progresses, trout that have been in the water a fair while begin to get nervous of lures. So you have more chance of sorting out a better quality resident fish by using a nymph fishing style.

1 Red Pearl Buzzer

COMMENT

Yet another buzzer nymph that will catch you a lot of fish at any time during the season. This nymph retains that hint of the bloodworm coloration which the natural has just hatched from. It works well in clear water fished on the point or middle dropper, and on a long leader. As with all nymph fishing a slow retrieve is in order.

DRESSING

Hook: Grub style size 10–12.
Tying silk: Black.
Tail: Tie right round bend; snip of white marabou.
Underbody: Red silk.
Overbody: Pearl lurex.
Rib: Fine copper wire.
Thorax: Bronze peacock herl.
Wing-cases: Orange globrite yarn.
Breathers: White marabou.
Head: Clear varnish.

2 Green Pearl Buzzer

COMMENT

Fish exactly the same as the Red Pearl Buzzer; it will give you similar success. This variant plays on the known fact that rainbows in particular go for bright greens. Scientists have proven that trout can see colours so be aware that regular colour nymphs or fly changes will give you a better chance. This is especially so if you are stationary on the bank or in an anchored boat, because then you will be covering the same fish regularly.

DRESSING

Hook: Grub style size 10–12.
Tying silk: Black.
Tail: Tie right round bend; snip of white marabou.
Body: Strand of green pearl flashabou.
Rib: 3lb breaking strain green/olive nylon.
Behind thorax: Red fluorescent floss.
Thorax: Bronze peacock herl.
Wing-cases: Orange Globrite yarn.
Breathers: White marabou.
Head: Clear varnish.

1 Red Pearl Buzzer   2 Green Pearl Buzzer   3 Mayfly Tinhead
4 Bob Church's Caenis Nymph   5 Potteries Superglue Buzzer
6 Fluoro Head Damsel   7 Dave's Stickfly   8 Scruffy Hare's Ear

3 Mayfly Tinhead

COMMENT

It had to happen, a tinhead mayfly! First I tried it as a point fly to hang my leader deep on the Irish mayfly loughs. Further up the cast I had other normal mayfly wet patterns. It did work but was not a major success. Where it happened to be very successful became apparent later when I first tried it at Dever. So it turned out to be a special for the small fisheries and impressive results came from Church Hill Farm and Lechlade before I realized that it worked at all of the small fisheries – whether mayflies were present or not!

DRESSING

Hook: Size 10–8 long shank tinhead.
Tying silk: Beige.
Tail: Brown marabou.
Body: Beige/cream mix of antron and seal's fur.
Rib: Gold oval thread.
Thorax: Same as body but built up.
Shellback: Natural cock pheasant tail fibres.
Wing-cases: Natural cock pheasant tail fibres.
Head: Eyes painted on: yellow with black pupils.

4 Bob Church's Caenis Nymph

COMMENT

After a whole day of not seeing a fish, I have several times at Pitsford witnessed a massive hatch of tiny Caenis flies (the anglers' curse) just as the sun was beginning to set. Trout do then come up and become preoccupied with their feeding on them, but what to put on when this happens has always been a head scratcher. I have found my own pattern B.C. Caenis Nymph to do the business. Fish it singularly on a 3lb low diameter nylon and floating line and hardly move it.

DRESSING

Hook: Size 16.
Tying silk: White.
Body: White tying silk.
Rib: Strand pearl crystal.
Thorax: Cream seal's fur substitute.
Hackle: One turn honey hen.
Head: Clear varnish.

5 Potteries Superglue Buzzer

COMMENT

International fly fisher Jeff Mason of Stoke gave me three of these to try when I met him at Rutland Water. I must admit it was some time before I tried them. But when I did I had a red-letter day. You need the right conditions – overcast with a light warm wind. Slow the boat right down with a maxi drogue and put up a light floating line outfit. Tie this fly on the point of a long cast and fish in a slow, very relaxed manner. Just concentrate on watching the floating line move in the wrong direction then lift the rod and the fish will be on.

DRESSING

Hook: Size 10–12.
Tying silk: Black.
Body: Black tying silk.
Rib: Fine pink copper wire.
Thorax: Black tying silk.
Wing-cases: Orange floss silk or raffine.
Whole fly: Coated with superglue, or three coats of clear varnish.

6 Fluoro Head Damsel

COMMENT

This is my competition fishing version of yet another damsel pattern nymph variant. It has been a lucky pattern in competitions when fished in conjunction with a team of three on a Hi-Di fast-sinking fly line. It works on a slow retrieve and long hang. As with many flies or lures that incorporate a fluorescent green (lime) target blob, it seems to work better than a pretty near copy of an actual damsel nymph.

DRESSING

Hook: Single or double size 10.
Tying silk: Olive.
Tail: Olive marabou.
Body: Olive marabou dubbed.
Rib: Gold oval thread.
Body hackle: Honey or white cock (tie some of each).
Head: Fluorescent lime-green Globrite floss.
Head finish: Clear varnish.

7 Dave's Stickfly

COMMENT

Dave Shipman is one of our best fly fishers whether competition or not. Although he has contributed dry flies to this book I have to mention this Stickfly of his. He gave me a couple to try a few years ago and it has become a steady consistent fish catcher throughout the main summer months. In particular it scores well at Grafham Water where it answers the question of what to put on the middle dropper when fishing a sunken line team of three.

DRESSING

Hook: Size 10–12.
Tying silk: Black.
Tag: Green flashabou strand.
Tail: Yellow floss silk.
Body: Bronze peacock herl.
Rib: Copper wire.
Thorax: Fluorescent green Globrite floss.
Hackle: Grey partridge.
Head: Clear varnish.

8 Scruffy Hare's Ear

COMMENT

This is a great all-round pattern and yet another Hare's Ear variant. Why does this nymph turn up with so many variants? – well I suppose it must be the world's best trout catcher when all its variants are considered. This scruffy pattern of mine has the lime-green touch again, and I get my best results when using it as part of a team fished on some kind of intermediate fly line. I have been favouring the clear slime line this past year and results prove it to be the right choice.

DRESSING

Hook: Size 10–12.
Tying silk: Olive.
Tail: Light brown hare's face fur.
Body: Hare's ear fur and a few fibres of orange seal's fur.
Rib: Fluorescent lime-green Globrite floss.
Thorax: Built up same as body mix.
Head: Clear varnish.

Dry Flies

Dry Flies

In the very first book on reservoir fly fishing, *Trout in Lakes and Reservoirs* by Ernest Phillips in 1914, very little was mentioned about dry fly fishing. The author was greatly in favour of wet fly fishing using all the great old traditional patterns, Wickham's Fancy, Greenwell's Glory, Mallard & Claret and March Brown, as the most successful approach by far to catching reservoir trout. He did however briefly make one observation – during summer in a flat calm, try a static dry fly. 'You can at these times tempt a big lusty fellow which would otherwise refuse all offerings.' His summing up was that dry fly on reservoirs was really rather monotonous and deprives us of the reservoir fly fishing's charm. We had to wait a long time for the next great book on reservoir fly fishing; here I refer to Tom Ivens's *Stillwater Fly Fishing* in 1952, revised in 1970 and again in 1973. Tom stated 'Dry fly fishing is the second best method for most of the time.' In general he hardly mentioned the method, by far preferring wet fly whether in lure, nymph or traditional wet form.

In 1977 my book *Reservoir Trout Fishing* came out, with a second edition in 1983. It was in fishing book terms a massive best seller and at last the dry fly began to get a mention. I talked about dry flies for Caenis time and the importance of having Pond Olive patterns in your box. I also picked out the seasonal Daddy Long Legs, Flying Black Ant, Floating Snail and Drone Fly as very important reservoir dry flies. I did also go into some detail on using sedge pattern dry flies for evening fishing in high summer.

The closest I came to using a chironomid pattern as a dry fly was with my own pattern, the Claret Hatching Midge. This I described as very effective when fished just under the surface because it looks very much like a midge pupa on the point of emerging. Slowly we were getting there.

Grafham expert dry fly fisher Bob Worts began the present craze of imitating the chironomid as a dry fly in its own right with his patterns known as Bob's Bits. This was in the mid-1980s, and very soon after Bob caught Grafham's first double-figure rainbow while using his dry emerging buzzer pattern all stillwater fly fishers wanted to know more. To put it in a nutshell a stillwater dry fly craze began. It spread from Grafham and the Midlands' reservoirs very quickly and soon the top fly fishers of the West Country were perfecting the technique and winning major competitions on these new dry flies – up until then this was unheard of. These days all top competition fly fishers have a special box of dry flies at the ready for when conditions are right. This doesn't always mean that there is a natural hatch and a rise taking place. Often, in my experience, some of the best stillwater dry fly fishing comes when there are no natural rises at all. Although this might sound strange, what happens is that the trout may be feeding out of sight probably in 20–30ft of water because conditions are right – that is, a dull grey cloudy day in July or August, with a fair wind creating a 6in to a 1½ft wave. At these times the trout leave their daphnia-preoccupied grazing and opportunistically rise and take your dry. I am of course referring to the traditional loch style drifting technique for many of my observations. However, an anchored boat or a good bank position can also work well for stillwater dry fly fishing. The growth in the use of stillwater dry flies has led to the introduction of groups of a type of pattern. A prime example are the Hoppers which have a resemblance to the crane fly family (daddies). There is a small delicate yellow-bodied summer crane fly which is present on the reservoirs from June onwards. A yellow Hopper imitates this one well, and I have taken some lovely catches at Grafham on it.

The hopper family means having all different sizes of hook from size 10 long shank down to a tiny size 16. Dave Grove proved how effective a size 16 rusty orange hopper could be when he won the English National at Bewl Water using one. This was on a most difficult day when there were 60 blanks out of 100 entrants – these had all qualified in previous knockout rounds and were the best in the country. Dave proved how skilful he was on that day, but he praised the fly for giving him six good trout. As well as sizes there are a variety of body colours and please check on Chris Howitt's hopper patterns in this book. Chris has won many major events on the reservoirs and even the mighty Loch Leven.

When putting this book together I was very impressed by the dry flies that came from our Irish contributors Brian Healy and Padraig Costello. Some of my best catches whilst fishing the Irish loughs have come while dry fly fishing, and as the years have rolled by I have become more expert at using them. A general observation is to try dry buzzer emerger patterns in March and April on Lough Corrib – the locals term this duck fly time.

Then comes that magical week in May which heralds the arrival of the mayfly. This brings most of the fish to the surface at some time over this period. On many of the Irish loughs the mayfly lingers on with occasional good hatches throughout July and August. I tend to fish a dry mayfly when I fish Lough Carra during the first week in August and I always do well with it. Also I have had browns to 3¾lb on a dry yellow Humpy on Lough Conn in August and this during a late season mayfly hatch. The fly which creates so much excitement is the autumn large daddy long legs; over the years this has produced such great sport for so many. This is a big dry fly pattern which often produces the specimen trout – it works on all stillwaters.

I really must end the dry fly introduction by stressing the importance of the dry chironomids (buzzers). The groups of dry flies that have now appeared to cater for this fishing are:- Suspender Buzzers in varying sizes and colours, Bob's Bits, Cul de Canard, and the same plus the seal's fur-bodied emergers which fish in the surface film. These patterns have proved a massive step forward in stillwater dry fly fishing and, after all, the chironomid is our most common hatching aquatic insect – so it all makes sense. When it comes to river or stream dry fly fishing this has never been in doubt with volumes on the subject. Things appear to stay fairly traditional as the old trusted patterns still work so well.

I have been fortunate enough to have fished the famous Test, Itchen, Kennet and upper Avon – all beautiful rivers on which to have a day's sport. As likely as not, there will be a hatch of some sort during the evening. Many fly fishers restrict themselves to dry fly only when fishing these rivers even though they may catch more by using the nymph. To see a trout rise up and take a well-presented dry fly is one of the most satisfying moments that any angler can experience.

Please note that some of the dry flies in this following chapter are hot off the secret list and well worth studying.

Brian Healy & Padraig Costello

Brian and Padraig met in a Dublin tackle shop a number of winters ago and found that they shared similar fly fishing tastes. Rivers such as the Suir, Boyne and Liffey hold great stocks of wary fish, some of them very large, in fact up to 5 or 6lb.

The lakes they mainly fish are Mask, Corrib, Carra and the Midland lakes; they are especially partial to the late night buzzering! They have concentrated on Corrib and Mask, lakes not normally associated with buzzer, and have been highly rewarded for their efforts. Ireland being a relatively small country puts

them in the enviable situation of being able to pick and choose the best waters for the type of fishing they prefer – Sheelin for the gnat, Mask for buzzer or Corrib for the duckfly.

Selecting flies for the submission was quite difficult, but on glancing at the flies that they did choose you will notice a common theme of softness and a touch of realism in them. Wild Irish trout are wary and therefore Brian and Padraig firmly believe in extended bodies for the larger fly species, and the usage of Cul de Canard and hen hackles on others.

1 Ethafoam Spent Mayfly

COMMENT

On reading Oliver Edwards' *Fly Tying Masterclass* I was struck by his extended body mayfly. I adapted his method slightly, switched the deer hair and parachute hackle to a normal hackle and came up with my spent. Fish love it! With the increasing fishing pressure on the Irish Midland lakes during the spent gnat, the fish in my opinion have responded by taking flies very softly and have in extreme cases changed their feeding times to avoid maximum boat traffic. This fly gives me an edge due to its realism and softness; fish will not spit this one out.

DRESSING

Hook: Kamasan B160 size 8–10.
Tying silk: Benecchi 12/0 white.
Tail: 3 microfibetts.
Body: Ethafoam – mark tail with pantone brown pen.
Wing: A pair of black & white hackles tied spent.
Head: Ethafoam pulled above and below wings – treated with epoxy for durability.

2 C–D–Z Spent Sedge

COMMENT

This is a truly great all-round fly. Padraig and I had been fishing 'F-Flies' to good effect for a number of years but I felt that they were lacking in certain situations – for example, when spent caddis were on the water. I added 'Z-Wing' material and this improved it and then began tying the body with a very bright green antron dubbing. I do not know why but fish love this colour, be it lake or river. Not only do fish take it well during sedge hatches but they rarely refuse it during B.W.O. hatches as well.

DRESSING

Hook: Kamasan B160.
Tying silk: Benecchi 12/0 white.
Body: Fluorescent green antron.
Wing: CDC + Z-wing strands.
Thorax: Dark ginger antron.
Antennae: Two pheasant tail feather fibres.
Head: Clear varnish.

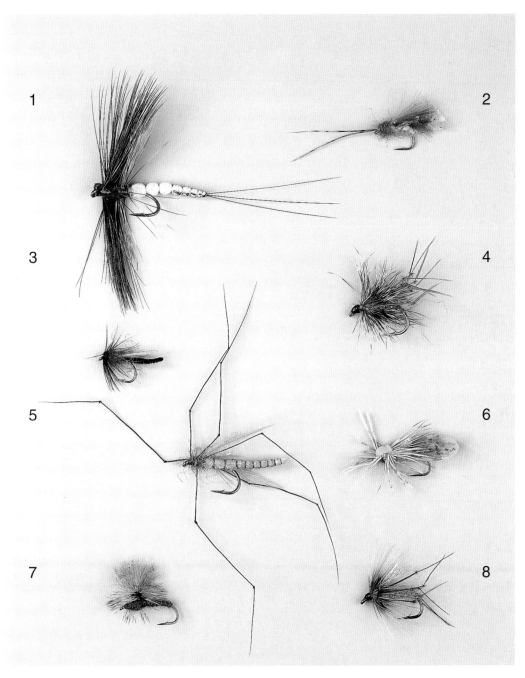

1 Ethafoam Spent Mayfly   2 C–D–Z Spent Sedge   3 Palomino Duckfly
4 Fox Squirrel Hopper   5 Ethafoam Daddy   6 Silkwing Sedge   7 Parachute Olive
8 Irish Ginger Hopper

3 Palomino Duckfly

COMMENT

I first gained information on Palominos five or six years ago when I read an article by Brett Smith in *Fly Fisherman*. Brett was cleaning up on the Bighorn with size 18 and 20 Palomino Sedges. After reading it I asked myself if these would work on Irish lakes to imitate the duckfly and buzzer. After an hour at the vice I came up with a fly which I thought would work well during the duckfly hatch. That dressing has since been refined and what you see in the photo is the stage it is at today.

DRESSING

Hook: Kamasan B160 size 12–14.
Tying silk: Benecchi 12/0 black.
Body: Micro black chenille burned to shape.
Wing: Two cream hackle tips.
Thorax: Orange antron yarn dubbed.
Hackle: Metz hen black.
Head: Black varnish.

4 Fox Squirrel Hopper

COMMENT

I have always had a high regard for hoppers due to their casual almost haphazard appearance with their scraggly legs indicating a troubled bug in the surface film. However, over the last two seasons I haven't been entirely pleased with cock hackles believing them to be too stiff. I tried changing to hen hackles greased up and was happier but then I couldn't see the fly so well when it was in a slight ripple. I then arrived at a happy medium by spinning hair in a dubbing loop. This gives the fly a 'buggier' appearance than hackles.

DRESSING

Hook: Kamasan B160 size 10–14.
Tying silk: Benecchi 12/0 black.
Body: Green antron.
Rib: Fine green lurex.
Thorax: Orange yarn.
Wing: Red fox squirrel spun in a dubbing loop and wound on hackle-like.
Head: Yellow yarn pulled up to head from underneath thus causing hair fibres to splay out.

5 Ethafoam Daddy

COMMENT

Traditional Irish Daddy patterns mostly include a long shank hook in the dressing. Trout do not like this particularly if the fly is offered in dry fly fashion. It doesn't matter much in wet fly fishing due to the speed of the retrieve. Trout will not spit this fly out when presented dry. I love to fish this pattern in the slicks during summer and autumn days when fish are cruising looking for nothing in particular but in a willing mood. Of course it fishes very well also when Daddies are around. I dress another bushier version with a brown hackle for wet fly fishing.

DRESSING

Hook: Kamasan B160 size 10.
Tying silk: Benecchi 12/0 brown.
Body: White ethafoam tinted with light brown marker pen.
Wing: Brown hackle tip.
Legs: Moose mane knotted twice for realism.
Thorax: Hare's ear coloured antron.
Head: Clear varnish.

6 Silkwing Sedge

COMMENT

This is one of my favourite sedge patterns for both rivers and lakes. I am indebted to Liam O'Broin for making me aware of the winging material that I now use in these flies, silk screen, which is used in the T-shirt printing industry. The first time I saw some of Liam's flies dressed with this wing I knew that it would be a winner due to the softness and ability to take colour. The imaginative fly dresser can imitate any sedge species with this style of fly by varying body and wing colour. I usually colour the wings with waterproof markers.

DRESSING

Hook: Drennan Emerger size 10–20.
Tying silk: Benecchi 12/0 fawn.
Body: Ginger antron dubbing.
Wing: Silk screen pre-cut and coloured brown mottled.
Overwing & Legs: Deer hair.
Thorax: Yellow ethafoam pulled back and tied in.
Head: Clear varnish.

7 Parachute Olive

COMMENT

I normally prefer to fish a *petit-jean* during olive hatches but I find that I get rejections to them during early-season hatches on both river and lake. Brian and I have had many a bankside discussion as to why this should be. Our theory is that due to the cooler air temperatures of early season it takes olives longer to hatch, and therefore the *petit-jean* sitting higher in the film is not as effective as usual. However, this parachute pattern of mine sits lower and fish take it very confidently. I had a lovely bag of four trout on Corrib last April.

DRESSING

Hook: Drennan Emerger size 14–16.
Tying silk: Benecchi 12/0 rust.
Post: Antron – cream painted grey with marker pen.
Hackle: Badger saddle.
Rib: Pearsall's silk – orange.
Tie in this order.

8 Irish Ginger Hopper

COMMENT

I tied this fly initially as a general wet fly that would look like food to trout and have movement. It has proved to be an effective fly for me in a number of situations. I love to fish it on the tail during olive hatches fished wet, or on the top dropper during buzzer hatches, particularly in light winds. Treated with floatant this is a deadly buzzer emerger, adult or cripple. The fish love it so who cares what they take it for? It doesn't look much of a dry fly but its buggy appearance and softness appeal greatly to trout.

DRESSING

Hook: Hayabusa size 12–14.
Tying silk: Benecchi 12/0 ginger.
Body: Ginger antron dubbing
Rib: Fine copper wire.
Thorax: ¾ turns of dubbing.
Legs: 6 dyed olive pheasant fibres.
Wing: 4 fibres of Benecchi mother-of-pearl thread.
Hackle: Badger hen.
Head: Black varnish.

David Shaw

David Shaw comes from Blythe Bridge in Staffordshire. He is looked upon by all his trout fishing friends as the master of the fly tying vice. He is currently the Captain of the Five Towns Fly Fishers. He has also fished for England twice in the Home International Competition. He won the prestigious Bob Church Classic in 1994 and has also been overall winner of the Benson & Hedges Fly Tying Competition run in the *Trout Fisherman* magazine. Over the last few years dry fly fishing on stillwaters, particularly the large reservoirs, has become increasingly popular. It is easy to see why as it is probably the most satisfying way to catch trout. Fishing from a boat and watching one of your flies disappear in a swirl, and hearing the 'hiss' of your fly line when it leaves the surface as you lift into a fighting bar of silver, is as good as it gets. The following patterns are a few of the most successful David has used over the past few seasons.

1 Fiery Shipmans

COMMENT

I am convinced that it is the particular blend of these two colours that make this fly such a killing pattern. On several trips to Blithfield Reservoir last summer both my boat partner and I caught limit bags, with 90 per cent of the trout coming to this pattern. Fished static and then left seems to attract smash takes, so make sure you tie up more than a couple when you try them.

DRESSING

Hook: Tiemco 921 size 10–12.
Tying silk: Claret.
Tail & head filaments: Polar bear.
Body: Medium claret and fiery brown seal's fur mixed 50/50.
Rib: Stretched Flashabou.
Head: Clear varnish.

2 Shuck Shipmans

COMMENT

This fly is a favourite of Lester Booth, who fished for the England World team in 1996. It works particularly well when the trout are being really difficult and feeding on buzzer shucks, and seem to be ignoring conventional patterns. One such day last season at Draycote, this pattern provided seven fish between my boat partner and myself, which was not too bad when most people were only catching one or two. To fish this fly just cast it out and leave it, hopefully the trout will do the rest.

DRESSING

Hook: Tiemco 921 size 10–12.
Tying silk: Primrose.
Tail & head filaments: Polar bear.
Body: 2/3 yellow seal's fur, 1/3 orange seal's fur blended.
Rib: Stretched Flashabou.
Head: Clear varnish.

1 Fiery Shipmans   2 Shuck Shipmans   3 Hawthorn Dry   4 Draycote Dry Olive
5 Mini-Hopper   6 Grey Emerger   7 Bill's Big Red   8 Scruffy Mo

3 Hawthorn Dry

COMMENT

In 1994 I was fortunate enough to win the Bob Church/*Angling Times* Classic at Rutland Water. At 2pm I had caught three fish in the Yacht Club area, so I suggested to my boat partner that we move to Sykes Lane. When we arrived a few fish were moving on top taking hawthorn flies. I changed to a floating line and a team of dries, with this fly on the point. Casting to rising fish then pulling, trout were bow-waving after the Hawthorn and as a result I landed a further seven fish, among which was the best fish of the day.

DRESSING

Hook: Tiemco 921 size 10–12.
Tying silk: Black.
Tail: Lureflash twinkle.
Body: Canadian dazzle dubbing (Black/Claret).
Rib: Stretched Flashabou.
Head: Ethafoam, doubled and black pantoned to match body.

4 Draycote Dry Olive

COMMENT

Draycote is a reservoir that generally has a good hatch of olives during the season. Not only that, but trout take the olive, which they don't seem to do at some other large waters. The parachute hackle makes this pattern sit high in the water and with the white ethafoam on top as a sight marker it is easy to spot when the fly is gulped down. Fishing over Musborough Shoal we have had great sport catching 3lb plus rainbows with this fly that seems to attract the better quality fish.

DRESSING

Hook: Tiemco 921 size 10–12.
Tying silk: Olive.
Tail: Grizzle hackle fibres.
Body: Olive dyed goose herl.
Rib: Stretched Flashabou.
Hackle: Grizzle tied parachute style.
Head: Ethafoam trimmed to shape.

5 Mini-Hopper

COMMENT

Sometimes these small hoppers work so it is always worthwhile having a few in your box. At Rutland Water in September we were fishing down the centre of the North arm over deep water. There was an easterly breeze with overcast conditions and a fine drizzle all day. The rainbows were up and feeding but proving to be very difficult. I managed to land seven trout during match hours, five of which took this fly. Using a WF6 line with 5lb to 4lb leader material the fish need to be played very gently.

DRESSING

Hook: Kamasan B400 size 14.
Tying silk: Primrose.
Butt: Globrite no. 6.
Body: Fiery brown seal's fur.
Rib: Stretched Flashabou.
Hackle: Pale ginger.
Legs: Six cock pheasant tail fibres, knotted.
Head: Clear varnish.

6 Grey Emerger

COMMENT

This pattern works well when the trout are feeding on buzzers just in the surface film, which usually means they are difficult to catch. As this fly needs to be fished static I usually fish it on the point, which means that the middle and top droppers need to be highly visible dries to act as sight indicators. At the sign of a slight movement of the droppers, just lift into the fish, or at least that is the theory! This fly has caught fish at Rutland, Draycote, Pitsford and Blithfield.

DRESSING

Hook: Partridge K2B size 14.
Tying silk: Primrose.
Tail: Lureflash twinkle.
Body: Pale grey fur (Russian giant vole) or substitute.
Rib: Stretched pearl flashabou.
Thorax: Orange seal's fur.
Thorax cover: Two CDC feathers tied in and pulled forward.
Head: Clear varnish.

7 Bill's Big Red

COMMENT

Devised by Bill Latham of the very successful Blagdon team, this pattern has won many competitions, particularly at Chew Valley Lake. When tying in the antron use open turns of silk, so that the antron shows through under the body. The secret of this pattern is the way that the antron is used as a 'post' for the parachute, and then pulled forward, making the hackle slope and giving the fly a tendency to fish the rear of the body sub-surface. The colour is again a blend of red and orange that a lot of trout find irresistible.

DRESSING

Hook: Kamasan B400 size 10.
Tying silk: Orange.
Tail & head filaments: White antron tied in and used as a post for the parachute, then pulled forward.
Body: Red seal's fur.
Rib: Very fine gold wire.
Hackle: Pale ginger, parachute style.
Head: Clear varnish.

8 Scruffy Mo

COMMENT

A silver medal for the Blagdon team at Rutland Water in the Benson & Hedges International Final came as a result of this fly. From a seemingly hopeless position at the end of Day One, they came from nowhere on the second day, and were unlucky not to win. The material for the body of the original pattern came from John Braithwaite's cat, hence 'Scruffy Mo'. I have used the pattern since and it comes into its own in September/October when the fish are feeding on grey/brown buzzer, particularly in dull, overcast conditions.

DRESSING

Hook: Kamasan B400 size 12.
Tying silk: Black.
Body: Pale grey fur (Russian giant vole) or substitute.
Rib: Single strand of black floss.
Hackle: Pale ginger.
Legs: Six cock pheasant tail fibres, knotted.
Head: Clear varnish.

Chris Guthrie

Although Chris had a full career as a top-class professional footballer he always found spare time for his favoured trout and salmon fishing. Being a Geordie, Chris has had to travel down to the Midlands Reservoirs for his top-class trout fishing.

He is a winner of many competitions and he was a founder member of the Northumbrian Badgers team. Chris has represented England in Internationals twice and truly loves the competitive side of fly fishing.

Always the keen fly tyer, he will tie up a quick half-dozen patterns on the eve of an important match. It's amazing how many anglers never seem satisfied with the thousands of flies they already have. Chris has selected the flies that have produced good results for him over the past eight years or so.

1 Summer Yellow Daddy

COMMENT

Fish this as a single fly lightly ginked to ensure it rides high on the surface. I first tied this fly for Grafham Water in the early 1990s where these small yellow daddies hatch and finish up on the water in good numbers during June and July. Naturally this dry fly works best at Grafham, but I have also had good success at Rutland Water. I took fourteen rainbows on it during the 1994 Benson & Hedges match. Do not confuse this pattern with the similar Yellow Hopper.

DRESSING

Hook: Drennan Sproat size 12.
Tying silk: Beige.
Body: A dubbing seal's fur mix of 60 per cent dark yellow and 40 per cent orange.
Rib: Flat gold tinsel.
Legs: Four pheasant tail fibres knotted – two forward, two behind.
Wings: Pair red game hackle points.
Hackle: Red game, two turns.
Head: Clear varnish.

2 Guthrie's Beetle

COMMENT

This is quite simply the easiest fly to tie. However, it remains one of the most effective in the north of England when waters are calm. This fly fishes well from May to December, especially when small black beetles or black smuts are on the water. This fly was featured in the *Trout Fisherman* magazine of September 1996. A big reservoir where this fly works well is Kielder, where it takes the little wild browns and the stocked rainbows.

DRESSING

Hook: Mustad 80000.
Tying silk: Uni-thread 8/0 black.
Body: Uni-thread half-way along the shank. Two turns of black SLF behind the eye of the hook.
Hackle: One and half turns black cock.
Head: Black thread and clear varnish.

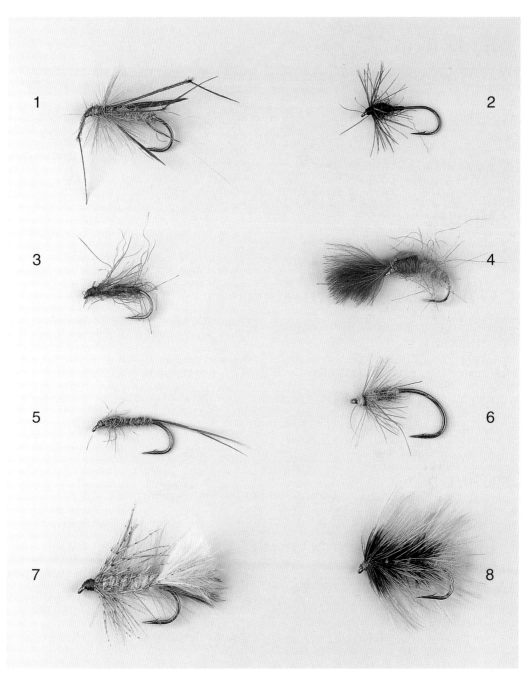

1 Summer Yellow Daddy 2 Guthrie's Beetle 3 Little Reden
4 Golden CDC Shuttlecock 5 Little Green Dry Nymph 6 Half Hare Dry Nymph
7 Parker's Partridge 8 Greenwell Palmer

3 Little Reden

COMMENT

This is one of my favourite dry flies to use when it is a dark and miserable day. I took eight fish for 33lb in the mid-1990s with this fly on Rutland Water. Obviously it is taken by the trout for the emerging buzzer; it is quite amazing how they take it just at the precise moment of emergence. An orange version of this little dry fly may also be worth having at the ready in the box. Keep your leader quite fine – no more than 4lb breaking strain and clear in colour.

DRESSING

Hook: Kamasan Emerger size 14.
Tying silk: Black Uni-thread 8/0.
Body: Fiery claret SLF.
Rib: Fine red tinsel.
Wing: A few strands of white deer hair.
Hackle: Two turns of red game.
Head: Whip finish black thread and clear varnish.

4 Golden CDC Shuttlecock

COMMENT

This is a fairly recent development of the Shuttlecock Buzzer. It fishes well in bright conditions. This fly helped me to win the overall heats of the Benson & Hedges in 1995. To fish this fly, cast four or five yards in front of moving fish. It is surprising just how quickly the trout will find the fly. Similar patterns did very well for the Scottish competitors from the Orkneys and one of their team won the Benson & Hedges International event using it.

DRESSING

Hook: Gold size 14.
Tying silk: Beige Uni-thread 8/0.
Body: Orange seal's fur, tied round the bend, followed by fiery claret SLF for the thorax.
Wing: 4 CDC feathers pulled over the thorax and whip finish.
Head: Clear varnish.

5 Little Green Dry Nymph

COMMENT

This fly catches fish all through the season and is again relatively simple to tie. It was this fly that took the best bag on both days for my team, the Northumbrian Badgers, in the 1993 Benson & Hedges International final on Rutland Water; it is also a tremendous fly in the north. The method of fishing is to cast to the side of the boat, 10–15yd, then give one long draw and hold. This is a dry nymph that fishes in the surface film. Once again keep everything very delicate.

DRESSING

Hook: Wet Fly Supreme size 12–16.
Tying silk: Beige Uni-thread 8/0.
Tail: Three strands of dirty green goose tail feathers.
Body: Green goose feather quill fibres.
Rib: Fine green wire.
Thorax: Hare's ear.
Wing-case: Green goose.
Head: Clear varnish.

6 Half Hare Dry Nymph

COMMENT

The method of fishing is either static or with a slow figure-of-eight retrieve. This is another variation of the Bath & Kent Lads anorexic theme. It helped me and my team-mates to win the Benson & Hedges National Final in 1996 at Rutland. Fish this fly in the surface film where the trout are used to taking the hatching nymph. Although it is very nice to be able to cast in front of a rising trout this is not often possible on the big reservoirs. So just fish this fly blindly and have faith – then see how it gets fish to rise up seemingly from nowhere.

DRESSING

Hook: Fine curved sedge size 10.
Tying silk: Fluorescent orange.
Tag: Fluorescent orange silk.
Body: Hare's ear tied sparse over the orange thread, half-way down the shank.
Rib: Fine copper wire.
Hackle: One turn red game.
Head: Whip finish the orange silk and clear varnish.

7 Parker's Partridge

COMMENT

I am indebted to my team-mate, Dave Parker, for this fly. Dave won first place from the bank at Draycote in the Trout Masters final in 1994. Dave finds the Parker's Partridge fishes best on the top dropper on a floating line where it creates quite a wake. It is also an obviously superb dry sedge pattern fished singly and static, or as part of a team (point fly) very slowly moved.

DRESSING

Hook: Anglian Water size 10.
Tying silk: Red.
Tail: Peach over brown marabou.
Body: Lamb's wool with honey hackle palmered through.
Rib: Fine gold thread.
Hackle: Grey partridge one turn.
Head: Clear varnish.

8 Greenwell Palmer

COMMENT

This is a great fly for all northern waters of England. I also tried it out on the western loughs of Ireland where it produced excellent results on Mask, Carra and Conn. Even the local ghillie experts Robbie and Kenneth O'Grady could not believe its pulling powers on Mask – usually a dour water. The fly is ginked up to fish dry on the top dropper of a team, cast 10–15yd then make three pulls and hold.

DRESSING

Hook: Drennan Wet Fly Sproat size 10.
Tying silk: Uni-thread 8/0 black.
Tail: Fluorescent pink tow wool.
Body: 4 Greenwell hen hackles palmered through.
Rib: Heavy embossed silver tinsel.
Head hackle: Two slightly bigger Greenwell hen hackles tied umbrella style.
Head: Clear varnish.

John Maitland

John has fished reservoirs for over fifty years, therefore most of his patterns in this selection started off with stillwaters in mind, but several have proved effective with river trout. The Cul de Canard Muddler has, in addition, been attractive to salmon when fished over the lies so as to make a wake as it skates across and through the ripples. Since John gets such a buzz from taking reservoir trout on dry flies, there is an understandable bias towards such patterns in this selection. Incidentally, do not think that dry flies attract only standard-size fish: his two best reservoir rainbows so far –

7½lb (Grafham) and 6½lb (Rutland) – both fell to seal's-fur emergers in the style of his Rutland Emerger. Cul de Canard has brought a new dimension into dry fly dressings and John now makes a lot of use of these feathers. Its ability to pop a fly back to the surface after it has been pulled under is amazing and some days this action is highly attractive to the trout. The two mayfly dressings have proved outstanding for John at the appropriate stages of the fly's life cycle. John has fished in the England International team once and has been a prominent member of the RAF team.

1 Hatching Mayfly

COMMENT

A super pattern based on one by Geoffrey Rivaz. The tail is tied less than an inch long and probably represents the shuck. When tying, secure the wing first, with the butt ends of the hair to the rear and overwound to form a foundation for the body. The fly seems more attractive if some short ends of this hair are left sticking out at the rear, perhaps looking like the legs of the shuck. The seal's fur front body is carried forward of the wing and the hackle palmered over it from front to rear and secured by the ribbing wire.

DRESSING

Hook: Longshank size 10–12.
Tying silk: Black or brown.
Tail: About 8 fibres of cock pheasant tail plus deer hair stubs.
Body rear: Wind on thick end of the pheasant tail fibres.
Body front: Dubbed seal's fur, olive, cream.
Rib: Fine copper wire.
Wing: An upright tuft of deer hair about ⅛ inch back from hook eye.
Hackle: Olive or honey cock, palmered.
Head: Clear varnish.

2 Cul de Canard Spent Mayfly

COMMENT

It is best to tie the wings on first, on to a silk foundation. If you can get them, the Cul de Canard feathers from a goose are ideal. These wings will remain flush on the surface and help float the fly; the hackle only represents legs. Alternatively, instead of a hackle, one can dub on a thorax of brown seal's fur around the wing roots and pick out some fibres. This pattern imitates the female mayfly that is dead or dying after egg laying is complete. It therefore works best during the spinner fall, normally during late afternoon or evening.

DRESSING

Hook: Long shank 10–12.
Tying silk: Black.
Tail: Cock pheasant tail fibres or badger hair.
Body: Sheep's wool (off fences or hedges).
Rib: Dark brown sewing thread.
Wing: Two big CDC plumes, tied spent.
Hackle: Two turns of short-fibred grizzle cock.
Head: Clear varnish.

1 Hatching Mayfly   **2** Cul de Canard Spent Mayfly   **3** Hare's Ear Cul de Canard Emerger   **4** Shuttlecock Cul de Canard Hatching Buzzer   **5** Rutland Emerger **6** John's Yellow Hopper   **7** Buoyant Damsel Nymph   **8** Cul de Canard Muddler

3 Hare's Ear Cul de Canard Emerger

COMMENT

Invaluable when the fish are taking midges in the process of hatching. The body is not greased and it fishes right in the surface film. In 1996 I found it extremely effective in sizes 12 and 14 for Rutland trout after corixa in the shallows. In this case the fly seems more attractive when tweaked along so that it is drawn under and pops back to the surface due to the buoyancy of the Cul de Canard wing. Also, on a size 16 or 18 hook and without the red thread it is a real killer of chalk stream fish sipping down hatching olives.

DRESSING

Hook: Size 12–18.
Tying silk: Black or to match body colour.
Body: Dubbed hare's ear fur; grey squirrel body fur can be substituted.
Rib: Narrow pearl, or gold wire.
Thorax: Two turns of fluorescent red thread just behind the wing.
Wing: Two to four CDC plumes; tied sloping over body and as long as hook shank.
Head: Clear varnish.

4 Shuttlecock Cul de Canard Hatching Buzzer

COMMENT

When tying shuttlecock style flies I find it easier to start by tying in the Cul de Canard plumes projecting over the hook eye. When the waste is cut away it leaves just the front of the body part thickened, a good foundation for the thorax. Aim to tie the remainder of the body slim so that it will penetrate the surface easily and then hang under water, unlike my Cul de Canard emerger that lies in the film. This pattern represents the black buzzers of spring, but variations on this theme with different colour thread to match the hatch all catch well.

DRESSING

Hook: Size 12–16 down eye.
Tying silk: Black.
Body: Wound from the tying thread.
Rib: Narrow pearl.
Thorax: Two turns of fluorescent red or orange thread.
Wing: Two or four CDC plumes over hook eye.
Head: Clear varnish.

5 Rutland Emerger

COMMENT

I have used this style of tying emergers, using varying body colours, for many years; the deer hair tag may give an impression of a shuck. This particular colour variation in size 12 or even 10 works well if the trout are after the big dark brown buzzer as it hatches at Rutland, usually between mid-May and mid-June. It has also worked well on other waters such as Chew Valley. If the water is fairly calm I trim off the hackle and body fibres below the hook, but in a big wind/wave it should be left more bushy.

DRESSING

Hook: Size 10–16, mainly 12 and 14.
Tying silk: Red or brown.
Tail: A short tuft of 8–10 deer hair fibres, cut off square.
Body: Dubbed seal's fur; rear quarter hot orange, remainder fiery brown.
Rib: Narrow pearl.
Hackle: Natural red or ginger cock.
Head: Clear varnish.

6 John's Yellow Hopper

COMMENT

Quite often in midsummer, from June to August, a fairly small yellowish daddy-long-legs blows onto stillwaters. If there are enough of them the trout take advantage and then this pattern yields good results. It is also worth trying when medium-sized ginger sedges are on the water in the evening. I have caught good Rutland trout on it, while a friend used it to attract a marvellous 6lb rainbow from Loch Leven. The yellow thread I use for ribbing is Madeira Neon (shade 1823) available from needlework shops.

DRESSING

Hook: 2x long shank size 10–12.
Tying silk: Yellow or orange.
Body: Dubbed ginger seal's fur.
Rib: Fluorescent yellow thread.
Legs: 6 or 8 knotted cock pheasant tail fibres.
Hackle: Natural red or ginger cock.
Head: Clear varnish.

7 Buoyant Damsel Nymph

COMMENT

When damsel nymphs are migrating ashore, a good imitation can be devastatingly effective. The basis of this pattern is a conventional damsel imitation by my friend Dick Stephen. However, it can fish deeper than the migrating nymphs that stay near the surface as they head for shore to hatch, and it then may catch on the silkweed often found at damsel time. Hence my modification of tying a foam slip as wing buds and thorax cover to keep the nymph near the surface.

DRESSING

Hook: Short shank size 10.
Tying silk: Olive.
Tail: Olive marabou.
Body: Olive dyed goose herl.
Rib: Olive-green twinkle (one strand).
Hackle: Grey partridge or same dyed olive.
Wing-case: Closed-cell foam, olive or fawn.
Head: Clear varnish.

8 Cul de Canard Muddler

COMMENT

This muddler is the ultimate in floatability and is intended to be used as a wake fly. If the Cul de Canard plumes are natural grey the whole fly has the sort of colours found in many sedges and stone flies. The bunch of Cul de Canard is tied onto the hook first, leaving the front third of the shank bare and then the deer hair is spun on to this and clipped in the usual muddler way. If more colour is desired a fluorescent floss tail tuft can be tied in before the Cul de Canard.

DRESSING

Hook: Size 10–12 wide gape.
Tying silk: Any colour, strong.
Wing: 5 or 6 CDC plumes.
Ruff: Flaired deer hair.
Head: Flaired deer clipped and finished with a spot of clear varnish at tie-off point.

Chris Howitt

Chris has represented England at World, Commonwealth and European level and is the current Commonwealth champion. He is particularly proud to have been a member at the last two Commonwealth Championships, with England winning the event in both Canada and Scotland. Chris has fished twelve times for the England Loch Style Home International team and once in the Rivers Home International team in the last decade, winning two Brown Bowls and several Grafham trophies in the process. Along with numerous other team events and individual achievements, he has won the Bob Church/*Angling Times* Classic twice. He is a dry fly enthusiast, but not a fanatic. He is also very keen on nymph fishing particularly since joining the crack Fulling Mill Weald of Kent team two years ago.

1 Fuzzy Hopper

COMMENT

Although the hopper works superbly as a static dry, many anglers quickly discover how effective it is when pulled. My loosely dressed and upwardly teased tying of John Moore's classic fly is meant for use as both. Lightly grease the top half of the fly and when left static it will fish in the film, but when pulled it will bulge just under the surface. The fiery brown Fuzzy Hopper helped the England Team win gold medals and me the individual title at the 1995 Commonwealth Championships at Loch Leven in Scotland.

DRESSING

Hook: Kamasan B830 size 12 and 14.
Tying silk: Uni-thread red 6/0 or 8/0.
Rib: Medium pearl mylar.
Butt: Pearl (optional).
Underbody: Pearl mylar.
Body: Seal's fur loosely and lightly dressed and stroked backwards with velcro.
Legs: Four knotted cock pheasant centre tail fibres.
Hackle: Chinese red game three turns. Stroke fibres backwards and upwards.
Head: Clear varnish.

2 Silver Invicta Muddler

COMMENT

I usually omit the blue jay throat hackle (mainly because it is awkward to tie in), and leave just a few strands of deer hair as the wing and the fly still works just as well as the original, if not better. Buff the mylar before tying in to give that extra sparkle, or alternatively overwrap with pearl. It works well in traditional muddler style or, as I prefer, like a wounded fry with a slow twitched retrieve, occasionally pausing for a few seconds. Try it when trout are chasing and mopping up stunned pinfry when anything from static to a ton-up retrieve may work.

DRESSING

Hook: Kamasan B830 size 12.
Tying silk: Un-ithread black 6/0.
Rib: Fine silver wire.
Tail: Golden pheasant topping.
Body: Silver mylar, palmered with red game.
Head: Pea-sized brown deer hair.

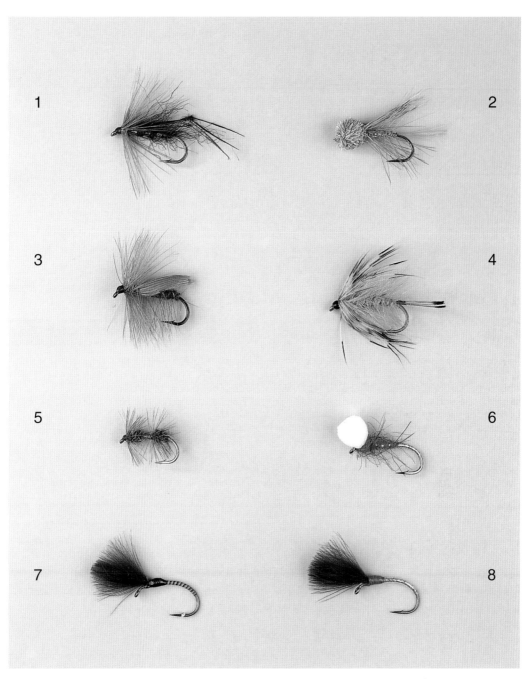

1 Fuzzy Hopper   2 Silver Invicta Muddler   3 Cinnamon Sedge
4 Fluorescent Partridge Mayfly   5 Hare's Ear Ant   6 Suspender Midge
7 Quill Proto-Cul   8 Pearl Proto-Cul

3 Cinnamon Sedge

COMMENT

I was introduced to this tying of the Cinnamon Sedge by Tony Hern when he was manager of Rockbourne Trout Fishery. For many years we shared a boat at Chew in June and Blagdon in October and Tony's Cinnamon Sedge was rarely off our casts. This pattern is an excellent general sedge imitation and was my first successful reservoir dry fly. Being well palmered, it is ideal for twitching and scurrying across the surface like the naturals. If left static it will pull up cruising and often deep-lying fish when no fish are rising.

DRESSING

Hook: Scorpion Down Eye Dry size 10–12.
Tying silk: Uni-thread black 6/0.
Rib: Medium oval gold tinsel.
Body: Cock pheasant centre tail fibres palmered with Chinese red game hackle.
Wing: Cinnamon dyed mallard primary folded and tied roof fashion over the body.
Hackle: Chinese red game.
Head: Clear varnish.

4 Fluorescent Partridge Mayfly

COMMENT

I will always experiment with patterns, even adding fluorescents to traditional Irish Mayfly patterns and this is one that paid off. This fly outperformed all my traditional Irish Mayfly patterns and combined with a Fulling Mill Silver Invicta double, helped the England team to win gold medals and myself the Brown Bowl individual title at the 1992 International at Lough Melvin. Fish it on the top dropper, traditional Irish style, short casting and stroking the surface – but watch out for those Sonaghan, they are devilishly fast!

DRESSING

Hook: Kamasan B830 size 12.
Tying silk: Uni-thread black 6/0.
Rib: Fine/medium gold wire.
Tail: Golden pheasant tippet dyed fluorescent orange.
Body: Golden olive and fluorescent yellow seal's fur, palmered with golden olive cock hackle.
Hackle: Yellow French Partridge with a stiff fluorescent lime-green cock hackle behind.
Head: Clear varnish.

5 Hare's Ear Ant

COMMENT

This fly will catch its fair share of fish when ants are on the trout's menu, but it also works very well as a general small beetle pattern. Small bugs and beetles are often blown onto the water during the warmer months and are eagerly taken by opportunistic trout. Fish it on the middle dropper position or as a single dropper with a shuttlecock cul de canard on the point (to aid turnover and accuracy), targeting individual fish that are selectively taking beetles or ants. Treat the fly with floatant.

DRESSING

Hook: Scorpion All-Purpose Lightweight size 14.
Tying silk: Uni-thread red 8/0.
Body: Oval-shaped and tightly bound short dark hare's ear fur.
Hackle: Small red game.
Head: Clear varnish.

6 Suspender Midge

COMMENT

This variation of John Goddard's Suspender Midge is simply an up-to-date 'Raider' style version. Tied short and slim, it will pierce the surface film for immediate effect. It is a good fly to fish in a wave when other emergers are being drowned. I prefer it as point fly whether fished on its own or with droppers. If you are getting refusals when fishing this fly static, try a fluorocarbon leader and when a fish swirls, pull the fly away with a smooth sweep of the arm and then leave it. The fluorocarbon leader should sink the fly and it will rise again slowly.

DRESSING

Hook: Scorpion All-Purpose Medium size 10–12.
Tying silk: Uni-thread red 6/0.
Rib: Fine pearl mylar.
Butt: Pearl mylar.
Body: Bright red seal's fur or substitute, with a few strands of dark claret.
Thorax: Same mix as body.
Head: Shaped cylindrical ethafoam.

7 Quill Proto-Cul

COMMENT

When I was a member of the Bewl Bridge Team, we came up with the idea of tying in a shuttlecock Cul de Canard wing 'short' from the eye on or above water level. I combined this idea with an imitative slim quill body and pronounced thorax on a curved grub/buzzer hook to create the Proto-cul profile. This fly was used to great effect when we won the 1994 Partridge competition at Bewl Water and has continued to be one of my most successful dries. It excels in calm conditions when trout are sipping green and olive midge.

DRESSING

Hook: Scorpion Super Grub or Mustad 80250 size 10–14.
Tying silk: Uni-thread olive dun 6/0 or 8/0.
Body: Stripped olive peacock herl.
Thorax: Flattened elliptical-shaped thorax built up with olive dun thread.
Wing: Three, four or five cul de canard feathers depending on hook size.
Head/thread: Superglue or varnish.

8 Pearl Proto-Cul

COMMENT

The Pearl Proto-Cul evolved after several months of experimenting with different colours and various materials following the success of the Quill Proto-Cul. Pheasant tail, silk and hare's ear bodies all worked on their day, but I discovered that using translucent pearl over a body of fire orange thread, with a fire orange thorax, was generally more consistent. It is deadly in flat calms or light ripples when casting to fish feeding on buzzers trapped by, and hanging in, the surface film.

DRESSING

Hook: Scorpion Super Grub or Mustad 80250 size 10–14.
Tying silk: Uni-thread fire orange 6/0 or 8/0.
Body: Fire orange thread overwrapped with medium pearl mylar.
Thorax: Flattened elliptical-shaped thorax built up with fire orange thread.
Wing: Three, four or five cul de canard feathers depending on hook size.
Head/Thorax: Superglue or varnish.

Clive Perkins

Clive Perkins' home water is Bewl, a reservoir that has bred a good number of today's top fly fisherman. Clive is also a member of the Bristol team which has won a number of top competitions this past decade.

Clive has represented England on two occasions and is quite versatile in his approach. Even so, Clive is known best of all for his expertise at dry fly fishing. It is when using some of his dry fly patterns shown here that he has achieved his most memorable successes.

It is very noticeable that his tyings show the great detail and neatness these little dries demand.

1 Le Shuttle

COMMENT

This is the original pattern I first tied about five years ago; since then there are too many variations to mention. After a great deal of time spent 'bench testing' (a bowl of water in my fly tying room) I worked out the best hook type and amount of Cul de Canard needed to make this fly sit correctly in the water. This pattern is most effective when fished on a single fly cast and used to target individual feeding fish, cruising in the top foot. I believe its success is due to the profile of the fly hanging vertically in the water makes it more visible.

DRESSING

Hook: Kamasan B170 size 12 .
Tying silk: Black.
Body: Black pheasant tail.
Tag: Globrite no. 4.
Rib: Fine copper or silver wire.
Wing: Three cul de canard feathers.
Head: Clear varnish.

2 Parachute

COMMENT

I normally fish this fly on the top dropper; this fly is made very visible at distance by the wool post that the hackle is wound around – in varying light conditions black rather than white is more visible. After ginking the hackle this fly is exceptionally buoyant and works either fished static or moved. If you cast at a fish and the fly is rejected, it is worth pulling the fly away from the fish; initially the fly will go under the water and the fish will follow, and when you stop, the fly will come back up to the surface more often than not inducing the fish to take.

DRESSING

Hook: Kamasan B170 size 12 .
Tying silk: Red.
Body: Mid-claret seal's fur.
Rib: Pearl flashabou.
Post: White fluorescent wool.
Hackle: Three turns ginger cock.
Head: Clear varnish.

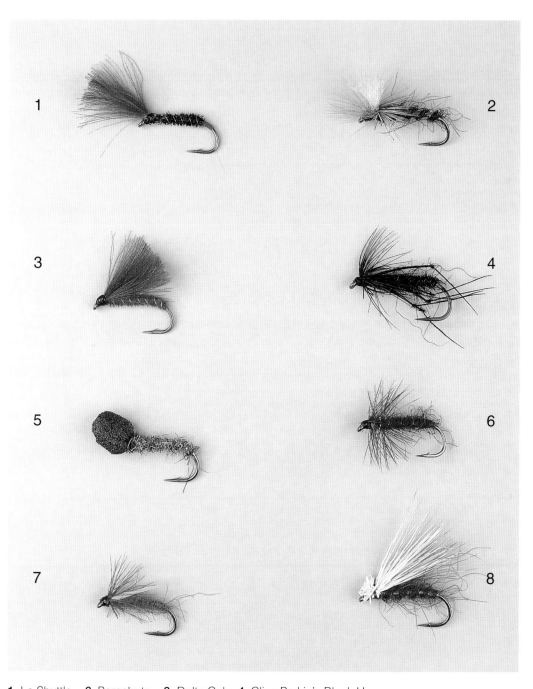

1 Le Shuttle   2 Parachute   3 Delta Cul   4 Clive Perkin's Black Hopper
5 Hare's Ear Suspender Buzzer   6 Semi-Palmer   7 U.F.O. Red Bits
8 Fiery Brown Elk Hair Sedge

3 Delta Cul

COMMENT

I normally fish this fly on the top dropper with a combination of hoppers and bits; it works better on smaller sizes 12, 14 and 16. I tie the body of this fly with either dyed turkey or pheasant tail rather than more buoyant material, because it will sit lower in the water and, as we are all aware, there are instances when dry flies sitting high in the water are rejected by fish because they are reluctant to stick their heads out; they would rather suck the fly down and so this is the time to try this fly.

DRESSING

Hook: Kamasan B170 size 12.
Tying silk: Red.
Body: Red dyed turkey.
Rib: Fine silver wire.
Wing: 3 CDC feathers.

4 Clive Perkins' Black Hopper

COMMENT

I normally fish this fly as my point fly; black is always a good bet to start with and it will often work. If casting to moving fish I personally prefer to tie this fly with a hen hackle, I believe that it sits better in the surface; however, if there are very few fish moving on top I will use a hopper tied with cock hackle, so that when it's either figure-of-eighted or pulled it will create a wake that might well induce a nearby fish to take. This pattern has been used to great effect on Llyn Brenig, the only difference was that the legs were tied with knotted dyed red tippets.

DRESSING

Hook: Kamasan B400 size 10.
Tying silk: Black.
Body: Black seal's fur.
Rib: Fine silver wire.
Legs: Knotted black pheasant tail.
Hackle: Three turns black hen.
Head: Clear varnish.

5 Hare's Ear Suspender Buzzer

COMMENT

I normally fish this fly as my point fly, but as with a shuttlecock cul, it can be used very effectively when targeting single feeding fish. When fishing single flies I fish a finer leader than with a team of flies. Suspender buzzers are less visible, to the angler, than most other dries due to the fact that the tip of the ethafoam is fust sitting in the surface film and fish will tend to suck them in without sticking their heads out of the water.

DRESSING

Hook: Kamasan B160 size 10.
Tying silk: Black.
Body: Hare's fur.
Rib: Pearl flashabou.
Wing: Black ethafoam teardrop.
Head: Clear varnish.

6 Semi-Palmer

COMMENT

This fly can be fished effectively on any part of your cast because it is palmered for one-third of the body length. It is more buoyant than a conventional hackled bit and fishes in a big wave. Les Toogood, one of my BRFFA team mates found out that this pattern was working when practising for the Benson & Hedges International Final at Rutland in 1993. Fortunately it worked also during the two-day competition and we won it.

DRESSING

Hook: Kamasan B400 size 12.
Tying silk: Red.
Body: Claret seal's fur.
Rib: Pearl flashabou.
Hackle: Red game.
Head: Clear varnish.

7 U.F.O. Red Bits

COMMENT

The name of this fly has a dual significance: it can mean unidentified fly object or as Chris Howitt and myself called it, UFO Red – because of its brightness fish will either take it with confidence or 'go away very quickly'. This fly works well in sizes 12 to 16, fished along with more sober coloured hoppers and bits, as well as being good for casting and leaving static for feeding fish. It works well in size 12 for pulling on the top and attracting fish that are not too keen to take static dries. I sometimes tie this pattern with a single goose biot.

DRESSING

Hook: Kamasan B170 size 12.
Tying silk: Red.
Body: FO Red seal's fur.
Wing: Goose biots.
Hackle: Red game.
Head: Clear varnish.

8 Fiery Brown Elk Hair Sedge

COMMENT

Yet another method of keeping the fly in the surface film; I will normally fish this fly either on the point or top dropper. The light-coloured elk hair makes it easier to see the fly and spot takes rather than waiting for the rod to be pulled out of your hand or, as often happens, the fish might take the fly and blow it out without pulling the line. As with the Parachute fly the Elk Hair Sedge works either fished static or moved. It is worth pulling and skating the fly away from a fish and more often than not it will induce the fish to take.

DRESSING

Hook: Tiemco TMC100 size 12.
Tying silk: Red.
Body: Fiery brown seal's fur.
Wing: Cream elk hair.
Head: Clear varnish.

Len Childs

Len Childs is a retired London fireman who now lives in Kent close to his beloved Bewl Water reservoir. It is here that he regularly fishes and in so doing has become quite an expert reservoir fly fisher. It follows that he needed to be a very competent fly tyer too, to keep him ahead of the game – this he certainly is.

Len's record is very good and after a most successful career as a coarse fisherman, when he specialized in big carp, he began fly fishing only ten years ago. Those ten years have been quite marvellous. He has fished for England in the Home Internationals three times and in 1997 captained the team on Loch Leven.

Len fishes for the Bewl Bridge Fly Fishers team which won the gold medal from 100 team entries in the 1996 Benson & Hedges event. The same team also won the national Wychwood trophy in 1996. It seems that Len is on a roll – study his dry flies well.

1 Hustler

COMMENT

This is a very good pattern when fished in a light wave on the point of a long leader – even if no fish are showing it will pull them up. It works best from July onwards on a warm, dull day just pulled through the surface. Its name came from my boat partner on one particular day when I was catching well on this fly and he begged me for one. I gave him one with a yellow head and it did not catch. When he saw mine with a white head his comments were not printable but the word 'hustler' was used.

DRESSING

Hook: Kamasan B170 size 10–12.
Tying silk: White.
Tail: Golden pheasant tippets.
Body: Hare's ear.
Rib: Pearl haberdashery thread (very strong).
Wing: Pine squirrel (sparse).
Head: White deer hair clipped short and round.

2 Basher

COMMENT

This is a super jelly fry pattern. I devised it after spending a day on Bewl trying to catch jelly fry feeders. I had only limited success using many patterns, the best being the grizzle palmer. At home that evening working at the vice, I replaced the hare's ear body with one of pearl and added a few strands of pearl flashabou to the tail. The next day I was back at Bewl. I found the fry feeders on top again so on went the new fly greased up on a long leader cast into the many rises. Fished static I soon had six trout in a short space of time.

DRESSING

Hook: Kamasan B170 size 12.
Tying silk: Black.
Tail: Pearl Flashabou.
Body: Pearl over white silk.
Rib: Fine silver wire.
Hackle: Top grade grizzle cock well marked.
Head: Black tying silk varnished.

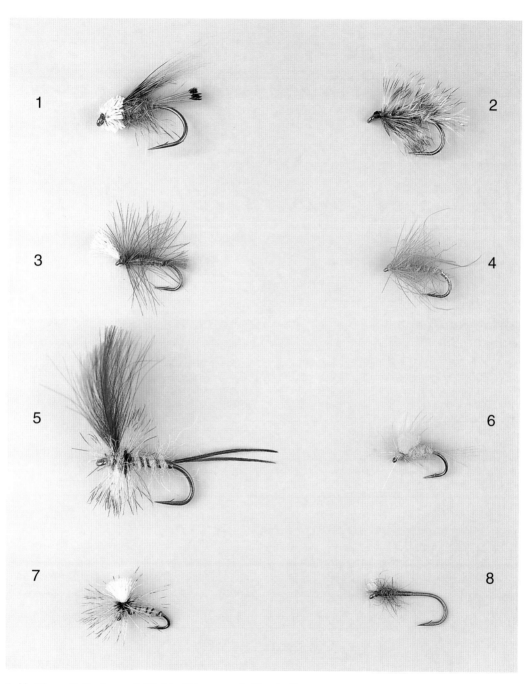

1 Hustler 2 Basher 3 Wickie Shippey 4 Simply Orange
5 CDC Mayfly 6 Greenfly 7 Paradrone 8 Sparse Arse

3 Wickie Shippey

COMMENT

Fish this pattern from July onwards in a light ripple on a dullish day. Just trundle it through the surface with a steady figure-of-eight retrieve. This pattern has won me a good few competitions. I use this fly on the point greased up, but fished in, not on, the surface with a small light nymph on the dropper.

DRESSING

Hook: Kamasan B170 size 12–14.
Tying silk: Brown.
Tail: Bright red floss (short).
Body: Gold tinsel.
Rib: Fine gold wire.
Hackle: Fiery brown cock.
Front breather: White polypropylene.
Head: Clear varnish.

4 Simply Orange

COMMENT

I just had to include this one on my list, as it was my most successful dry in 1996–97 and has taken many trout in many waters throughout the country. The fish will always pick it out from a team of three. Fish it fast, slow or dead stop – it's brilliant! I fished this fly on its own on a long leader in the 1996 National Final at Bewl on a very hard day and it took five fish thus qualifying me for the 1997 England team.

DRESSING

Hook: Kamasan B170 size 14.
Tying silk: Orange.
Butt: Pearl over orange.
Body: Orange seal's fur (or sub) mixed with hot orange SLF.
Rib: Pearl haberdashery thread (very strong).
Hackle: Hot orange cock clipped under to sit in the film.
Head: Orange tying silk varnished.

5 CDC Mayfly

COMMENT

This fly is the brainchild of my good friend Baz Reece who is a Rivers International. He perfected this fly over two years and it is superb. The fly is most effective fished bone dry. The CDC gives the image of wing but does not aid buoyancy. Rolling the wing over the thorax forms a ball and imitates a hatching mayfly. Baz says he is not boasting about it but the male mayflies want to mate with it before it hits the water!

DRESSING

Hook: Wet Fly Supreme/Emerger size 10–12.
Tying silk: Cream.
Tail: Three pheasant tail fibres.
Body: Cream seal's fur (or sub) picked out.
Rib: Brown floss.
Wing: Two long CDC feathers faced front to front.
Hackle: Two cock badger hackles.
Head: Clear varnish.

6 Greenfly

COMMENT

Every now and then we have a fall of green fly on Bewl and the fish go mad for them. They get so preoccupied with them that they will not look at anything else. I designed this simple pattern and it is taken readily. The first time I used the fly I cast to a moving fish, the fish moved about ten feet sideways to the fly and took it. It's great to be out on the water and get a few fish that are so set on one insect. Never go out in the summer without one in your fly box. You may only use it once but you will catch when nobody else will.

DRESSING

Hook: Size 14–16 Emerger/Midge.
Tying silk: White.
Tail: Honey hackle (sparse).
Body: Insect green easy dub or midge floss.
Wing: Post of yellow foam to aid buoyancy.
Hackle: Sparse honey cock 1½ turns.
Head: Clear varnish.

7 Paradrone

COMMENT

This fly was invented by my fellow team mate and fishing partner Mick Betts. Mick is a superb angler and fly tyer. He also fishes small stillwaters where he uses his Paradrone on midsummer days. When the fish wise up and refuse most offerings, the Paradrone comes into its own. He fishes it on a long fine tippet and catches more than his share. We have also caught on this fly on the big reservoirs.

DRESSING

Hook: Mustad 80080 size 20.
Tying silk: Cream.
Rib: Black horse hair.
Body: Yellow herl.
Post: Polypropylene.
Hackle: Cock badger.
Head: Clear varnish.

8 Sparse Arse

COMMENT

I use this pattern in flat calm conditions when lots of fish are up and smutting. Dress this fly short, hence the name, and use buoyant material; it is a must to use seal's fur to aid the buoyancy, and in conjunction with the polypropylene front breather add a small amount of floatant so that it will stay up long enough to get a take. Use a light rod and lightweight line, resist playing the fish hard and the light hook will hold. Try it at Bewl or Rutland if you have the nerve!

DRESSING

Hook: Size 12 Emerger.
Tying silk: Any colour to match the hatch.
Body: Seal's fur any colour to match the hatch (same as silk).
Breather: White polypropylene.
Head: Clear varnish.

Dave Shipman

Dave owns a tackle and gun shop in Whittlesey, Peterborough, which is close to his beloved Rutland Water. One of the most successful competitive fly fishers, his record over the past decade speaks for itself. He captains the well-known Cormorants team which won the Benson & Hedges final when it took place on Rutland a few years ago.

In the 1996 season Dave won both the Hanningfield Masters events, when 100 top fly fishers battle it out for top rod. To win two on the trot shows fantastic consistency. Dave has fished for England on a couple of occasions and I am sure more caps will follow.

Many would say Dave is best known for inventing his famous Shipman's Buzzer. It was the simple style of the dressing and how the fly appeared on the water's surface as the perfect silhouette that captured most tyers' imaginations. A lot of variants have been developed from Dave's original.

1 50/50 Shipman's Buzzer

COMMENT

Once the water starts to warm up on the larger waters from the end of May onwards I use this brighter version of my buzzer to great effect. The red back end is a popular colour and with the hot orange thorax imitating the orange burst of colour as most buzzers hatch, the pattern works well. I fish this pattern on the dropper of a two-fly cast or singly if the fish are wary.

DRESSING

Hook: Kamasan B405 size 10–16.
Tying silk: Orange pre-waxed 8/0.
Tail: White floating floss.
Body: Rear half, bright red seal's fur; front half, hot orange seal's fur.
Rib: Flat gold tinsel: medium 10–12 hook, thin 14–16 hook.
Head: White floating floss breathers tied up.

2 Shipman Fiery Brown Buzzer

COMMENT

This was the original colour for my buzzer and still the best all-rounder. By using the new modern white floating floss I can tie the fly slimmer. I've made the shape more tapered but still only use two turns of tinsel. I gink the front end only – in a big wind the fly can be pulled and with the front breathers pointed up the fly will 'pop'. In a flat calm I fish it static. I fish this pattern on the point of a two-fly cast.

DRESSING

Hook: Kamasan B405 size 10–16.
Tying silk: Brown pre-waxed 8/0.
Tail: White floating floss tied pointing slightly down.
Body: Fiery brown seal's fur.
Rib: Gold flat tinsel (two turns): medium 10–12 hook, thin 14–16 hook.
Head: White floating floss breathers tied up.

1 50/50 Shipman's Buzzer **2** Shipman Fiery Brown Buzzer **3** Dry GRHE
4 Olive Green Shipman's Buzzer **5** Peacock & Orange **6** Mountford's Blue Damsel
7 Dave's Ginger Hopper **8** Flexi Emerger

3 Dry GRHE

COMMENT

This pattern was first shown to me by John White of Bewl Water, who is an excellent imitative fisher. The hook is very important in that it is very strong but light and has a straight eye. Many other size 16 hooks just open up when putting pressure on the fish. When fish are taking corixa over weed beds, fishing this pattern with a quick figure-of-eight retrieve can be very effective. This pattern hardly needs ginking because being quite bushy and light it is very buoyant.

DRESSING

Hook: Kamasan B980 size 16 only.
Tying silk: Brown pre-waxed 8/0.
Body: Light-coloured dubbed hare's mask.
Rib: No. 1 gold tinsel.
Head: Clear varnish.

4 Olive Green Shipman's Buzzer

COMMENT

Whenever there is a hatch of pond olives and trout are taking them off the surface I use this pattern, fished with a slow figure-of-eight retrieve. The best session I remember was at Rutland at the mouth of Dickinson's Bay in 1992 when I had 13 fish for 39lb 9oz, proving that this pattern is effective on both browns and rainbows. Jeremy Herrmann used this pattern to great effect to take the Brown Bowl Trophy at Draycote in 1993 on mature fish over the open later during a May International.

DRESSING

Hook: Kamasan B405 size 12–14.
Tying silk: Olive pre-waxed 8/0.
Tail: White floating floss.
Body: Olive seal's fur.
Rib: Silver tinsel medium.
Head: White floating floss breathers tied up.

5 Peacock & Orange

COMMENT

This is a variation of a pattern shown to me five years ago and I put the hackle in front and behind the CDC feather for greater stability. The back two-thirds fishes sub-surface. It is very effective when cast accurately to rising fish and pulled away or fished static in a flat calm when fish are taking dark buzzers.

DRESSING

Hook: Kamasan B170 size 12–14.
Tying silk: Black.
Tail: Globrite no. 4 floss.
Body: One strand bronze peacock (underbody varnished).
Rib: Extra fine red wire.
Wing: Natural CDC feathers (two plumes).
Hackle: Stiff dark brown cock tied behind and in front of CDC. Cut off underneath.
Head: Clear varnish.

6 Mountford's Blue Damsel

COMMENT

This is a useful pattern on a lot of waters where there is a prolific hatch of damsel flies such as at Elinor fishery near Thrapston. Fish become preoccupied with taking the adult even out of the air! My friend Gordie Mountford, who ties flies for me, has a season ticket at Elinor and has tried to imitate the adult male damsel. The body fishes subsurface with only the wing above water. Takes can be explosive or mere sips. Gordie has spooned as many as twenty adult damsels from fish. Fish this fly static.

DRESSING

Hook: Kamasan B400 size 12.
Tying silk: Black.
Body: Blue seal's fur.
Rib: Fine embossed silver.
Wing: White floating floss.
Hackle: Teal blue cock (cut underneath).
Head: Black tying thread and clear varnish.

7 Dave's Ginger Hopper

COMMENT

Use from June onwards on a two-fly set-up with this Hopper on the dropper 5ft up from the point fly, a dry or nymph. I quite often fish a nymph with a dry or hopper. In a Benson & Hedges English Final at Grafham when there was a large ginger buzzer hatch, I had eleven fish for 27lb – the best fish was 5lb 12 oz; eight took the Hopper and the other three took a single size 14 Stick fly on the point.

DRESSING

Hook: Kamasan B400 size 10–12.
Tying silk: Brown 8/0.
Butt: Pearl tinsel tied round bend.
Body: Ginger seal's fur.
Rib: Medium pearl tinsel pulled to fine diameter and twisted for strength.
Legs: Hen pheasant tail knotted.
Hackle: Ginger cock (cut underneath).
Head: Clear varnish.

8 Flexi Emerger

COMMENT

Tony Monroe imported Flexi-Floss two years ago and after experimenting came up with this pattern with obvious variations in colours. Fished singly on a 10ft cast when fish are wary, it has been very effective. I prefer the gold hook on bright days and feel the gold represents the shuck.

DRESSING

Hook: Kamasan B100G (gold hook) size 14–16.
Tying silk: Claret.
Body: Flexi-Floss black or claret.
Hackle: Claret.
Thorax: Claret seal's fur mixed with red lite brite (cut underneath).
Head: Clear varnish.

Dave Grove

Dave was born in Essex in 1955. On leaving school he moved to Dartmoor from where he now runs the family business and a fly fishing English and International consultancy and guiding service. Among his list of successes are: twice winner of the National Rivers' Championship, winner of the National Loch Style Championship and winner of the Natwest Bank Stillwater Championship. Dave is also a regular member of the European Grand Slam teams. Dave was the European Grand Slam champion in 1991 and 1992, captain of the English Rivers' team in 1993, member of the England team in the Commonwealth Championship in Canada, member of the England team in the World Championship in Norway, regular member of an English Loch Style and River Fly Fishing teams since 1987. He also has four Benson & Hedges individual titles.

He ties a lovely dry fly and this is what he has chosen for his selection – four reservoir dries and four for rivers.

1 GBH (Reservoir)

COMMENT

I call this fly the GBH because it has really done the damage for me when the going gets difficult. The fly was devised by me one night, when fishing a Benson & Hedges Final at Chew. The lake was a flat calm and the fish were very selective, picking off those large adult midges that are seen at Chew. On the practice day I only had three casts with the fly, the result . . . three fish! We then went on to win our day, thanks to the GBH. Cast the fly out and just let it sit there; it will do the rest. Make a lot of them as they are not durable.

DRESSING

Hook: Partridge, Oliver Edwards Nymph or any similar shape in size 12–14.
Tying silk: Red, micro fine wispa.
Body: Bright orange seal's fur.
Rib: Red silk.
Wing: Two grey cock hackle points tied flat along the body.
Legs: Natural cock pheasant centre tail fibres, knotted, tied two forwards and four backwards as in the natural insect.
Head: Clear varnish.

2 The King's Bug Fly (Reservoir)

COMMENT

This little fly comes out when we see those little black beetles on the water. A few years ago I clinched a European Grand Slam Individual title with this fly. Black beetles were blown into a corner of the lake at Ghent in Belgium and in the afternoon fishing was very difficult with hardly any fish caught. I had a few fish rising to my left, in the corner. I could see that they were taking little beetles and I knew I only needed one fish to win the title, so on went the KBF, and with just ten minutes to go I lost three fish and landed two.

DRESSING

Hook: Kamasan B160 size 14.
Tying silk: Black micro fine wispa.
Body: Black seal's fur.
Rib: White or silver fine thread.
Wing: Natural CDC cut short.
Legs: Dyed black cock pheasant tail fibre, knotted and left untrimmed.
Head: Clear varnish.

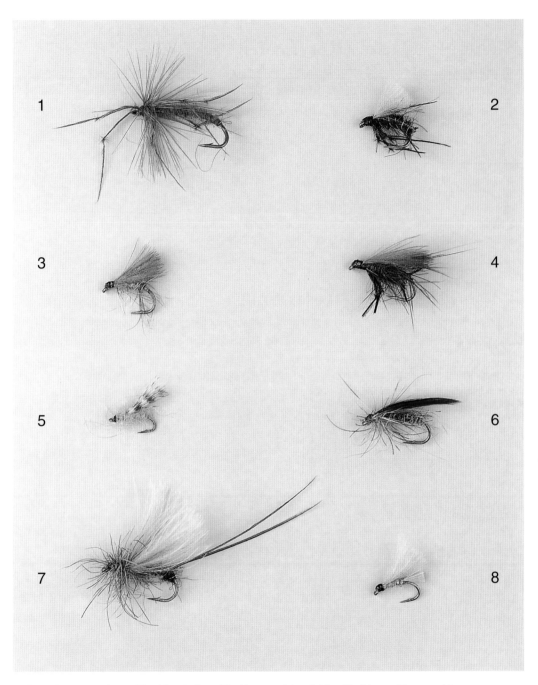

1 GBH (Reservoir)   2 The King's Bug Fly (Reservoir)   3 The No Name (Reservoir)
4 The House Fly (Reservoir)   5 Green Fly (Aphid) (River)
6 Stone Fly (*Plecoptera*) (River)   7 Large Dark Olive Dun (*Baetis rhodani*) (River)
8 The Clayton (River)

3 The No Name (Reservoir)

COMMENT

I am sure this fly is known to everyone, but my favourite sizes are 16 and 18. Do not be afraid to use small hooks. The wide gape on the B160 is useful in these small sizes. It was this fly that won the National Final for me at Bewl and the Individual title at an International Benson & Hedges at Rutland. Use it as a single fly on a long leader when the fish are just nebbing the surface. It is rarely refused when cast in front of feeding fish.

DRESSING

Hook: Kamasan B160 size 12–18.
Tying silk: Black micro fine wispa.
Body: Hare's fur dubbed.
Rib: Gold tinsel flat.
Wing: Natural CDC.
Head: Clear varnish.

4 The House Fly (Reservoir)

COMMENT

This is a good all-round fly, and has won more competitions for me at Wimbleball than I can remember. I find it is best fished close to the bank or trees, when the wind is blowing the naturals on to the water. It makes a good imitation of the cow dung when tied in amber. It sometimes works better with a little movement added.

DRESSING

Hook: Kamasan B400 size 12–14.
Tying silk: Black micro fine wispa.
Body: Black rabbit.
Wing: Natural CDC, flat on body.
Legs: Dyed black cock pheasant centre tail fibres trimmed short.
Head: Clear varnish.

5 Green Fly (Aphid) (River)

COMMENT

Out of all my river flies, this one in green or black has produced the most fish. How many times have you been to a pool that has hardly any flow on it, but has feeding fish? Once again do not be afraid of using the small hooks. Cast the fly at a feeding fish and nine times out of ten he will take it. Be warned! do not strike, just tighten into it and he will be hooked. It was this fly that won me top English rod on the River Wharfe in a Home International and it has seen me through many qualifying heats. The grayling love it as well.

DRESSING

Hook: Size 18–20.
Tying silk: Black micro fine wispa.
Body: Bright green seal's fur or SLF.
Wing: Barred teal fibres.
Head: Clear varnish.

6 Stone Fly (*Plecoptera*) (River)

COMMENT

This is a rough water fly that can be used the whole season. It has never produced fantastic results but can turn a bad day into a memorable one. It fishes best at the top of the stickles and will produce a lightning fast splashy rise. Only fish it on warm days when the naturals are drifting in the air.

DRESSING

Hook: Kamasan B170 size 14–16.
Tying silk: Black micro fine wispa.
Body: Hare's ear fur ribbed with stripped peacock herl.
Wing: Four dark brown to grey cock hackle points tied flat.
Hackle: Hare's fur.
Head: Clear varnish.

7 Large Dark Olive Dun (*Baetis rhodani*) (River)

COMMENT

This fly is common on my local Devon rivers. It can be quite large and can seen on cold days when there is nothing else hatching. This pattern has done very well for me in the past when there is any sort of large olive on the water. It seems to achieve best results on rough fast-flowing streams. It caught my largest ever grayling on the Wharfe at just over 3lb.

DRESSING

Hook: Kamasan B400 size 12–14.
Tying silk: Black micro fine wispa.
Tail: Two cock pheasant centre tail fibres tied split.
Egg shuck (female): Black seal's fur.
Body: Claret or olive seal's fur.
Rib: Stripped peacock herl.
Wing: Two CDC tied split.
Hackle: Olive hare's fur.
Head: Clear varnish.

8 The Clayton (River)

COMMENT

This is a grayling fly, mainly for our southern Chalk streams where it works at its best. Use it when the grayling are rising. When they are taking this fly it is possible to catch fish all day long. It fishes well right into the cold weather months of autumn and early winter.

DRESSING

Hook: Size 12–16.
Tying silk: Black micro fine wispa.
Tail: Fluorescent pink marabou cut short.
Body: CDC.
Rib: Flat gold mylar tinsel.
Wing: CDC.
Head: Clear varnish.

Guido Vinck

Guido Vinck is from Belgium, he is forty-eight years old and is the chief editor of the fishing magazine *BEET*, translated 'a take'. He has been fishing since he was six years old and has been tying flies for twenty-five years. He says flies are easy to tie and catch fish with.

Guido's success record is as follows: Belgian Champion for reservoir fishing in 1994, seven times world champion fly caster, one European champion fly casting win, winner of European Open in 1989 at Grafham, winner of the Partridge competition on Bewl Water in 1995, member of the winning team in the European Open (Grand Slam) in 1995 and 1996, winner of the Open International in Dreux in 1989, 1992, 1993 and 1995, winner of the Marathon Fly International in Belgium 1995 and Bronze medal as a team member in the World Championship in Ireland in 1995.

1 Thymallus Sedge

COMMENT

This imitation of an egg-laying sedge seems to be very attractive to grayling and trout, especially on rivers where there is a lot of angling pressure. The CDC feather keeps the fly in the surface and the honey colour helps the angler to see the fly during the evening rise. It is a killing pattern from June to September. Fish the fly on a long leader, about 16ft, and a thin tippet (10mm).

DRESSING

Hook: Size 16–22.
Tying silk: Dark brown.
Tail: Orange poly yarn.
Body: Numidis herl (small ostrich).
Wing: Honey CDC feather.
Head: Clear varnish.

2 Last Hope

COMMENT

A very easy fly to tie and very effective when there are mini black beetles, small black ants or small black midges sitting on the water. Sometimes a last-hope fly when everything else has failed. It is a fly that imitates nothing and everything. It gives me good results for grayling and brown trout on rivers as well as some nice rainbow trout from Grafham and Bewl Water. Use a long leader of about 16ft on the river or 20ft on the reservoir and use on a single-fly cast.

DRESSING

Hook: Size 18–22.
Tying silk: Black.
Tail: White cock hackle fibres.
Body: ½ peacock herl, ½ flat silver tinsel.
Head: Clear varnish.

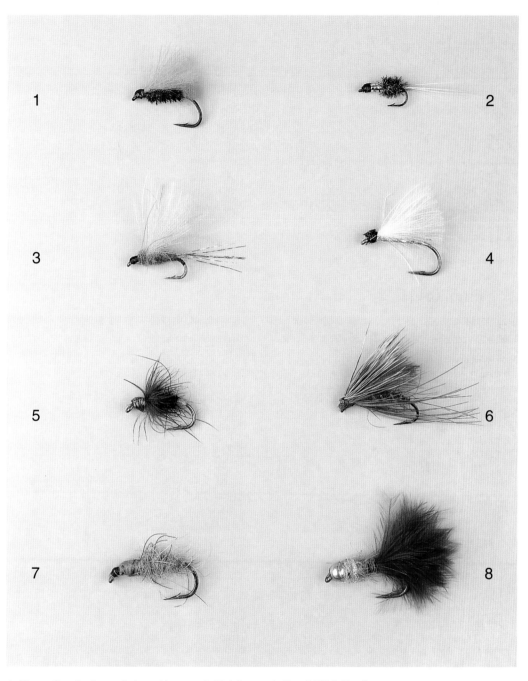

1 Thymallus Sedge   2 Last Hope   3 Uni-Dun   4 Pearl CDC Devil
5 Black Magic   6 Happy Hopper   7 Sticky Grub   8 Belgian Brownie

3 Uni-Dun

COMMENT

I love to fish with a fly that imitates a dry emerger or a wet dun. This fly is floating in the surface but doesn't sink because of the CDC, and imitates all kinds of dun flies. This is a fly that has taken fish for me in competitions on rivers and reservoirs, in Europe and in the USA when I was fishing for fun. It is a universal dun for trout and grayling. Fish it as a single fly on rivers all year or as a point fly with a sinking emerger on the dropper on reservoirs.

DRESSING

Hook: Size 12–18.
Tying silk: Black.
Tag: Black silk.
Tail: Grizzle hackle fibres (V-form).
Body: ⅔ 'rusty' CDC dubbing, ⅓ light brown CDC dubbing.
Wing: Light grey CDC feathers.
Head: Clear varnish.

4 Pearl CDC Devil

COMMENT

This white surface fly was developed as a fry imitation particularly for when you have 'followers' who turn away when they come close to the boat. As a top dropper it works, twitched, pulled or static. I won the Partridge Challenge on Bewl Water in 1995 with this fly. Fished static I think that the trout not only take the fly as a fry but also as an emerger. Use a long leader of 20ft; the fly works well in sunny conditions.

DRESSING

Hook: Size 12–14.
Tying silk: Black.
Body: Pearl Flashabou.
Wing: White CDC feathers with a few strands of pearl.
Head: Clear varnish.

5 Black Magic

COMMENT

This is a fly that I use a lot on small reservoirs, especially on 'dog days' when the rainbows are lazy. Very good on cold days, fished as a point fly in a team with two nymphs on the droppers. Fish the flies on a floating line and with a slow retrieve along the surface.

DRESSING

Hook: Size 10–14.
Tying silk: Black.
Tag: Pearl lurex.
Body: ⅘ black baby squirrel fur dubbing, ⅕ copper wire varnished.
Hackle: Black hen.
Head: Clear varnish over tying off.

6 Happy Hopper

COMMENT

I love flies that are easy to tie and catch fish. This type of hopper works well on a long leader in windy and sunny conditions. It is a happy fly that plays in the wind and imitates a sedge or an emerger. The body can be tied in different colours. Works well on the Irish lakes tied as a mayfly emerger. You can use it as a bob fly or on the point.

DRESSING

Hook: Size 12–14.
Tying silk: Black.
Body: Dark red or light claret seal's fur dubbing.
Rib: Fine gold wire.
Wing: Mixed grey CDC and cream-tipped deer hair.
Legs: Red neck strands from golden pheasant.
Head: Clear varnish.

7 Sticky Grub

COMMENT

Imitation of a caddis larva (river) but works also as a stick fly for reservoirs. Fish it on the bottom (river) from June until September, or as a point fly on reservoirs during the spring or autumn. Fish it on a floating line and fish it back with a very slow retrieve.

DRESSING

Hook: Size 10–14 leaded (optional).
Tying silk: Black.
Body: ⅔ grey hare's ear, ⅓ insect green floss.
Rib: Copper wire.
Head: Clear varnish.
Note from Bob Church: Guido misunderstood my 'all dry' guideline instructions for his chapter, but the two grubs he has slipped in are too good to leave out.

8 Belgian Brownie

COMMENT

This is a nymph, a mini tinhead or a small streamer. The most important thing is that the fly catches fish, especially rainbow trout. As a point fly on a long 20ft leader from the bank or from the boat, it was the Belgian Brownie that won for the last two years at the Belgian Marathon and French Open International. A fly that 'seduced' a lot of stockies in Rutland, Grafham and Bewl Water.

DRESSING

Hook: Size 10–12 with an appropriate sized gold-plated brass ball threaded onto the hook to stop at the eye.
Tying silk: Larva lace nylon thread.
Tail: Brown marabou.
Body: ½ hot orange seal's fur, ½ swan pearl flash dubbing.
Head: Clear varnish over tying off.

Julie Emerson

For the past four consecutive years Julie has fished at international level for the England Ladies team and in 1997 qualified for the England Senior team (men's) for the Autumn squad. This was competing against 100 of the country's top anglers for a place.

Julie is a member of the Mid-Northants Trout Fishing Association as well as a local club, the Rutland Kingfishers, with whom she spends most of her fishing time practising for events and competitions and just having fun.

Julie's favourite method of fly fishing is the dry fly purely because it is so 'visual' and possibly because of the patience it takes. Unfortunately most of the competitions are fished early season where dry fly fishing does not always work, but at the back end of a season Julie can think of no more pleasurable way to tempt the fish. 'When I'm fishing dry flies there are a few patterns that I wouldn't want to be without . . .'

1 Julie's Orange Hopper

COMMENT

The Orange Hopper for me is a classic dry fly pattern that I find works at many different venues including my local water, Rutland. In 1995 I was practising at Bewl Water in Kent for the ladies' national competition. I found that fish were rising and investigating my hopper but wouldn't take it. I inadvertently pulled the hopper, creating a wake on the surface; this was instantly followed by a huge bow wave and a tightening of the line. Several more fish took the hopper using this pulled method, although theoretically dry fishing is static.

DRESSING

Hook: Kamasan B170 or B400 size 10–12.
Tying silk: Red.
Body: Fiery orange seal's fur.
Rib: Gold Flashabou.
Legs: Knotted pheasant tail fibres (2 each side).
Hackle: Light orange cock (clipped underneath).
Head: Clear varnish.

2 Amber Hopper

COMMENT

In 1994 I was fishing the Rutland Fours Competition with perfect conditions for dry fly fishing and I approached using two orange hoppers, and although I had very many follows I could not induce a take. I swopped the point fly for an Amber Hopper and got an instantaneous take which turned out to be a lovely fin-perfect brown of 3lb. I won the top lady's rod on the day. Interestingly my boat partner Graham Wright was also getting action but no takes, and after I had given him an Amber Hopper he caught five fish as well.

DRESSING

Hook: Kamasan B170 or B400 size 10–12.
Tying silk: Claret.
Body: Amber seal's fur.
Rib: Stretched Flashabou tinsel.
Legs: Knotted pheasant tail fibres (4 each side).
Hackle: Dark brown or yellow.

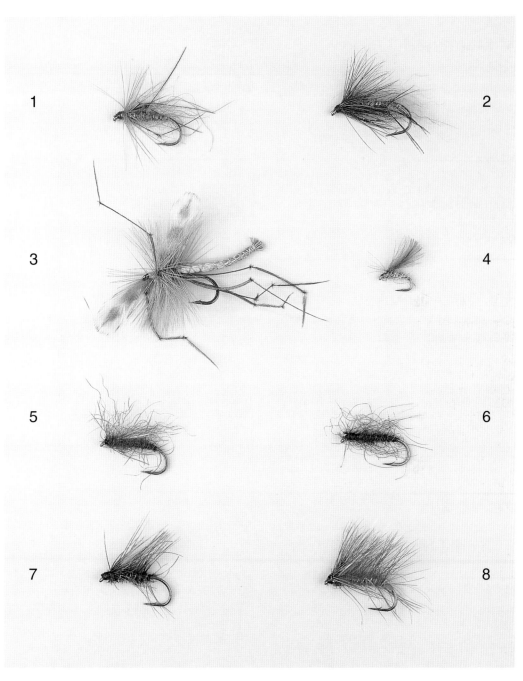

1 Julie's Orange Hopper   2 Amber Hopper   3 Detached Daddy
4 Hare's Ear Cul De Canard   5 Red Dry (Bob Worts)   6 Claret Dry   7 Black Mohican
8 Red Mohican

3 Detached Daddy

COMMENT

Believe it or not, it wasn't until late season 1997 that I had ever used a Daddy, preferring to use my hoppers when daddy-long-legs were about. I spent one of my most memorable days fishing with Jeanette Taylor on Draycote Water in 1997. Jeanette was using a detached daddy and the water surface came alive with bow waves and follows. The strange part is that once we had caught a few fish the detached body literally became detached – that is, it fell off! This, however, didn't put the fish off, in fact they seemed to like it better.

DRESSING

Hook: Kamasan B400 size 10.
Tying silk: Fawn.
Body: Tube of deer hair pre-tied on a thick dubbing needle.
Legs: Six knotted pheasant tail feather fibres.
Wings: Two natural cree cock hackle tips.
Hackle: Ginger cock.
Head: Clear varnish.

4 Hare's Ear Cul De Canard

COMMENT

This fly holds many memories for me because without it I wouldn't have qualified for the ladies' team in 1995. The ladies' national competition was held on Bewl Water and on this day the drifting boats became stationary and casting became almost impossible. I decided to drop down to a single fly in an attempt to gain some accuracy in casting. On the first cast I had another fish to add to the three from earlier. I lost another and caught one more positioning me third and securing a place in the 1996 squad.

DRESSING

Hook: Drennan Buzzer size 18.
Tying silk: Black.
Body: Hare's ear mask.
Rib: Thin pearl flashabou.
Wing: 2 CDC feathers.
Head: Clear varnish.

5 Red Dry (Bob Worts)

COMMENT

I used Bob's Red Dry on Grafham Water to take my first ever limit there. The following year I decided that I would enter the ladies' national competition for the first time. I set out armed with my dry flies and found that I wasn't prepared fully for the amount of fish that showed interest. I managed to catch only four of them which made me second reserve. I did learn, however, that Bob's Red Dry fly was a weapon that I would use later in my fishing career with confidence.

DRESSING

Hook: Kamasan B400 size 12.
Tying silk: Black.
Body: Red seal's fur.
Wing: Four to five white cock hackle fibres.
Rib: Globrite no. 5 (twisted).
Head: Clear varnish.

6 Claret Dry

COMMENT

Another infamous fly of Bob Worts is this Claret Dry. My husband John and I were out on Pitsford one day in 1995. I had caught well in the morning but John had failed to tempt any fish at all. After changing his flies to claret it was as if someone had turned on the fish to his dries. At this point, I could not even get a pull. I swopped to claret and found the action first class. On another trip I was using nymphs and struggling to get many takes, whereas John put on Bob's Claret Dry and caught a limit of rainbows that weighed over 24lb.

DRESSING

Hook: Kamasan B400 size 12.
Body: Claret seal's fur (dark).
Rib: Globrite no. 5 (twisted).
Wing: 4 or 5 white cock hackle fibres.
Head: Clear varnish.

7 Black Mohican

COMMENT

This fly was a joint invention of Bob Worts and my husband John. It was tied specifically for Pitsford Water when sedge are predominant. Fished singly it can be deadly, with a static approach or pulled, especially from the bank. At an evening's bank fishing in June, although fishing was difficult and many bank anglers were struggling to get one or two, both Bob and John caught well. After meeting up and supplying tactics and flies I set out armed with the Mohican and started to catch consistently.

DRESSING

Hook: Kamasan B170 size 10.
Body: Black seal's fur.
Rib: Fine oval gold tinsel.
Hackle: Palmered dark brown cock (trimmed underneath).
Wing: 4 or 5 white cock hackle fibres.
Head: Clear varnish.

8 Red Mohican

COMMENT

The Red version of the Mohican was tied by my husband John. It acts as an attractor, which is just what it does as well as catch. In 1997 John and I fished at Draycote Water; no fish were rising at all. I had caught three or four on a slime line with damsel nymphs and John wanted to prove a point that a fish will rise to a dry fly even when there's no surface activity. A fish came out of nowhere and took his Red Mohican. John caught a further six fish on this fly, so it goes without saying that I do use the fly.

DRESSING

Hook: Kamasan B170 size 10.
Tying silk: Black.
Tag: Globrite no. 5.
Body: Fluorescent red seal's fur.
Rib: Fine oval gold tinsel.
Hackle: Palmered fluorescent red cock.
Wing: 4 or 5 white cock hackle fibres.
Hackle: 3 turns light brown cock.
Trim fly underneath.
Head: Clear varnish.

Bob Church

I have made my dry fly selection purely from American patterns. Their dry flies travel well and work marvellously with all European trout on rivers and stillwaters. Most of the American flies are high riding, heavily hackled designs. This obviously means that they float much better and even in turbulent water conditions they don't get sucked under by the strong currents as some sparser dressed patterns would.

These dry flies will give your box a variety of choice throughout the season. Rather than trying to make exact copies of the real hatching fly, these patterns are more generally suggestive.

1 White Wulff

COMMENT

Part of a set of Wulff dry flies designed by the late Lee Wulff. Lee had a great reputation not only in the United States but all over the fly fishing world. This particular white pattern is an excellent dry fly for when the Mayfly is hatching and is best as a river pattern rather than for lake or lough. In its very small dressing on size 18 and 16 hooks, it makes a good Caenis dry fly. We all know how difficult it is to tempt trout when this 'anglers' curse' is on the water.

DRESSING

Hook: Kamasan B140 size 10–18.
Tying silk: Black or white.
Tail: White calf tail hair.
Body: White fur or antron.
Hackle: Badger.
Wing: White calf tail hair.
Head: Clear varnish.

2 Grey Wulff

COMMENT

I have often used the Grey Wulff to very good effect on the rivers of southern England, mostly at Mayfly time. Cast accurately upstream to a rising trout it will take this artificial nine times out of ten, if the fish has been taking newly hatched flies coming downstream. Other places where this fly works are Loughs Mask, Corrib, Carra and Conn in the west of Ireland. The mayfly hatch continues throughout the summer on these loughs, just enough to keep the brown trout interested. As such times try this fly – the locals do.

DRESSING

Hook: Size 8–10.
Tying silk: Black.
Tail: Grey squirrel tail hair.
Body: Grey antron or musk rat.
Hackle: Medium dun cock.
Wing: Two bunches grey squirrel tail hair.
Head: Clear varnish.

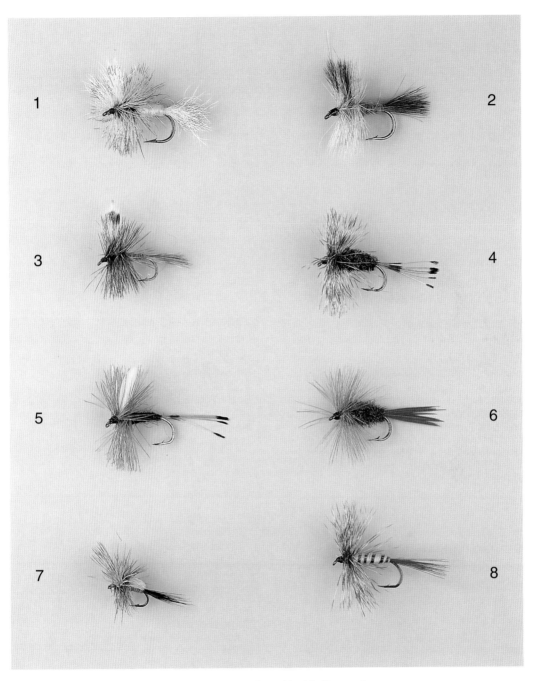

1 White Wulff   **2** Grey Wulff   **3** Adam's   **4** Grey Hackle Peacock
5 Rio Grande King   **6** Brown Hackle Peacock   **7** Orange Humpy   **8** Grey Hackle Yellow

3 Adam's

COMMENT

A much admired general pattern of many river trout and grayling fishers. I have fond memories of fishing the Welsh Dee with Brian Leadbetter and practising for the World Championships. We were down to size 24 and even size 26 hook patterns of the Adam's and this is the smallest fly I have ever used. It was very successful used on a 2lb nylon leader and a very soft rod. In this situation only the gentlest of lifts was needed to set the hook.

DRESSING

Hook: Size 14–26.
Tying silk: Black.
Tail: Mixed brown and grizzle hackle fibres.
Body: Musk rat.
Hackle: Mixed brown and grizzle cock.
Wings: Grizzle cock hackle tips.
Head: Clear varnish.

4 Grey Hackle Peacock

COMMENT

A most simple fly to tie but a great hatching buzzer pattern; it fishes well on the big reservoirs from April to September. Fish two on the cast, well-spaced and leave them to fish static or to just bob along with the breeze. It can also be fished in conjunction with a slimline nymph that is tied on a dropper and fished just under the surface. The fly will then act as an indicator if the nymph gets taken; a good method to remember.

DRESSING

Hook: Size 12–14.
Tying silk: Black.
Tail: Golden pheasant tippets.
Body: Bronze peacock herl (carrot-shaped).
Rib: Tying silk.
Hackle: Grizzle cock.
Head: Clear varnish.

5 Rio Grande King

COMMENT

One of the most successful well-travelled American flies. I know that this dry fly version was a great favourite on the New Zealand rivers when I spent three weeks fishing on North Island. The same fly is tied as a streamer lure, but the one I have used incorporates a yellow tail. As far as this dry pattern is concerned, use it with confidence on any of our little wild brown rivers anywhere in the UK or Ireland.

DRESSING

Hook: Size 10–14.
Tying silk: Black.
Tail: Golden pheasant tippets.
Body: Black floss silk tied carrot-shaped.
Wing: White duck feather slips.
Hackle: Ginger brown cock.
Head: Clear varnish.

6 Brown Hackle Peacock

COMMENT

Similar to our Red Tag pattern which we know works very well on rivers throughout the country. This then is basically a river fly, but I know it would be a great fly for the Tasmanian central lakes where gum beetles get on the water's surface in high numbers. I imagine too it will be a good fly for the English reservoirs when the snails rise to the surface for migration.

DRESSING

Hook: Size 12–16.
Tying silk: Black.
Tail: Bright red cock hackle fibres.
Body: Bronze peacock herl tied carrot-shape.
Rib: Black tying thread.
Hackle: Ginger or honey and ginger cock.
Head: Clear varnish.

7 Orange Humpy

COMMENT

This fly originated from the western rivers of America. Many of these rivers have fast turbulent currents that simply drown many conventional dry fly patterns. The Humpy series were specially designed to withstand these currents and remain buoyant and floating high – it's a success in this respect. This fly also has travelled well and I once had a marvellous catch on it on Lough Conn and this during a mayfly hatch. Jeanette also boated a 4lb brown trout from Conn on a yellow-bodied version.

DRESSING

Hook: Size 10–14.
Tying silk: Orange.
Tail: Black deer hair.
Body: Orange synthetic fur (various will do).
Shellback: Natural light deer hair.
Hackle: Grizzle cock.
Wings: Two bunches of fine tips from light deer hair.
Head: Clear varnish.

8 Grey Hackle Yellow

COMMENT

An out-and-out general dry pattern much favoured and used by the Americans. With the thickly tied grizzle hackle at the head of this fly it has a very high floating profile. This helps it perform well during hatches of mayfly or sedges. Normally it is used as a single fly, but I have found that for the UK fishing situations on the reservoirs or lochs, two flies can be worked on a cast to good effect. First, after casting, fish static, then after about five seconds slowly retrieve to cause a slight wake.

DRESSING

Hook: Size 10–14.
Tying silk: Black.
Tail: Bright red cock hackle fibres.
Body: Yellow silk.
Rib: Gold tinsel.
Hackle: Grizzle cock heavy.
Head: Clear varnish.

Lure Fishing

Lure Fishing

It was during the early 1960s that I became labelled as a lure fisher. I championed the cause, with my writing, because in those days I liked to catch specimen trout from the reservoirs. I had found out that small coarse fish fry were high on the menu of specimen trout and I began to tie up some new patterns that imitated small fish. For example, the Church Fry was meant to look like a small perch, the Appetizer and Jack Frost small roach – to cut a long story short these patterns worked very well and still do. The point I am trying to make is that lure fishing became far more acceptable from that time on and I am glad I was able to help it on its way.

Some of the fish-imitating patterns of today are very realistic creations as the synthetic materials now available help the imaginative tyer more than ever. If you make a careful study of Dave Barker's lure collection you will appreciate what I mean, and Dave holds the Grafham Water rainbow trout record caught on one of these designs.

Most of the others also fall into the popular lure mood of the time, that is, smaller lure patterns than ever before on size 10 hooks. This is due to the influence of competition fly fishing where this maximum hook size is one of the rules. These little lures have proved highly successful and have become match winners in many big events.

Then we have the weighted lure patterns that can come in any colour. Some have bodies weighted beneath their dressing as in Kevin Garn's collection. Others are weighted with brass ball goldheads, tinheads or leadheads but most usually have the flowing marabou tail, perhaps mixed with a few strands of crystal hair or Flashabou. Fluorescent materials are big in lures just now, where the new chenilles and fritz are very popular.

Most of today's modern lure fishing on reservoirs is carried out with some sort of sinking fly line. Fast-sinking line techniques have developed into an art form and my method of lift and then 'hang' with the lure is a well accepted successful style. You will hear anglers say 'I was fishing on the hang'. This is when they have cast a long line, usually with three mini lures on, or two well-spaced if the water is gin-clear, then they have retrieved steadily along the bottom, after which comes a long lift of the rod and a pause for up to around ten seconds. During that time the lures are held static and this is when a nervous trout that has followed the lure will often pluck up courage and take. As it turns down on the lure you usually secure a good hook hold. You will notice several of these mini lure patterns are tied on double hooks, or that the tying instruction says that you can dress it on a single or double hook. These doubles are very popular used on size 10s, for they give the extra weight to the point lure and therefore help with the 'hang' technique acting as a sort of anchor. Double hooks are also the only legal additional weight allowed in international competition rules.

Although sinking fly lines dominate on the reservoirs this has not always been the case. Fly fishers pray for more fly life to get the fish used to coming up in the water more, like they once did. I well remember the golden days at Grafham when floating lines and surface-fished big Muddler Minnow patterns was the trend everyone was into – now they are seldom used simply because the fish are not up close to the surface as they were. I hope those days will return because it was such a visually exciting sport. Kevin Garn's long-tailed lure selection must be mentioned, not so much because they are all killing lures, but because of the style in which they are tied. Some years ago Peter Cockwill advocated long-tailed lures of the Nobbler style for the smaller fisheries. He did have tremendous success with them and I watched him win the Wilcon Classic at Dever Springs while using them. It convinced me at the time and so it was a natural move to try various extra long-tailed lures out at the reservoirs. I can personally vouch for this collection of Kevin's – I've tried most of them and they are quite deadly; I cannot praise them enough.

There is one family of lures I know can be fished so slowly that it is like nymph fishing rather than lure fishing; I refer to the tinhead range often tied on a size 10 normal shank wet fly hook. For a start the weight is quite delicate and it is soldered onto the hook with an equal amount of weight above the shank as below; this means that when the lure is tied on this mount it will always swim evenly and upright as it is retrieved. Ex-Lady Champion, Jeanette Taylor, has popularized these tinhead patterns on a national basis and they are now well known. Ex-World Fly Fishing Champion, Jeremy Herrmann, quoted 'If I had to use just one fly on any type of water in any part of the world it would have to be Genie's Olive Tinhead' – a compliment indeed.

Uses of tinhead patterns are versatile as they work well on both large and small waters. Usually for the small fisheries when seeking the larger fish and stalking them, a single olive eye pattern is very good. This is fished with a leader the length of the fishing depth on a floating fly line. When I am fishing blind and casting a long line on a big gravel pit trout fishery or a reservoir I lengthen the leader. I often fish one or two buzzer nymph patterns on droppers, so giving my cast presentation a lure – nymph retrieving, or slow twitches, the presentation is right for either fly.

I would like to end by saying that lure fishing is now no longer looked down upon with a snobbish attitude, as once it was. It is a modern attractor fly or imitative method, which is essential to use if you are to call yourself a good all-round trout fly fisherman. As they say, 'Horses for courses' – choose the right conditions to try your lures out and give them equal importance along with the wets, nymphs and dries.

Dave Barker

Dave has fished for the England team on several occasions. He is a major competitor on the National scene and regularly takes a high position in the big events. He is an innovative fly tyer. Dave has a long reservoir history and his early buoyant foam floating patterns were leaders in the dead fry field. Dave was the first-ever individual winner of the Benson & Hedges National competition. He was Trout Masters Champion in 1993. In 1995 he was individual champion in the European Grand Slam event. In 1997 he was a member of the four-man team that won the Wychwood event and he was third in the individuals.

Although these are very impressive results, Dave is at his best as a lone bank fly fisher. Grafham is his local water and he holds the record for the best ever wild rainbow caught from there on his Minky Lure pattern. It weighed a massive 13lb 13½oz. Dave likes to put something back into the sport he loves and works tirelessly as chairman of the Grafham Water Fly Fishers Club.

1 Silver Fox Minky

COMMENT

Fish this fly on a long leader and floating fly line. Best areas, around shallow weed beds where the small coarse fry congregate. There are times when the trout are mad on feeding on these small fish. Keep to a steady, slow, jerky retrieve, to imitate a small fish on its travels.

DRESSING

Hook: Longshank 6–10 leaded at head end.
Tying silk: Black.
Body: Pearl sparkle yarn – fritz.
Rib: Fine silver wire.
Tail & wing: ⅛inch strip of silver fox or long-haired mink twice the length of the hook, tapering towards the tail end. The mink strip is matukared along the body with the rib and secured at the head.
Hackle: Few strands badger cock.
Eyes: Jungle cock.
Head: Clear varnish.

2 Minky (The Original)

COMMENT

Best fished on a long leader and floating line especially when bank fishing, this lure has gained a very good reputation since it began its life at Grafham Water. It caught many big trout to slow figure-of-eight retrieves. Also, as Dave points out, many takes come quite confidently as the lure drops after casting. Very good during early season when fished in deeper water.

DRESSING

Hook: Long shank 6–10 leaded at head.
Tying silk: Black.
Body: Brown wool dubbed.
Rib: Gold thread.
Tail & wing: ⅛inch strip of brown long-haired mink twice the length of the hook and tapering towards the tail end. The mink strip is matukared along the body with the gold thread.
Hackle: Few strands of silver mallard.
Eyes: Jungle cock.
Head: Clear varnish.

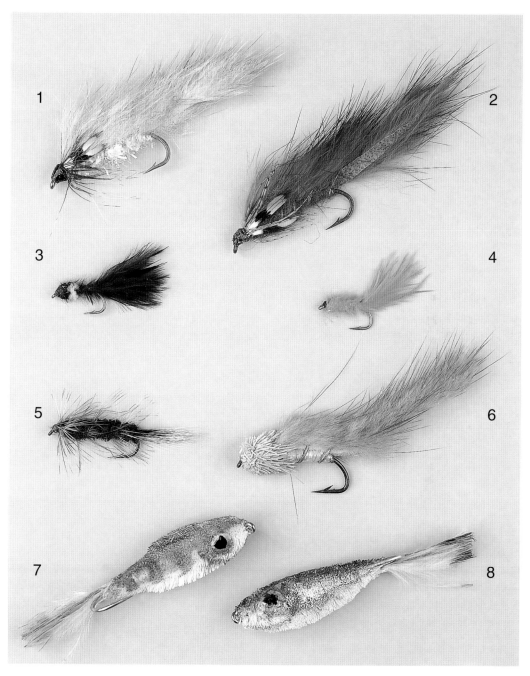

1 Silver Fox Minky   2 Minky (The Original)   3 Black Competition Taddy
4 Orange Competition Taddy   5 New Zealand Fuzzy Wuzzy   6 Muddler Minky
7 Floating Fry (Perch)   8 Floating Fry (Roach)

3 Black Competition Taddy

COMMENT

Adapted from the large tadpoles to suit the rules of competitions. This takes advantage of the new hook and fly length rules. The hook and tail reaches the maximum allowable length. The largish head creates a mini vortex when retrieved. In that vortex the tail pulsates quite vigorously adding attractive movement to the fly.

DRESSING

Hook: Kamasan B175 size 14.
Tying silk: Black.
Tail: Black marabou.
Body: Black marabou.
Rib: Black tying silk.
Thorax: Black tying silk.
Head: Build up with black tying silk and layers of varnish, finally dub a little black marabou over wet varnish.

4 Orange Competition Taddy

COMMENT

We all know that orange can be absolutely devastating more often than not where warm-water rainbows are concerned. This mini lure has been quite deadly for me at Grafham. The best results have come when using either a Hi-Di or Di 7 fast-sinking fly line and a steady slow retrieve.

DRESSING

Hook: Kamasan B175 size 14.
Tying silk: Black.
Tail: Orange marabou.
Body: Orange marabou slightly tapered.
Rib: Orange tying silk.
Head: Clear varnish.

5 New Zealand Fuzzy Wuzzy

COMMENT

The first self-tied lure Dave ever used, it was very successful in the early days at Grafham. It still works well today when I eventually get round to tying one on, probably for sentimental reasons. I cannot help but point out that drab, black-based lures have invariably worked best over the passing years.

DRESSING

Hook: Long shank size 12.
Tying silk: Black.
Tail: Squirrel tail hair.
Body: Black chenille.
Rib: Silver wire.
Body hackle: Badger hen palmered down length of body.
Head hackle: Badger hen.
Head: Clear varnish.

6 Muddler Minky

COMMENT

Fished on a floating fly line – grease the head well with gink then retrieve the lure slowly through the surface film. The head action creates a V-wake vortex and the tail pulsates beautifully. Another great lure for fry feeders. It has a good record at all the major Midlands reservoirs. One tip – use strong leader nylon because it tempts the big fish.

DRESSING

Hook: Size 6.
Tying silk: White.
Body: Pearl lurex.
Rib: Silver wire.
Tail & wing: Silver fox mink ⅛in strip.
Head: Light-coloured deer hair clipped to ball-shape.

7 Floating Fry (Perch)

COMMENT

Tie in white marabou tail onto very back end of hook – keep tying as short as possible. Apply superglue to silk overlay. Allow to dry, then varnish smooth to allow deer hair to spin over the tail tying. Spin white deer hair packed very tight all the way down the hook shank (through experience little and often is best). Tie off at the head and superglue. Trim into shape with new razorblade. Colour to your taste. For base of eye add a blob of superglue then add gold paint. Allow to dry, add black and allow to dry, then coat with varnish. Fish static or short pulls.

DRESSING

Hook: Long shank nickel finish Sparton size 4–6.
Tying silk: White.
Tail: White marabou.
Body: Natural white deer hair clipped to shape.
Colouring: Pantone waterproof pens of light green, grey, yellow and red.
Eyes: Humbrol model paint, gold and black pupils, cover in layer of clear varnish. Remember with this floating lure you present it sideways on to the trout's window.

8 Floating Fry (Roach)

COMMENT

When trimming shape this differently from the perch. It pays to have pictures of fry to use as a model when shaping. Dave uses magazine photos. Fry fishing methods are possible all the year round but are at their best from the beginning of September onwards. Fish the areas with plenty of weed – this will pay off.

DRESSING

Hook: Long shank nickel finish Sparton size 4–6.
Tying silk: White.
Tail: White marabou.
Body: Natural white deer hair.
Colouring: Pantone waterproof pens: silver and grey.
Eyes: Humbrol model paint, gold and black pupils, cover in layer of clear varnish.

Jeanette Taylor

Jeanette is a professional fly dresser with some eight years' experience of running her own business. She may be known for her specialist fly tying where she pioneered her tinhead patterns with their painted heads; however, she is even better known for her competition fly fishing results.

Jeanette has qualified to fish for the England Ladies' team eight times and on two of those occasions won the individual Four Home Countries International event. Apart from that, she has been European Grand Slam winner in 1993 over three legs, Benson & Hedges Individual Midland Final winner, Leeda Pairs individual winner and Mid-Northants Fly Fishing Club champion of the year. To prove her versatility she won the Small Fisheries Friendly International between England and Wales held at Dever Springs with nine big trout.

Finally she fished for England in the Commonwealth fly fishers match held in New Zealand where she received a runners-up medal. Quite a record for a lady fly fisher mixing with the top men. Her selection of tinhead lures shown here are both imitative patterns and lure types.

1 Mini Pink Zonker Tinhead

COMMENT

This pale shade of pink seems to be very attractive to both rainbow and brown trout. Tied in this fashion it represents a small fry of perch or roach which, as we know, trout feed well on. On reservoirs it fishes best on the point on some sort of sinking line, retrieved in short, sharp, jerky movements with pauses in between; takes can come at any time, even during the pause. For the small fisheries use a floating or sink-tip fly line and a 12 ft leader of 6lb breaking strain clear nylon.

DRESSING

Hook: Kamasan B175 size 10 Tinhead painted with yellow enamel eyes and black varnish pupils.
Tying silk: Black.
Body: Pearl.
Wing: Bunch of pink rabbit fur.
Hackle: Grizzle at head only.
Head: Clear varnish at tying off only.

2 Green-Headed Daddy Tinhead

COMMENT

Fly tyers have experimented with crane fly (daddy-long-legs) patterns for many years, and this is one of my favourites. Many years ago I discovered that at daddy-long-legs time trout could be caught just as easily below the surface as they could on top with a dry pattern. This Green-Headed Daddy has been quite excellent bringing in big catches and some specimens too from the main small fisheries. Fished with a floating line or sink-tip and a long leader, just the single fly is best. Double-figure rainbows have fallen to this pattern.

DRESSING

Hook: Kamasan B175 size 10 Tinhead painted with fluorescent green enamel paint.
Tying silk: Black.
Body: Yellow wool.
Rib: Black tying silk.
Legs: Three natural pheasant tail fibres knotted and tied in each side.
Wings: 2 cree hackle tips tied in at '10 to 2'.
Head: Clear varnish at tying off only.

1 Mini Pink Zonker Tinhead **2** Green-Headed Daddy Tinhead **3** Bibio Tinhead
4 Hawthorn Tinhead **5** Monday's Child Tinhead Mark II **6** Orange Fritz Tinhead
7 White Viva Tinhead **8** Red-Headed Cat's Tinhead

3 Bibio Tinhead

COMMENT

This is an imitation of the land-born heather fly that naturally finds its way onto the water's surface where it is carried by the wind. Trout love them and both browns and rainbows feed on them during late summer. This goes on year after year on many loughs/lochs in both Ireland and Scotland. I have also encountered them in Wales on Llyn Brenig. I have found this tinhead many times to be as good as a surface floating pattern when it is too bright a day for trout to rise up for them. When such conditions exist try my sinking tinhead pattern.

DRESSING

Hook: Kamasan B175 size 10 Tinhead painted with fluorescent red enamel paint.
Tying silk: Black.
Body: Dubbed-on black marabou with fluorescent red in centre.
Rib: Fine silver wire.
Hackle: Black cock palmered.
Legs: Three red pheasant tail fibres knotted and tied in each side.
Head hackle: Black cock.
Head: Clear varnish at tying off only.

4 Hawthorn Tinhead

COMMENT

The hawthorn fly appears at the time of the May blossom and gets onto the surface of many English trout waters in good numbers. Trout are very partial to them and I have known some preoccupied in feeding on this large black fly. Now having established that both the tinhead Daddy and the tinhead Bibio heather fly worked so well – it was time to find out how a tinhead hawthorn fly would work. It worked superbly, and I am now convinced that trout do not know the difference between a fly having to float or unnaturally sunken.

DRESSING

Hook: Kamasan B175 size 10 Tinhead painted with black varnish.
Tying silk: Black.
Body: Black midge floss.
Legs: Three knotted black pheasant tail fibres each side.
Wings: Two white feather points tied in at '10 to 2'.
Hackle: Black cock.
Head: Clear varnish at tying off only.

5 Monday's Child Tinhead Mark II

COMMENT

This pattern came to my notice several years ago as a wet fly pattern that had a history which began at Chew Valley Lake. I had two or three seasons of great success while using it and won a few competitions as well. It was a natural move for me to try the pattern out in a tinhead form. Now, instead of just a surface wet fly, I had a sort of mini lure that took lots of trout on sinking fly line methods. A good all-round pattern that will not let you down.

DRESSING

Hook: Kamasan B175 size 10 Tinhead painted with fluorescent orange enamel paint.
Tying silk: Black.
Tail: Fluorescent red marabou.
Body: Orange seal's fur.
Rib: Gold oval tinsel.
Hackle: White at front of fly.
Head: Clear varnish at tying off only.

6 Orange Fritz Tinhead

COMMENT

An out-and-out stripping lure pattern. Excellent when fished on a fast-sinking line on the reservoirs particularly in the months of April and May and then again when daphnia blooms become predominant in July and August. This mini lure has also proved very good at the gravel-pit type of trout fishery. Try fishing it on the new slime fly line. It also has its uses at the small fisheries where a long leader and floating line approach is best. It is one you must keep at the ready in your box.

DRESSING

Hook: Kamasan B175 size 10 Tinhead painted with fluorescent orange paint.
Tying silk: Black.
Tail: Fluorescent orange marabou.
Body: Orange fritz.
Head: Clear varnish at tying off only.

7 White Viva Tinhead

COMMENT

I suppose this mini lure must be considered a small coarse fish imitation. As we are all aware, trout feed quite regularly on small fry and this pattern fished sunk on a floating fly line is deadly. It will work equally well on any trout water in the country – reservoirs, small fisheries, gravel pits. You can put your faith in it. Perhaps it's the fluorescent painted head that gives this white lure the edge.

DRESSING

Hook: Kamasan B175 size 10 Tinhead painted with fluorescent green enamel paint.
Tying silk: Black.
Tail: Fluorescent white marabou.
Body: Fluorescent white marabou dubbed on.
Rib: Silver oval tinsel.
Hackle: Grizzle palmered.
Head: Clear varnish at tying off only.

8 Red-Headed Cat's Tinhead

COMMENT

The Cat's Whisker pattern is one of the great modern lures of our time. But, like all top patterns, anglers invent variations that they swear works better than the original. Just by adding a red head to this pattern it turned into a big trout catcher for Bob Church. Browns of over 5lb from Grafham, and a 24½lb rainbow from Earith fishery, fell to his rod while using it. Try this variant for yourself and perhaps it will tempt a specimen trout for you.

DRESSING

Hook: Kamasan B175 size 10 Tinhead painted with fluorescent red enamel paint.
Tying silk: Black.
Tail: Fluorescent white marabou.
Body: Fluorescent green marabou dubbed on.
Rib: Oval gold tinsel.
Hackle: Grizzle palmered.
Head: Clear varnish at tying off only.

Gareth Headland

Gareth Headland has lived at the centre of the stillwater trout fishing scene in Northampton all of his life.

Gareth still fishes the same waters now as he did then – Pitsford, Draycote, Rutland, Grafham, and so on, and has worked in the fishing tackle trade for most of his working life.

Gareth was one of the youngest ever members of the English Loch Style team when, at the age of 23, he qualified to fish the Home International on Llyn Brenig, and won a team gold. Since then Gareth has fished constantly for the successful 'Bob Church Tackle Team', has won a Benson & Hedges Midland Final with a then record 23 fish at Grafham, and looks forward to realizing his ambitions one day of fishing for England in the World Fly Fishing Championships and captaining the England team in the Home International Championship. He has also fished several times in the Général des Eaux Grand Slam European events, in keeping with his interest in world-wide fishing trends and styles.

1 Tangerine Man

COMMENT

Trying black and orange instead of black and the usual lime green came into the minds of myself, Jeremy Herrmann and ex-Youth International Jonah Clarke at Grafham several years ago. I once caught 25 trout in two matches a few years back on this exact dressing at Grafham, including fishing the annual event of the Pro-am match. It's a great sinking line fly, and works with all usual Hi-Di methods of retrieve.

DRESSING

Hook: Scorpion Wee Double size 10 .
Tying silk: Regular black thread waxed.
Tail: Black marabou.
Body: Back part dubbed black marabou, front thorax orange Globrite chenille.
Wing: Black marabou, tied in heavy and picked back to form an international size wing.
Head: Black varnish over black thread.

2 Crystal Cat

COMMENT

This fly has caught me dozens of trout every season for the past six seasons. I thought of it after having had such success with Jeanette Taylor's Baby Doll variant, that is practically the same fly without a wing, but as it looks like a Cat's Whisker I called it Crystal Cat. I have caught fish on it on all types of lines, but find it best as a top dropper fly rather than on the point. It has accounted for trout at all of the Midlands waters, in Wales, at the Bristol waters such as Chew, and also Bewl Water.

DRESSING

Hook: Partridge Captain Hamilton Wet size 10–12.
Tying silk: Black.
Tail: White fluorescent wool.
Body: Back part white fluorescent chenille, front thorax fluorescent lime chenille.
Wing: White marabou, fluorescent if possible, and 6–10 strands of pearl crystal hair.
Head: Usually black varnish over black thread but can be substituted with red fluorescent thread with clear varnish.

1 Tangerine Man   **2** Crystal Cat   **3** White Fritz Cat   **4** Reversed Flo-Jo
5 Orange and Gold Muddler   **6** Black and Pearl Double
7 Wickham's Fancy double   **8** Green Tag Wingless Wickham's

3 White Fritz Cat

COMMENT

Martyn Adams was the first to introduce me to competition-size fritz lures. I fished with his fishing companion Terry Griffiths in an England Team Eliminator at Draycote and he had me 6–0 down on a black and green fly similar to this idea. I knew I had caught in practice on Appetizers, so put the Appetizer on the top dropper, a J.C. Viva in the middle and the White Fritz Cat on the point. As he was catching on the black and green I expected to catch on the J.C. Viva, but I went on to catch Terry up, pass him and win the match.

DRESSING

Hook: Kamasan or Scorpion Wee Double size 10.
Tying silk: White (fluorescent if possible).
Tail: White marabou, tied long and cut back to form a short heavy stub.
Body: Green fritz.
Wing: White marabou, sometimes with a few strands of pearl crystal hair.
Head: White silk, clear varnish.

4 Reversed Flo-Jo

COMMENT

When fishing the original Flo-Jo, first tied by Florence Green of Bewl Fly Fishers, I caught many fish on it and decided to reverse the colours whilst with the England team at Llyn Brenig (actually the reversing was done by Jeanette Taylor whilst the rest of the team and I talked tactics – in the bar of course). Making the wing orange instead of black worked wonders and I caught while practising on it at Brenig and in the match too.

DRESSING

Hook: Kamasan B175 size 10–12.
Tying silk: Black.
Tail: Black floss tied long and cut back to form a short butt.
Butt: Silver flat tinsel at bend of hook.
Body: Fluorescent lime-green chenille.
Wing: Fluorescent orange marabou.
Throat: Black floss, tied in same way as tail.
Head: Black varnish.

5 Orange and Gold Muddler

COMMENT

I was introduced to this fly about eight years ago when acting as boatman for the Home International at Grafham. One of the anglers I was looking after had this fly on his top dropper on a Hi-Di line, and caught 7 or 8 fish on it. At the end of the day he gave it to me as I was fishing a match the next day. I took a few fish on it in a very hard match. Since then I've caught well on it as a top dropper fly on the Hi-Di, also on intermediate lines and, but not quite so successfully, on a floating line in the old muddler style of fishing.

DRESSING

Hook: Captain Hamilton Wet Fly size 10–12.
Tying silk: Light brown.
Tail: 4–5 strands gold crystal hair.
Body: Orange floss, ribbed with fine gold oval tinsel.
Hackle: Deer hair left long behind the spun head.
Wing: Orange squirrel hair dressed sparsely and 8–10 strands of gold crystal hair.

6 Black and Pearl Double

COMMENT

This is a great point fly to fish on a medium sink line such as a Wet Cel II or a Hi-Di line, and I first used it about 14 years ago at Grafham, but with pearl flashabou in the wing, as crystal hair was unheard of then. Going back through my fishing diary I see I took 7 trout on this fly in a match at Grafham in 1984 to get into the Midland Final which greatly excited me at the time. It really is only a move on from a Viva with the green moving from the back to the front of the fly, and the pearl dazzlelure gives it great visibility.

DRESSING

Hook: Kamasan or Scorpion Wee Double size 12.
Tying silk: Fluorescent lime-green.
Body: Pearl dazzlelure.
Wing: Black marabou with 6–8 strands pearl crystal hair.
Head: Fluorescent green thread, clear varnish.

7 Wickham's Fancy Double

COMMENT

I have used double-hook wet flies for many years now and this is one of my favourites. It catches lots of fish fished slow on a floating or wet-tip line as you can inch it back so, so slowly. Also it catches well on intermediate lines. I know my team-mate Terry Oliver uses double-hook wets a lot, the Silver Invicta double being his favourite, and not many anglers in England can match Terry for expertise in floating line and wet fly fishing. This fly is an excellent summer pattern.

DRESSING

Hook: Scorpion Wee Double size 10–12.
Tying silk: Fine black.
Tail: Red game or ginger cock hackle fibres.
Body: Medium flat gold tinsel.
Hackle: Palmered red game or ginger cock.
Wing: Two wing slips cut from starling feather.
Head: Black thread, black varnish.

8 Green Tag Wingless Wickham's

COMMENT

The amount of various methods on which this fly has caught me fish amazes me. As well as its traditional use – that is, on a floating line pulling loch style, I have also caught a lot of fish on it as a top or middle dropper fly when fishing deep on Hi-Di lines. Here it seems that perhaps the fish that follow a more gaudy, bright point fly that has attracted them go past it to get to the dropper flies that look more natural to them. The tail floss or wool can be substituted for red or orange to provide a different colour combination that might work.

DRESSING

Hook: Bob Church Wet Fly size 10–14.
Tying silk: Fine black.
Tail: Lime-green floss or yarn.
Body: Fine gold flat tinsel.
Hackle: Ginger cock palmered.
Head: Fine black thread, black varnish.

Martyn Adams

Martyn started fishing at the age of seventeen on Welsh rivers and Midlands reservoirs. After a long rugby career he took up competition fishing in 1988. He won the English National in 1990 and the Rivers National in 1991. He also won the first Rivers International on the Welsh Dee in 1992.

He has been a member of the English team on three occasions winning gold every time and was a member of the European Grand Slam winning team of 1992 and 1993. He has fished in the Benson & Hedges International final twice and has won or been in the top positions in many competitions including the Leeda Pairs, Airflo Pairs, League matches. He won the Bob Church/*Angling Times* Classic in its tenth year. He has also qualified again for the England team in the 1998 Home International.

1 Adams' Abortion

COMMENT

This is my variation on a new fly of the last two seasons. A great point fly on the Hi-Di line with a fast retrieve but also works well on a figure of eight or very slow pulls. Always hold it in the water after the retrieve because a lot of fish take it on the hang. It is a good fly for all Midlands waters and has even caught sea trout in Scotland. You can vary the tail colour to green, pink, and so forth.

DRESSING

Hook: Kamasan B175 or B270 size 10.
Tying silk: Orange fluorescent.
Tail: Fluorescent orange yarn.
Body: Olive fritz.
Wing: Gold and silver mix flash material.
Head: Clear varnish.

2 The Simple One

COMMENT

Soon we will not need birds, the feathered kind I mean, because all the flies I catch fish on nowadays seem to have no feathers in them, all man-made fibres. There are many colours you can tie in this fly, orange being a good one on all Midlands reservoirs – but I have caught on green shade no. 12 as well. I tie all my flies to competitions size.

DRESSING

Hook: Kamasan B175 or B270 size 10.
Tying silk: Fire red.
Tail: Globrite no. 5 multi-yarn.
Body: Pearl tinsel lureflash.
Rib: Silver wire.
Wing: Globrite no. 5 multi-yarn.
Head: Clear varnish.

1 Adams' Abortion   **2** The Simple One   **3** Martyn's Viva Variant
4 Cat's Whisker Variant   **5** Adams' Orange Tadpole   **6** Martyn's Olive Booby
7 Adams' Pink   **8** Adams' Black & Silver Knight

3 Martyn's Viva Variant

COMMENT

The combination of fluorescent green and black seems to work well on all waters. This fly has caught me a lot of fish on the middle dropper on a Hi-Di line at all reservoirs in England, Scotland and Wales. I never leave it off my cast. It can be tied with jungle cock cheeks – both dressings work very well.

DRESSING

Hook: Kamasan B175 or B270 size 10.
Tying silk: Black.
Tail: Fluorescent lime.
Body: Black wool dubbed.
Rib: Flat silver.
Wing: Black marabou.
Hackle: Black hen tied at throat.
Head: Clear varnish.

4 Cat's Whisker Variant

COMMENT

Try this Cat's Whisker when fishing a Hi-Di line at the start of the season or the back end. It can best be used as a point fly tied on a double hook, or as a single on the top dropper. It works on all lines from a Hi-Di to a floater with most retrieves from slow pulls to the 'roly poly'. When trout are taking fry it is good on a floater with a silver thorax pheasant tail as a dropper. Can be fished on all lakes, reservoirs, and so on. I know people in Internationals who have even used it on a river and won.

DRESSING

Hook: Kamasan B175 or B270 size 10.
Tying silk: Fluorescent red.
Tail: Fluorescent lime yarn.
Body: Globrite chenille no. 11.
Wing: White fluorescent marabou.
Overwing: Four strands of ripple flash silver or gold tinsel.
Head: Clear varnish.

5 Adams' Orange Tadpole

COMMENT

If you want an orange fly go no further! This is the one, good on all Midlands reservoirs, on all lines from Hi-Di to a floater. Always have it on when the water is coloured, that is why orange always works well at Grafham at the start of the season. Even tied on a treble hook for salmon it works. Never be without your Orange Taddy!

DRESSING

Hook: Kamasan B175 or B270 size 10.
Tying silk: Fluorescent orange.
Tail: Fluorescent orange marabou plus four strands of ripple flash silver.
Body: Globrite chenille no. 5.
Head: Clear varnish.

6 Martyn's Olive Booby

COMMENT

We have all seen big boobies. This one is a little cracker on a flat calm day when the boat is only just moving. Cast this out on a Hi-Di line and let it sink and lie on the bottom with about 18in of leader nylon from the fly line and slowly figure-of-eight back. The trout will swallow it with confidence.

DRESSING

Hook: Kamasan B401 size 12.
Tying silk: Olive.
Tail: Medium olive marabou.
Body: Medium olive marabou chopped up and dubbed on to hook.
Eyes: Yellow plastazote.
Head: Clear varnish.

7 Adams' Pink

COMMENT

When I started trout fishing thirty years ago, if someone had told me that one day I would catch a trout on a pink fly I would have told them to go away. But now thirty years later I would apologize and buy them a pint. It is a good fly at the start of the season, fished on the point or top dropper on a Hi-Di to a floater. Browns at Rutland like them, in fact they fight with each other to take them. Also as I have found out, this season's salmon like pink too.

DRESSING

Hook: Kamasan B175 or B270 size 10.
Tying silk: Pink.
Tail: Fluorescent pink marabou.
Body: Flat silver.
Rib: Silver wire.
Wing: Fluorescent pink marabou.

8 Adams' Black & Silver Knight

COMMENT

While sitting at the vice one day tying Abortions, I was thinking that the Viva was a good fly; green, black and silver. I had some black and silver mix so I made a few Knights. I visited Grafham the next day, put one on and caught three fish on a Wet Cel II line so I've tied some more for next season.

DRESSING

Hook: Kamasan B175 or B270 size 10.
Tying silk: Black.
Tail: Fluorescent green yarn.
Body: Black fritz.
Wing: Black and silver mix of flashabou.
Head: Clear varnish.

145

Kevin Garn

Regular Midlands reservoir fly fisher Kevin is very successful as a sunken-line lure fisherman. His catches at Pitsford, Ravensthorpe, Grafham, Draycote and Rutland are very consistent, his results including a lot of specimen trout.

Kevin belongs to the Mid-Northants Trout Fishers where he has been their club champion. A keen and inventive tyer of all types of fly, he claims that this is one of the main reasons for his success. This particular set of lures are his long-tailed highly mobile variety; they are rather special.

1 Fluorescent Special

COMMENT

A lure devised for Ravensthorpe and Pitsford, fish singularly on a long leader from the bank. During early season use it with a slow-sinking fly line, but as summer approaches often a floater will be best. When boat fishing on dour days try using it on the fastest sinking fly line, then allow it to sink right to the bottom before stripping back very fast.

DRESSING

Hook: Long shank leaded at head only, size 8–10.
Tying silk: Olive.
Tail: Long orange marabou.
Body: Orange fluorescent chenille.
Rib: Gold oval thread.
Thorax: Two turns fluorescent lime-green chenille.
Head: Clear varnish.

2 Olive Sparkle Tinhead

COMMENT

During the 1997 season I fished Draycote quite a lot and this was my first choice for the point; it was quite outstanding. Fished on a Wet Cel II fly line, I made long casts and retrieved 'roly-poly' style. Later I tried the pattern elsewhere and similar limit bags followed at Pitsford and Rutland. There is no doubt that all my lures with these added long marabou tails have that extra wiggle action that induces the take.

DRESSING

Hook: Long shank tinhead special hook size 8–10.
Tying silk: Olive.
Tail: Long olive marabou and four strands of gold holographic.
Body: Olive micro-fritz.
Rib: Gold oval thread.
Hackle: Palmer grizzle cock.
Head: Paint on eyes, yellow outer with black pupils.

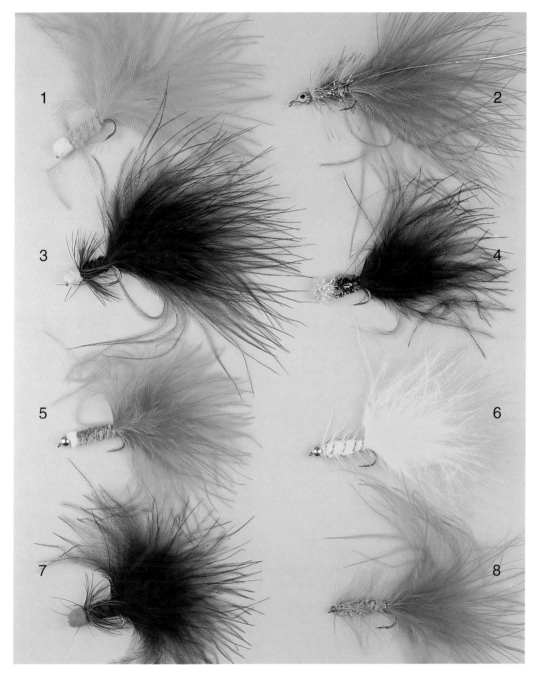

1 Fluorescent Special   2 Olive Sparkle Tinhead   3 Bombhead Pea
4 Fritz Pea   5 Fluorescent Damsel   6 Cloudy Water Special   7 Red Breast
8 Oliver's Favourite

3 Bombhead Pea

COMMENT

I (B.C.) can certainly vouch for this lure, having made some great bank catches with it while using a sink-tip shooting head. When fishing the bank at Elinor Fishery, I landed an 8lb 10oz rainbow that was the best fish there for over a year. This is a great all-round lure that is excellent during early season and then again later on in September. I often use a single dropper unweighted fly with this one. Kevin's best fish on it is a 10¼lb rainbow from Ringstead Grange.

DRESSING

Hook: Kamasan leaded at the head.
Tying silk: Black.
Tail: Long black marabou.
Body: Black chenille.
Hackle: Black hen.
Thorax: Two turns fluorescent lime-green chenille.
Head: Clear varnish.

4 Fritz Pea

COMMENT

For whatever reason, this lure fishes much better when retrieved very slowly – almost at nymph fishing speed; therefore it works well at both the small fisheries and the reservoirs. The best line with this pattern has been the floater. If ever you are in doubt about what pattern to tie on, try this one – I promise it will not let you down.

DRESSING

Hook: Kamasan B175 leaded at head size 8–10.
Tying silk: Black.
Tail: Long black marabou.
Body: Black fritz.
Thorax: Fluorescent lime-green fritz.
Head: Clear varnish.

5 Fluorescent Damsel

COMMENT

A great midsummer lure pattern that obviously works well at damsel fly time. For the best results, fish it slowly on a floating line as you would a nymph. Although most of my descriptions for fishing these lures seem very simple, this is the secret. Slow twitches makes the long tail work even more tantalizingly so concentrate on this.

DRESSING

Hook: Long shank with goldhead bead size 8–10.
Tying silk: Olive.
Tail: Long olive marabou.
Body: Olive chenille.
Rib: Gold oval tinsel.
Thorax: Two turns fluorescent yellow chenille.
Head: Clear varnish.

6 Cloudy Water Special

COMMENT

The most deadly of all lures for cloudy waters – why? Because, as salmon fishers will confirm, bright yellow stands out best in brown flood-water conditions. The same can be said for the coloured algae-stained waters of some reservoirs during midsummer heatwaves. At this time water visibility can go down to a few inches and most normal flies get lost in the murk. This lure stands out best so the trout see it and take it.

DRESSING

Hook: Long shank with goldhead bead size 8–10.
Tying silk: Yellow.
Tail: Fluorescent yellow long marabou.
Body: Fluorescent yellow chenille.
Rib: Gold oval thread.
Hackle: Palmered yellow cock.
Head: Clear varnish.

7 Red Breast

COMMENT

A specialist lure for Ravensthorpe where results have been good. The good limit bag catches with this lure have fallen to sunken line tactics. This is just another pattern I fall back on for reliability. A good one to try when all else seems to be failing.

DRESSING

Hook: Kamasan B175 leaded at head only, size 8–10.
Tying silk: Red.
Tail: Long black marabou.
Body: Black chenille.
Hackle: Black hen.
Thorax: Fluorescent red chenille two turns.
Head: Clear varnish.

8 Oliver's Favourite

COMMENT

Although this is one of my favourite lures it is even more so for my England International fishing friend Terry Oliver. Terry uses it a lot for all his summer fishing, especially at Toft Newton and Rutland Water. It is always fished slowly on a floating fly line – where the fly is tweaked back with a figure-of-eight retrieve. It has the ability to tempt an old resident trout into making a mistake.

DRESSING

Hook: Long shank leaded at head only, size 8–10.
Tying silk: Olive.
Tail: Long olive marabou.
Body: Olive chenille.
Rib: Gold oval thread.
Hackle: Olive cock.
Head: Clear varnish.

John Emerson

Like many other fishermen John spends quite a few of his winter evenings attempting to invent new fly patterns to tempt the fish at my local waters which are Pitsford, Grafham and Rutland Water. The flies he uses also work well at most of the other reservoirs throughout England.

His twenty years of fishing and fly tying have seen a lot of improvement in fly-tying materials, so much so, that we are almost spoilt for choice when creating new patterns. It's always very satisfying to find that a brainwave at the vice becomes a successful pattern in the new season. He is constantly on the look-out for new fly patterns to complement his fly box. Most early competitions work consists of fast-sinking lines teamed with traditional mini lures. These are the patterns that John turns to when all the well-known killing flies cease to work.

1 Searcher

COMMENT

I find this a superb fly for deep buzzer feeding trout. Use it on a Hi-Di line on the top dropper with two buzzers behind for the best effect. Ideally I like to use it in gin-clear water where its effect can be devastating. In the 1996 Benson & Hedges eliminator on Rutland Water I caught five fish on this fly giving me second place overall. My team came first with ten fish so, in effect, the Searcher caught half of the team's total catch.

DRESSING

Hook: Kamasan B175.
Tying silk: Globrite no. 4.
Tail: Yellow marabou.
Body: Bi-visible yellow.
Head: Globrite no. 4 varnished.

2 Daphne

COMMENT

Great fly for catching daphnia-feeding fish especially at Grafham Water from June onwards. I find the best position for Daphne is the point from, floating lines to fast sinkers. I first gave this fly to Jeanette Taylor the day before the Ladies Home International at Grafham Water in June 1995. Jeanette used it and caught ten fish making her top lady at the event and securing gold for the England Ladies. In the same year Daphne gave me second place in the Confederation Final at Grafham Water.

DRESSING

Hook: Kamasan B270 Double.
Tying silk: Black.
Tail: Twelve strands Globrite no. 4.
Body: Medium pearl lureflash over black tying thread.
Hackle: Palmered light orange.
Rib: Thin silver wire.
Head: Black tying silk varnished.

1 Searcher **2** Daphne **3** Major Murk **4** T Shirt Fly **5** The Classic
6 White & Orange Killer **7** Pink Lady **8** The Surprise

3 Major Murk

COMMENT

I tied this fly specifically for dirty, murky water at Grafham. I find it works best when fishing deep and slow and is especially useful in tempting fish to the 'hang'. I use it on either the top dropper or the point. In 1996 I fished the final round of the Major League competition at Grafham and this fly saved my day by catching eight fish when all the usual patterns wouldn't work. I also caught well on this pattern at Grafham and Pitsford during the early part of the season.

DRESSING

Hook: Kamasan B175.
Tying silk: Black.
Tail: Lime-green marabou.
Body: Black micro fritz.
Hackle: Lime-green fritz.
Head: Black silk varnished.

4 T Shirt Fly

COMMENT

I called this fly the T Shirt Fly because the fabric paint used on the body is designed for T shirt motifs. This fly is another great all-rounder that will work well on buzzer and daphnia feeding fish. In 1995 Dave Shipman used the T Shirt Fly to catch a double limit of sixteen fish by 2pm in the Bob Church open competition, easily securing him first place. It works best as the point fly from fast-sinking lines through to floaters. The pattern works just as effectively when tied on a single Kamasan B175 and fished on the top dropper.

DRESSING

Hook: Kamasan B270 Double.
Tying silk: Globrite no. 7.
Tail: Light orange marabou.
Body: Orange slick fabric paint (available from art shops), allow 3–4 hours to dry.
Rib: Medium oval tinsel.
Hackle: Light orange.
Head: Globrite no.7 varnished.

5 The Classic

COMMENT

The first time I used this fly was in the Bob Church Classic in 1996 and it caught me three fish up the North Arm on what turned out to be a very difficult day. Incidentally, the winner on that day caught five fish, and my three placed me eleventh. This fly also worked again this season at Rutland for an angler, new to the sport, who stepped in at the last minute in the Bob Church Classic. He fished with Paul Davison up the North Arm and caught fourteen fish on the Hi-Di.

DRESSING

Hook: Traditional Wet size 8 & Kamasan B275 Double size 10.
Tying silk: Globrite no. 7.
Tail: Light orange marabou.
Body: Orange bootlace.
Wing: Light orange marabou and 4 strands of copper Globrite.
Head: Globrite no. 7 and three coats of clear varnish.

6 White & Orange Killer

COMMENT

I used this fly for the first time at Hanningfield when I first entered an eliminator in 1989. I caught three fish to gain a place in the Confederation Final which was to be fished again at Hanningfield. In the final I was drawn with the famous old World Champion Brian Leadbetter. On the day I caught three fish using this fly and Brian had two. Being a little nervous, I managed to lose four fish that had all come to this fly. I qualified in twelfth position and gained a place at my first National Final. This fly works well on all sinking lines.

DRESSING

Hook: Kamasan B175.
Tying silk: Black.
Tail: 10 strands Globrite no. 7.
Rib: Medium oval silver tinsel.
Body: Fluorescent white chenille.
Wing: White rabbit & orange rabbit over the top.
Head: Black silk + 2 lureflash black and red eyes superglued on.

7 Pink Lady

COMMENT

This is a new fly that I have started to experiment with this year. I have used it at both Rutland and Grafham on a Hi-Di line using a fast retrieve and it seems to hammer the stock fish. I have also had an over-wintered rainbow of 3lb 10oz from Rutland's North Arm on this fly. I have yet to use it in a competition but I am totally convinced it will prove popular in my competition box for many seasons to come. I had noticed that pink was very popular for early season competitions; most of the 'top names' in the sport were using pink.

DRESSING

Hook: Kamasan B270 Double.
Tying silk: Globrite pink.
Tail: Fluorescent pink marabou.
Body: Pink T shirt paint.
Rib: Medium oval silver tinsel.
Wing: White marabou.
Head: Pink Globrite floss and three coats of varnish.

8 The Surprise

COMMENT

This is another of my 'new' fly patterns that I have been experimenting with this season (1997). So far I have caught well at Rutland on two outings using this pattern on the top dropper on a Hi-Di line followed by either black buzzers or black mini lures on the middle and point. I merely use it on the top dropper as an 'attractor' and I was quite surprised to find that the fish came from the depths on the 'hang' and took this pattern as opposed to the buzzers. I am also convinced that this pattern will feature well in the competition box.

DRESSING

Hook: Kamasan B175.
Tying silk: Globrite no. 12.
Tail: Lime-green marabou.
Body: Lime-green micro fritz.
Head: Globrite no. 12 floss and three coats of varnish.

Nicola Church

My daughter Nicola has a fine record for a young female fly fisher. She has qualified to represent the England Ladies team seven times and she is still only 26 years of age.

Nicola was captain of the England Ladies team in 1995 when the team won gold at Grafham Water. She is also the 1997 Ladies International Champion after winning the individual title on Lough Melvin in Ireland. Nicola also has a second overall under her belt at the Ladies International at Loch Fitty, Scotland in 1992.

Competition fly fishing holds an interest for her and she has been a member of a Benson & Hedges team that won a Midlands heat. In 1997 she made her way through the various eliminators to the English National Final (Senior) held at Grafham. Although she boated ten fish she finished 32nd out of the country's top 100. Nicola's best wild fish was a 7lb 6oz rainbow from Grafham caught on her Pink Panther Tinhead. Nicola's fly tying has developed due to her competition fishing.

1 Pink Panther Tinhead

COMMENT

Pink is a favourite colour of mine for fishing at Grafham, especially when the water colours up. This fly took my best ever rainbow of 7lb 6oz from Gaynes Cove at Grafham on opening day when Anglian Water took management over back in 1990. It is best fished slow and long in coloured water on a Hi-Di and 'hung' for at least 30 seconds to give the fish time to see it. Depending on how coloured the water is I might shorten my nylon leader to keep my flies close together so if they turn away from one they immediately see the one behind.

DRESSING

Hook: Size 10 Tinhead.
Tying silk: Pink.
Tail: Fluorescent pink marabou.
Body: Dubbed fluorescent pink marabou.
Rib: Silver oval thread.
Hackle: Pink and white cock.
Head: Painted yellow eyes with black pupils.

2 Kev's Puller

COMMENT

This fly was given to me by Kevin Garn about four seasons ago. It has proved very successful for me as a point fly on a double hook on all lines. It is a fly that I would put on as first choice when going out on any water as it will always pick up one or two fish. It can be fished either with long, slow pulls then 'hung' or with a typical lure retrieve of varied twitches and pulls giving the marabou life-like movement. The cheeks, in my view, are essential to this tying as the pattern tried without has limited advantages.

DRESSING

Hook: Size 10 double.
Tying silk: Black.
Tail: Pearl crystal hair.
Body: Pearl crystal hair.
Wing: Black marabou to bend of hook.
Cheeks: Jungle cock.
Head: Clear varnish.

1 Pink Panther Tinhead   **2** Kev's Puller   **3** Goalie   **4** Yellow Fellow
5 Cobblers Away   **6** Jelly Belly Fry   **7** John's Pea   **8** Feather Duster

3 Goalie

COMMENT

This fly was thrown together as an experiment at the back end of the 1997 season. It gave both myself and my father, Bob, great success, especially at Grafham and Rutland Waters. It seems to work well on daphnia-feeding fish cruising at about 5ft below the surface – easy to reach on a slime line. During the English National Final held on Grafham I took seven of my ten fish to this fly in quick succession. Again the retrieve should be varied and twitchy to create a natural look.

DRESSING

Hook: Size 10.
Tying silk: Black.
Body: Fluorescent green marabou dubbed on roughly.
Rib: Fine silver wire.
Wing: Black marabou and a few strands of pearl crystal.
Head: Clear varnish.

4 Yellow Fellow

COMMENT

This has turned out to be another coloured water pattern, also good for tempting the brown trout in reservoirs. When the reservoirs have a stir-up because of strong winds the water takes on a milky colour, especially at Grafham. Trout have difficulty picking out our various lures at this time but this one stands out and continues to work. The key is to keep everything slow. In the 1997 season this lure became excellent for catching brown trout especially at Rutland where it accounted for many 3lb+ fish. Incidentally, we normally return browns.

DRESSING

Hook: Size 10 double or single.
Tying silk: Black.
Tail: Fluorescent yellow marabou.
Body: Yellow fritz.
Wing: Fluorescent yellow marabou.
Head: Clear varnish.

5 Cobblers Away

COMMENT

This is really a Kev's Puller but due to my other passion, football, I have named it after my local team as their away strip is orange. This is a good pattern for early season stock fish, which makes it a must for competition fishing. Best fished as a point fly on a double hook on a fast sink Hi-Di line and 'hung' at the end and in the middle of the retrieve. Will arouse rainbows' natural aggression and induce takes. Again the eyes are essential to this pattern.

DRESSING

Hook: Size 12 double or single.
Tying silk: Black.
Tail: Bunch orange crystal (long enough to continue with body).
Body: Orange crystal.
Wing: Fluorescent hot orange marabou.
Cheeks: Jungle cock.
Head: Build up big, clear varnish.

6 Jelly Belly Fry

COMMENT

Each July the reservoirs and gravel pits become alive with coarse fish fry and they soon grow to about half an inch long. Trout become preoccupied with feeding on these swarms of pin fry or jelly fry as fly fishers know them. This is a good pattern for such times. It caught a lovely brownie for me at Grafham in 1997 and I shall use it with great faith in the seasons ahead. Best fished on a slow sink or slime line around the shallows when pin fry are still quite small.

DRESSING

Hook: Size 10–12.
Tying silk: Black.
Tail: White marabou.
Underbody: Pearl lurex.
Overbody: Stretched clear polythene strip.
Head: Clear varnish, painted-on eyes.

7 John's Pea

COMMENT

Never go on Grafham without this on your top dropper when lure fishing! This is John Emerson's tying of the popular Green Pea and although many fly fishers have their own version I just had to include this purely for its consistency in catching trout. I always have it on the top dropper and hardly ever take it off. I find it serves different purposes each time, as an attractor with nymphs or as a take inducer when lure fishing. Can be fished on any line with any retrieve.

DRESSING

Hook: Size 10–12.
Tying silk: Black.
Tail: Black marabou.
Body: Dubbed black marabou.
Rib: Black tying thread.
Thorax: Fluorescent yellow chenille.
Head: Clear varnish.

8 Feather Duster

COMMENT

Paul Davison of the Ospreys from Newcastle upon Tyne must take credit for this pattern. He scored a double limit with its help at the 1997 Bob Church/*Angling Times* Classic. Andy Eyre was his last-minute boat partner to whom Paul kindly gave a copy of this pattern. Andy caught fifteen rainbows and finished sixth in the event, Paul third. Since then the pattern has passed to me and it is a great top dropper fly. The hackle and marabou have a lovely action in the water which induces take after take. We weren't sure of its original name so we made one up!

DRESSING

Hook: Size 10–12.
Tying silk: Red.
Tail: Pale pink cock hackle fibres.
Body: Flat silver tinsel.
Wing: Fluorescent pink marabou.
Hackle: Pale pink cock hackle long fibres tied cloak-style.
Head: Built-up clear varnish.

Paul Grevett

The first waters Paul fished in England when he moved here were in the north including Clowbridge Reservoir near Burnley, now closed, Barnsfold near Preston and Patshull Park in Staffordshire. He met Derek Webster from Wolverhampton at Gailey on the bank – he was catching, Paul was not. Derek gave Paul a Cove's Nymph and he started to catch. This was the start of a fast learning curve. Derek sent him flies and instructions on how to use them on a regular basis. Derek was then forced to give up tying due to a back injury and Paul had to take up the craft for himself. Paul formed the Lancashire Spartons with some other flyfishing friends to take part in competitions and to try loch-style fishing. This year they were delighted with a fifth-place finish in the Benson & Hedges National Final.

Nowadays he ties some of his own flies when time permits but also receives flies from Sid Knight, who regularly sends Paul patterns to try. His selection is a mix of his own and some from others. The selection includes his favourites for loch style and small waters.

1 Jammy Dodger

COMMENT

Good early and late season lure, also very effective in coloured water. I have caught fresh stockies and residents with this lure. In a competition on Patshull Park I moved into a bay just as a well-known nymph fisherman was moving out claiming that the area was devoid of fish. I had four trout in as many minutes. Try it on an intermediate, counting down to find the taking depth. I usually give this lure a bit of speed when retrieving, so the fish don't have a chance to think twice. Originator of this lure is Derek Webster.

DRESSING

Hook: Long shank size 10 leadhead or tinhead.
Tying silk: Orange.
Tail: White and fluorescent orange mixed.
Body: White chenille.
Rib: Oval silver.
Hackle: Fluorescent orange dyed partridge.
Head: Painted eyes.

2 Sequin Damsel

COMMENT

Excellent all-year Sid Knight original pattern. The sequin sets up turbulence to give extra movement to the hackle and tail. Fishes at all depths, will catch on a slow figure-of-eight or stripped retrieve depending on the trout's mood. It works everywhere from the smallest of small waters to the big reservoirs. Use a slow sink and find the depth. The takes are usually very positive but if you get nips just keep retrieving until the trout hooks itself.

DRESSING

Hook: Kamasan B170 size 10.
Tying silk: Olive.
Tail: Olive marabou with few strands of pearl tinsel.
Body: Green and brown mottled chenille.
Hackle: Olive partridge.
Head: Gold or silver bead backed up by a sequin.

1 Jammy Dodger 2 Sequin Damsel 3 Olive Leach Gold Head Stinger
4 White Fritz Mini Nobbler 5 Olive Fritz International 6 Paul's Fritz Viva
7 Pearly Damsel (Mini Lure) 8 Eye Spy

3 Olive Leech Gold Head Stinger

COMMENT

Usually used when fish are deep and tail nipping. Figure-of-eight retrieve with varying speeds on a sinker. You can obviously use any colour rabbit, i.e. black or white. This lure seems to work when other large lures don't, this could be because it is so mobile or because we don't always feel if a fish is tail nipping. If they nip this one's tail they'll get a surprise.

DRESSING

Hook: Size 10–12.
Tying silk: Olive.
Body: Strip-dyed olive rabbit and 15lb nylon from head to hook.
Head: Gold bead to hook cut at bend.

4 White Fritz Mini Nobbler

COMMENT

This is my favourite back end of season white lure for small waters. I usually fish it with an intermediate line and a fairly quick jerky retrieve. The trout seem to come out of nowhere and take it with real confidence, sometimes only a couple of inches below the surface. I keep the tying as sparse as possible so as to give a slim profile. I find that many fritz lures available commercially are very bulky and definitely 'scare' a lot of fish off.

DRESSING

Hook: Tinhead or leadhead with painted eyes.
Tying silk: White.
Tail: White marabou long.
Body: White fritz, only a couple of turns.
Butt: Lime-green twinkle or chenille.

5 Olive Fritz International

COMMENT

Olive is my favourite colour for lures. Also I find myself incorporating fritz in a lot of my flies these days, hence this olive fritz mini lure I designed for international rules fishing. It is one of those flies that is either deadly on the day or does nothing. I fish it usually on the point from a figure-of-eight to a fast retrieve. This year in Barnsdale Creek at Rutland this fly accounted for six fish in a bag of ten in the Benson & Hedges when the rod average was just over two.

DRESSING

Hook: B175 Kamasan size 10.
Tying silk: Olive.
Tail: Olive marabou.
Body: One or two turns olive fritz.
Butt: Lime-green twinkle.
Rib: Fine gold oval.
Hackle: Olive partridge.
Head: Clear varnish.

6 Paul's Fritz Viva

COMMENT

I think everyone has a Viva version of their own. This is my favourite and an early season must. I also tie it on a double for early season loch-style dredging on the likes of Rutland. Quite often I will use this fly on the dropper with a white lure on the point. When the early season trout are lying deep, as they usually are, I catch a lot of trout 'on the drop' while counting down with the Viva on the dropper.

DRESSING

Hook: Sprite wide gape size 10.
Tying silk: Black.
Tail: Globrite green floss.
Body: Black fritz two or three turns clipped across back so that marabou lies flat.
Wing: Black marabou.
Head: Clear varnish.

7 Pearly Damsel (Mini Lure)

COMMENT

This is a fly sent to me originally by Sid Knight for use in a competition at Draycote. I did not like the look of it at first and thought it was a bit too flashy. After three hours with only one fish I thought I might as well try it. I ended up with thirteen fish in the boat and qualified for the English Loch Style Final at my first attempt. I fished it on the slime line with a jerky figure-of-eight retrieve. It has also caught fish at Rutland and various small waters. It seems to work best when the water has a touch of colour to it. I also use a smaller single hook version.

DRESSING

Hook: Size 10 international double.
Tying silk: Brown.
Tail: Pheasant tail fibres.
Body: Mix of olive and red seal's fur.
Rib: Gold wire.
Wing/hackle: Few strands pearl tinsel.
Thorax: Lite brite.
Thorax cover: Pearl tinsel.
Head: Clear varnish.

8 Eye Spy

COMMENT

Another variation on the green/white theme. Designed for international rules fishing either as a dropper or on the point. I often use this instead of the mini Cat's Whisker; whether the painted eyes play a part I don't know but it seems that they may well do. Again mainly an early and late season fly, but then aren't most lures? It has a slim profile for a lure but just a little bit of flash to attract the trout. Usually works pulled on a sinker but will also catch 'on the hang'.

DRESSING

Hook: Kamasan B170 size 10.
Tying silk: Black.
Tail: White marabou and a few strands pearl tinsel or Krystal Flash.
Body: Fluorescent yellow chenille.
Rib: Silver flat tinsel.
Head: Built up with black thread then painted eyes.

Gareth Hancock

I've included 17-year-old Gareth in this book of experts for a very good reason. Gareth is a keen young coarse fisherman from our village who asked if I would help him to start up fly fishing for stillwater trout. This was only two years ago and he has progressed extremely well with his fly tying and trout catching. He is a perfect example for any beginner or improver to follow. The lesson to be learnt from this is that if you can tie and invent your own flies, then go and fish at several different top stillwaters; you can get good very quickly. If you have the will to do well you certainly can achieve a great deal. Here are Gareth's own tied lures that catch him a lot of trout.

1 Brown Sedgebrook Lure

COMMENT

This fly was one of my first designs and fished very well in unfavourable conditions at Ringstead Grange fishery. On days when there is bright sunshine this lure can produce fish when others may fail. I prefer to fish this fly using short sharp pulls of the line; the response is often a violent take. It is best suited to clear water fished mid-depth – this is because if the water is cloudy the Sedgebrook Lure is not all that visible due to its lack of bright colours. The thorax made of Lite Brite is very effective on this pattern.

DRESSING

Hook: Bob Church long-shank lure/nymph leaded under body size 12.
Tying silk: Black.
Tail: Brown marabou.
Body: Natural pheasant tail fibres.
Rib: Medium gold tinsel.
Thorax: Pearl Lite Brite.
Hackle: Ginger cock.
Head: Clear varnish.

2 Olive Sedgebrook Lure

COMMENT

This is very much the same lure as the previous pattern with the only difference being the colour. If the natural-coloured Sedgebrook Lure does not produce a response from the trout, the olive version may just do so. The olive lure can be very productive when fished near to weed beds on a floating line. This pattern is only lightly weighted with a few turns of fine lead wire underneath the body material. It has caught me a number of fish when the main food source is damsels. Best fished with a figure-of-eight retrieve.

DRESSING

Hook: Bob Church long shank lure/nymph leaded underbody size 12.
Tying silk: Olive.
Tail: Olive marabou.
Body: Olive pheasant tail fibres.
Rib: Medium gold tinsel.
Thorax: Chartreuse Lite Brite.
Hackle: Ginger cock.
Head: Clear varnish.

1 Brown Sedgebrook Lure   2 Olive Sedgebrook Lure   3 Bright-Eyed Booby
4 Red & Black Attack   5 Hancock's Hammerer!   6 Church Hill Chomper
7 Black & White Cat   8 Pitsford's Prowler

3 Bright-Eyed Booby

COMMENT

In the short period of time I have been fly fishing I have found myself attracted to fishing the booby; I was amazed at how effective it is. I made this pattern because I believed that the booby needed to stand out even more in the water: I changed the eyes to orange, to replace the regular white ones, and added some twinkle to the main body and tail. This pattern proved most successful for me when I was fishing at Rutland. Best fished with a short leader with a fast sinking line.

DRESSING

Hook: Kamasan B175 size 10.
Tying silk: Black.
Tail: Black marabou with twinkle fibres.
Body: Black antron.
Rib: Black twinkle.
Head: Orange plastazote shaped into spheres.

4 Red & Black Attack

COMMENT

This lure works at its best when the fish are feeding deep down. Twitched along the bottom this lure can often induce very fierce takes. I used this pattern at Grafham Water with pleasing results. I have had most success using this lure on a very fast sinking line. This method came into its own when fishing the dam wall at Grafham. The blend of red and black antron gives the lure quite a unique appeal. Many lure patterns I have come across in my short time in fly fishing had a solid colour body, therefore I wanted to see a change in style.

DRESSING

Hook: Tinhead short shank size 10.
Tying silk: Black.
Tail: Black marabou.
Body: Blend of red and black antron.
Hackle: Throat hackle made of orange hackle fibres.
Head: Clear varnish.

5 Hancock's Hammerer!

COMMENT

This lure is very useful in the early months of the season for obvious reasons – its bright colours make the lure very attractive to the trout. It fishes well on either a floating or medium sink line with quite a fast jerky retrieve. The fast retrieve makes the wings on the lure create a lot of disturbance in the water which can often trigger a response from a trout that is not actually feeding. An added bonus on this fly is that the tail has 'glow in the dark' fibres in it. This is a lure that glows in the dark, creates disturbance and sinks quickly.

DRESSING

Hook: Kamasan B175 size 10.
Tying silk: Black.
Tail: Orange marabou with luminous twinkle.
Body: Red antron.
Rib: Medium gold tinsel.
Wing: White long saddle hackles.
Head: ¾mm gold bead, apply clear varnish.

6 Church Hill Chomper

COMMENT

I first used this pattern at Church Hill Farm with great success. This lure may represent an injured fish with the red tag at the tail end of the fly. The speed at which it sinks requires a jerky retrieve, imitating a prey fish. Best fished on a floating line. This lure seems to produce fish when the sun is shining, which may be due to the sparkling effect given off by the fritz. It is very quick and easy to tie and catches fish – perhaps an ideal one for beginners to start off with.

DRESSING

Hook: Tinhead long shank size 10.
Tying silk: Black or olive.
Tail: White marabou.
Body: Red antron, white chenille.
Thorax: Olive fritz.
Head: Clear varnish.

7 Black & White Cat

COMMENT

This is a superb early season lure that produces well if fished relatively deep using a sinking line. It is a variation of the original Cat's Whisker. This, in my opinion, is one of the best lures for early season trout. The chain bead eyes on it get the lure down the water very quickly. It can be retrieved in either steady pulls, stripped back or even a slow figure of eight, they all seem to catch. The Black & White Cat is an extremely versatile lure that can be fished on reservoirs or smaller waters and will almost always attract the attention of a fish.

DRESSING

Hook: Kamasan B175 size 10.
Tying silk: Black.
Tail: Black marabou.
Body: White chenille.
Wing: Black marabou.
Thorax: Peacock herl.
Eyes: Bog chain eyes.
Head: Clear varnish.

8 Pitsford's Prowler

COMMENT

The Pitsford's Prowler lure is a variation of the Pitsford Pea, and with the addition of the gold bead and the fluorescent bead I have had a more successful catch rate. This lure is best fished on either a floating or medium sink line retrieved in long pulls or even a quick figure of eight. It produces well when there is a slight breeze with a little cloud cover. The fluorescent bead at the head of the lure gives the trout a hitting point therefore resulting in confident, savage takes.

DRESSING

Hook: Kamasan B175 size 10.
Tying silk: Black.
Tail: Black marabou.
Body: One turn of fluorescent green chenille, one ¾mm gold bead.
Hackle: Black cock.
Head: Fluorescent green hot head bead.

Bob Church

I suppose I was a bit of a trailblazer as regards modern lure fishing. I was in at the off of the lure revolution that began in the early to mid-1960s. It was the opening of Grafham Water in 1966 that really brought lure fishing to the fore. My Church Fry, and Dick Walker's Sweeney Todd and Polystickle set the ball rolling, soon to be followed by the Black Chenille lure, Appetizer, Jack Frost, and so on, all on no. 6 hooks.

Along with the lures came the specialized fishing techniques of fast sinking lines, the two together giving fantastic results to a band of Northampton specialist reservoir fishers. It is interesting for me to observe how the patterns are now commonplace for autumn fishing.

It is, however, for competition fly fishing that the small mini lure has now become very popular. Modern materials mean that highly colourful lures can be developed and I can assure you that they are very successful at catching lots of trout.

1 Pink Concrete Bowl

COMMENT

I had tried this Concrete Bowl variation a few times prior to the 1995 Midlands Confederation Final. It had shown quite consistent catches so I tied it on my middle dropper with an ordinary Concrete Bowl on the point. The day's method in bright sunshine was fast sink Hi-Di line fishing, slow and deep with the maxi drogue out to slow the boat down to a minimum, and the trout came steadily. I finished with seven good rainbows on a very difficult day to win the 100-strong event on Grafham.

DRESSING

Hook: Size 10.
Tying silk: Black.
Tail: Black marabou.
Body: Black chenille.
Body hackle: Ginger cock palmered.
Thorax: Fluorescent pink chenille.
Head: Clear varnish.

2 Len's Pink and Pearl

COMMENT

In the early Summer of 1997 I fished in a boat at Bewl Water with local expert Len Childs. Len was helping with the practice sessions of the England team who were about to take part in a Four Country International competition. While I was disproving that we need not bother with a fast sink Hi-Di line method, Len coolly knocked out a quick two-hour limit on this Pink and Pearl pattern of his. He fished it on the point of a slow-sinking slime fly line.

DRESSING

Hook: Size 10–12.
Tying silk: Fluorescent red.
Tail: Pale pink marabou.
Underbody: Red tying silk.
Overbody: Pearl lurex.
Hackle: Long-fibred honey.
Head: Clear varnish.

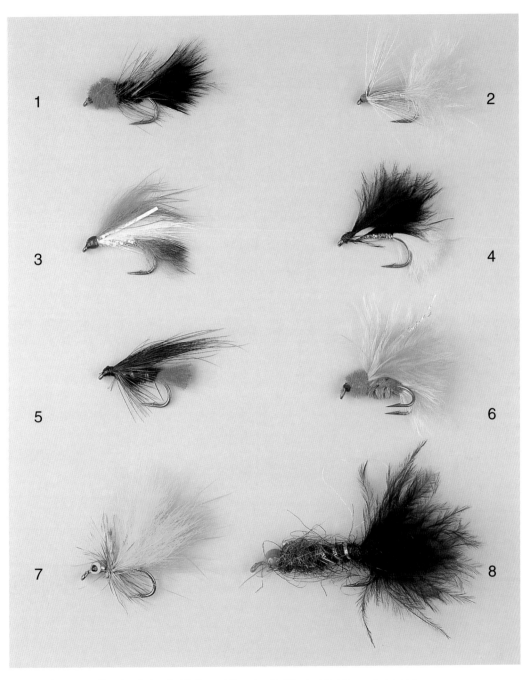

1 Pink Concrete Bowl   2 Len's Pink and Pearl   3 Glyn's Mini Fry   4 Leven
5 Modern Sweeney   6 Coogan's Winner   7 Orange Tinhead Zonker   8 Lite Brite Lure

3 Glyn's Mini Fry

COMMENT

In the very hot Summer of 1996 I was fishing in the European Grand Slam on Bewl Water. I had caught six in an afternoon's practice the day before and was feeling very confident. I was drawn to fish with Paul Vekemans from Belgium and we both agreed to fish the deep water out from the dam wall. While I struggled to catch two fish Paul took seven fish very quickly. We were both fishing fast sink line tactics but Paul had this secret mini-lure on and that was doing the damage. It was tied for him by local tackle shop owner Glyn Hopper of Lamberhurst.

DRESSING

Hook: Size 10.
Tying silk: Red.
Tail: Natural brown rabbit fur.
Body: Pearl holographic tinsel.
Underwing: White rabbit fur.
Overwing: Dyed olive rabbit fur.
Cheeks: Two strands of pearl holographic tinsel.
Head: Clear varnish.

4 Leven

COMMENT

Designed originally for the algae-cloudy waters of Loch Leven, this mini-lure has turned out to be a great all-rounder. It has worked well on all Midlands reservoirs and on all types of fly line. I have great faith in catching a fish on this lure no matter what the conditions. It was particularly good with the browns on Grafham and Rutland during 1997.

DRESSING

Hook: Size 10–12.
Tying silk: Black.
Tail: Yellow marabou.
Body: Pearl lurex.
Wing: Black cock.
Cheeks: Jungle cock.
Head: Clear varnish.

5 Modern Sweeney

COMMENT

In the mid-1960s that great angler the late Dick Walker invented a big lure on a no. 6 long shank hook called the Sweeney Todd. It proved a top trout catcher for a number of years before eventually losing its popularity with the passage of time. The combination of black and red has always been successful in many patterns of fly or lure. With this in mind I came up with this competition size mini modern Sweeney. I think Dick would have approved – I don't know about trout competitions though.

DRESSING

Hook: Size 10.
Tying silk: Black.
Tail: Fluorescent red Globrite floss.
Body: Black antron.
Rib: Silver tinsel.
Hackle: Bright red cock.
Wing: Black squirrel hair.
Head: Clear varnish.

6 Coogan's Winner

COMMENT

A few years ago I encouraged Steve Coogan to take up fly fishing. He regularly went to Ravensthorpe and started to do very well and, when it came down to it, he was catching most on his home-tied fly. The particular blue fly shown here was his pride and joy and he proved to everyone how good it was. We soon realized it was a stockie-basher fly and ideal for competitions where new fish were present. Kevin Garn won a match using it at Grafham and Jeremy Herrmann cleaned up in an International on the Lake of Menteith.

DRESSING

Hook: Double size 10.
Tying silk: Black.
Tail: Fluorescent blue marabou.
Body: Fluorescent blue chenille.
Wing: Fluorescent blue marabou and three strands of pearl crystal.
Thorax: Fluorescent pink chenille.
Head: Clear varnish.

7 Orange Tinhead Zonker

COMMENT

There are certain conditions when trout are up fairly high in the water on the reservoirs yet there are no signs of a rise. Usually they will be gorging on daphnia and will be 10ft down one minute and 4ft the next. My successful method in this last season was to use a floating line, a long leader and this little weighted lure. Takes come on the drop, on the twitch retrieve and on the fast stripping retrieve. Although a real rainbow method for the reservoirs, it is also a very good lure for the small fisheries.

DRESSING

Hook: Size 10 Tinhead hook.
Tying silk: Black.
Body: Pearl lurex.
Wing: Hot orange rabbit fur.
Hackle: Grizzle cock.
Eyes: Painted yellow with black pupils.

8 Lite Brite Lure

COMMENT

Like all black lures of the nobbler style this is another good trout catcher. I was given it to try by an angler at Farmoor Reservoir and promptly caught six fish on it. Since then I have used the lure quite often and it works virtually everywhere. I got to thinking, if this colour combination is that good I must tie a few competition size double mini patterns up. They have worked well to the hang method on the Hi-Di fly line. The blue Lite Brite seems to have something special that the trout want to bite.

DRESSING

Hook: Size 8 long shank tinhead.
Tying silk: Black.
Tail: Black marabou.
Body: Black antron.
Rib: Pearl lurex.
Thorax: Blue Lite Brite prominent.
Head: Painted red.

Wet Flies

Wet Flies

Wet fly fishing is the traditional approach method to use when boat drifting on any of the large waters in the four home countries. There is no doubt that it is a most pleasurable way to fish 'just stroking the water's surface' as it was once described to me. The method can also be used in streams, rivers, lakes, loughs and reservoirs.

As its name implies it is used to separate the technique from dry fly fishing. In wet fly fishing the fly or flies can be fished on or across the surface or at any depth you choose all the way down to the bottom. This can be achieved by using different density sinking fly lines.

Traditionally a longer soft rod in the 10½ to 11½ft range was used, so as to allow the top dropper of three or four flies to be dibbled in the waves at the end of the retrieve. This still applies very much where wild brown trout are concerned and I refer to the lochs of Scotland and the wild loughs of Ireland. However, on the English and Welsh reservoirs the situation has altered considerably in the past twenty years. Stocked rainbow trout for much of the time are feeding deep down on daphnia and this has meant developing a completely new style of sunken line wet fly fishing. As algae problems have increased on many big waters so the daphnia (which feeds on the horrible stuff) has increased in its billions. This has now become a major food source and probably is even more important than the once dominant chironomid. Therefore it is important that you equip yourselves with the new flashy wet fly patterns and learn this newer technique because I cannot see things changing as far as the big reservoirs are concerned.

For wet fly fishing on reservoirs or lochs a leader is tied up usually using 5lb or 6lb breaking strain nylon or fluorocarbon material – the latter is becoming more and more popular. This is normally about 4m in length and carrying two droppers. My personal set-up is for a leader of 5m: the top dropper being 2m from the fly line tip, followed by the middle dropper a further 1½m away and then the same distance again to the point fly. This is excellent for clearwater conditions when the flies need to be well separated. If the water is well stirred up and murky, only then would I fish my flies much closer together, sometimes as little as 0.6m.

Continuing with the theme of boat drift fishing, I have to confess that my greatest pleasure in all forms of fly fishing is to fish one of the big Irish western loughs, probably Mask, because it's the most difficult. I like to fish with the services of an experienced ghillie who just uses the back oar to bring me down over all the shallow rocky areas. If you were in a boat without a ghillie you would be forever running aground on the rocks. As it is, they simply follow the contours of an island keeping you in the trout holding zones. Catching those lovely wild browns is super wet fly sport and coupled with scenery that is second to none anywhere in the world and the 'crack' afterwards in the local bar to end the day, what else could a man ask for in our chosen sport. When it comes to stream or river wet fly fishing remember that trout or grayling will be facing the direction from which the water is flowing. It is quite possible to stealthily creep very close to a fish provided you are moving quietly upstream. Try also to keep the sunlight in your face to avoid casting body shadows across the water as this will scare fish before you have a chance to get a cast in. For this reason in most instances upstream casting wet fly fishing is my choice. When fishing a big wide river an alternate of casting square across then allowing the flies to sweep downstream can also be very good. This is also the style as used by sea trout wet fly fishers for their night-time sport. Only on special occasions do I get to try this, but it is a very exciting sport. To get the rod almost pulled out of your hand by a wild leaping sea trout in total darkness makes the heart beat that much faster.

Now on to the flies themselves. In the olden days fly tyers used to tie wet flies with all sorts of rare bird natural feathers, and no one seemed to object. Could you imagine today, going out and shooting a blackbird to get the right feather for an original Greenwell's Glory? The fact is we have not missed using original rare bird feathers in our dressings and substitute materials are as good or even better.

The great named historic trout wet flies like Greenwell's Glory, Blae and Black, Claret and Mallard, March Brown, Butcher, Alexandra, Invicta, and so on, still do get used and have a part to play in today's fly fishing approach. In truth though it is mostly for the wild fish rather than for reservoir rainbows. If those perfect days ever return when shoals of rainbows used to cruise upwind on or just below the surface picking up buzzers then the use of these old flies may return to the reservoirs.

You will notice that most of today's modern wet flies are lure-like and to be honest they are virtually impossible to separate. Mostly they are tied to catch rainbows, because even our most famous trout lake, the mighty Loch Leven, now holds a good head of lovely rainbow trout up to double figures in weight, whereas only drab wet flies would have been used there when it was a wild brown trout fishery only. During the past five years stockings have taken place with small fingerling rainbows and these have given the loch a good head of fish. These rainbows have grown on well and become like wild fish, but they are daphnia-feeding and the wet flies that are catching them best are those incorporating the new synthetic and fluorescent materials.

You will notice in this section of wet flies that contributors from England, Scotland and Wales all use attractor type wet fly patterns in their collections. However, the four Irish contributors still favour the natural fly whether it be mayfly, sedge, olive or land blown flies.

Joe Creane

Joe has been fishing since the age of seven and was taught by his father, Paddy Creane, who was himself a master angler. It is to him that Joe is indebted for his success.

Originally he started fishing the small mountain lakes around Roundstone (his home town) and Clifden. Then he fished for sea trout on the Ballina hind fishery and also Gawle Fishery and Inver.

Brown trout fishing being Joe's first love, he bought a boat and engine and took on the massive loughs of Corrib and Mask, that in the beginning seemed like oceans.

Competitions followed: he won the Irish Masters on the third attempt. The International Irish Team followed and he went on to qualify for Ireland in some eight Internationals that included two World Championships.

His wish for the future would be to see all the Irish lakes return to their former glory. 'To achieve this I would strongly recommend that anglers adapt to a catch and release system.'

1 The Kilbeg Thing

COMMENT

This fly has certainly got a very short lifespan on Corrib and Mask. I have been fishing this fly for twenty years at least and the story is still the same. It fishes on a dirty day during early duckfly season when the hatch does not appear because of wind or cold. It's best fished on top of the stones and in shallow ground, but its main time is between the duckfly and the olive hatch when fishing becomes difficult and slow. This fly has come to my rescue many times in competitions held during this period. I owe this fly great respect.

DRESSING

Hook: Kamasan B830 size 10–12.
Tying silk: Black.
Tag: Globrite no. 6 and flat gold tinsel.
Body: Three strands peacock herl.
Rib: Fine gold wire.
Hackle: Greenwell's hen.
Wing: Hot orange squirrel topped with red bucktail.
Head: Clear varnish.

2 The Birchall Secret

COMMENT

A fly to be fished on the tail or in any of the middle positions. From the opening day right up to Mayfly and again in September. Fishes best on Corrib and Mask on a dirty windy rainy day and fished slowly along the shore margins. It was originally fished without the bucktail, but after introducing it the fly really became a great one. One strange characteristic is its capability to dominate your whole catch on certain days not giving any other fly a look in. Very much an Easter fly on Corrib for the Masters Competition. Best on an intermediate line.

DRESSING

Hook: Kamasan B830 size 10–12.
Tying silk: Black.
Tag: Gold flat tinsel (small tag).
Body: Claret floss.
Rib: Fine gold wire.
Hackle: Claret cock palmered.
Wing: Four fibres hot orange bucktail and three turns of brown partridge.
Head: Clear varnish.

174

1 The Kilbeg Thing   2 The Birchall Secret   3 The Tourmakeady Lady
4 Byrne's Sedge   5 Colton's Bumble   6 Creane's Murrough   7 Inis Lee Olive
8 Roundstone Bumble

3 The Tourmakeady Lady

COMMENT

This fly came to fame while fishing Lough Mask with Irish International Toby Bradshaw. Fishes best on the tail during mayfly, and when fish are feeding on daphnia I rib the fly with Globrite no.12 but this fly really shines fishing the Tourmakeady side of Lough Mask especially after a big flood when the water rises on the sands. This fly can be fished anywhere on a team of four flies and will produce. If a big fish is to be caught this fly is your man! Undoubtedly this fly ranks very close to the top of my favourites.

DRESSING

Hook: Kamasan B175 size 10.
Tying silk: Black.
Tail: Six fibres cock pheasant tail.
Body: Copper rib, ⅔ hare's ear, ⅓ scarlet seal's fur, palmered grizzle cock.
Wing: Hen pheasant wing.
Hackle: Four turns red game.
Head hackle: Three turns of grey partridge.
Head: Clear varnish.

4 Byrne's Sedge

COMMENT

I found this fly very effective especially during August and September and is a must during the World Cup held on Mask on August Bank Holiday weekend. A very good fly on Corrib, Mask, Carra and Conn. Fishes best on the bob size 10 or on a size 12 on the point, fished on an intermediate line. This fly may look like a standard sedge but mark my words it just can not be compared. This fly has a permanent place on my cast of flies in every competition.

DRESSING

Hook: Kamasan B175 size 10–12.
Tying silk: Light red.
Body: ½ dark grey, ½ dark brown mixed.
Rib: Light copper.
Hackle: Dark red brown cock palmered.
Wing: Cinnamon dyed duck.
Head hackle: Red brown cock.
Head: Clear varnish.

5 Colton's Bumble

COMMENT

This fly was given to me by a friend of mine from Dromore, Mark Colton. It is possibly the best bob fly you will fish on Lough Melvin any time of the year. Bob this fly for as long as possible along the top of the water. It always has a place on the cast of four flies when fished next to the point. This fly is normally taken by the Melvin sonaghan with a vicious take. It also fishes well in the west of Ireland but especially in the pristine waters of Lough Carra. This fly is certainly one of the best bumbles I have ever fished.

DRESSING

Hook: Kamasan B175 size 10–12.
Tying silk: Black.
Tag: Gold tinsel.
Tail: Golden pheasant crest.
Body: Golden olive SLF.
Rib: Oval gold tinsel.
Hackle: Golden olive and hot orange palmered together.
Head hackle: Golden pheasant red neck feathers three turns, blue jay to finish.
Head: Clear varnish.

6 Creane's Murrough

COMMENT

A fly for August and September fished on a floating line. The method to fish this fly is very important. Fish when murroughs are blowing out from the shore and fish rising but coming short to the standard murrough. Fish short and jerked with a slow short retrieve, then static. Do this repeatedly and at the end of the retrieve hold the fly quite still keeping in touch with the raised rod. The little pinch of yellow seal's fur in the body imitates the female murrough. A great fly on Lough Arrow and the western lakes including Lough Ennell.

DRESSING

Hook: Kamasan B400 size 10–18.
Tying silk: Black.
Tag: Gold flat tinsel and scarlet seal's fur.
Body: Claret seal's fur, pinch of yellow seal's fur, claret seal's fur.
Rib: Oval gold tinsel.
Body hackle: Chocolate brown cock.
Wing: Speckled hen under spade wing of flank feather of guinea cape (CYB or black).
Head hackle: Five turns furnace cock.
Antennae: Two horns pheasant tail fibres.
Head: Clear varnish.

7 Inis Lee Olive

COMMENT

This pattern is an excellent fly fished on the tail before and during olive hatches and fished all during mayfly. Fishes best on a sunny windy day when olives and mayfly are hatching. This fly fishes best on the Lower Corrib but is an all-rounder including on Mask and Lough Conn. I have seen this fly totally dominate in the middle of a big mayfly rise when fish were taking them down. It would also be advisable to have this fly tied with a soft dark blae wing. A must for the west of Ireland loughs. Fishes equally on either intermediate or floating line.

DRESSING

Hook: Kamasan B830 size 10–14.
Tying silk: Black.
Tag: Gold.
Body: Mix furs – $\frac{1}{3}$ hare's ear, $\frac{1}{3}$ sooty olive, $\frac{1}{3}$ green olive.
Rib: Gold wire fine.
Hackle: Sooty cock.
Wing: Blae wing jay.
Head hackle: Three turns grey partridge black varnish.
Cheeks: Pair olive biots.
Head: Clear varnish.

8 Roundstone Bumble

COMMENT

I call this fly my own and my fishing friends reckon it's the best bumble of all. It's not like every other bumble which in my opinion are way too heavily palmered. I deliberately palmer this fly lightly; it fishes like all golden olive bumbles. This fly has won more competitions for me than any other fly. It fishes the whole year round but is best when mayfly are hatching and trout just coming on them. A good fly on the tail because of its sparse dressing. You just cannot be without this simple bumble.

DRESSING

Hook: Kamasan B175 size 10–12.
Tying silk: Black.
Tail: Golden pheasant tippet.
Body: Scarlet tag and golden olive seal's fur.
Rib: Fine gold oval.
Hackle: Golden olive cock palmered lightly.
Wing: One strand golden pheasant crest.
Head hackle: Five turns golden olive cock finished with blue jay.
Head: Black varnish.

Frank Reilly

It was only in 1990 that Frank set his sights on the 'Green Blazer'. In 1991 he fulfilled his ambition, sooner and more spectacularly than he had ever dared hope, by winning the 'National' on Lough Sheelin with ten trout. Winning the National was a wonderful achievement in itself but it was further enhanced by the fact that it ensured him a place on the Irish International team for the following year. He fished his first International on Lough Melvin in the Spring International of 1992. 1993 was a very rewarding year for Frank; his appointment as captain of the Irish team for the Autumn International was a tremendous honour which he did not take lightly. He spent many long hours researching Llyn Brenig in preparation for the autumn match.

The Bank Holiday in August of the same year saw him winning the 'World Cup', the mammoth international competition organized annually by Ballinrobe and District Anglers on Lough Mask. Frank caught four fine trout to 8½lb. Frank loves competition fishing, he enjoys the buzz, camaraderie and good-natured banter of the big competitions.

1 Olive Mayfly

COMMENT

I have many tyings of mayfly, wet and dry, however I have decided to include this pattern as one of my favourites for the west of Ireland. In 1992 I won the Connaught Cup on Lough Conn with this fly catching seven trout for 8½lb. I have also done well with this fly in other competitions on loughs Corrib and Mask. I like to fish this mayfly on the top dropper; however it can also be fished on the tail as some of my friends do, and to great effect. It is best fished early in the day and when fish are moving.

DRESSING

Hook: Long shank size 8–10.
Tying silk: Black.
Tail: Three or four cock pheasant fibres.
Body: Natural raffia.
Rib: Light gold wire.
Hackle: Olive cock palmered down the body.
Shoulder hackle: Dark olive cock.
Head hackle: Grey French partridge.
Head: Clear varnish.

2 Claret Mayfly

COMMENT

This is one out of many of my wet mayflies that have done me proud over the years on loughs Corrib, Mask, Carra and Conn. It works best naturally enough during the mayfly season. We all know how hard it is to find a fly to work on the middle dropper, well this is it! This fly will catch fish on a floating or intermediate line when nothing else is working, particularly on a showery overcast day.

DRESSING

Hook: Long shank size 8–10.
Tying silk: Black.
Tail: Three cock pheasant tail fibres.
Butt: Two or three turns of peacock herl.
Hackle: Grey French partridge.
Head: Clear varnish.

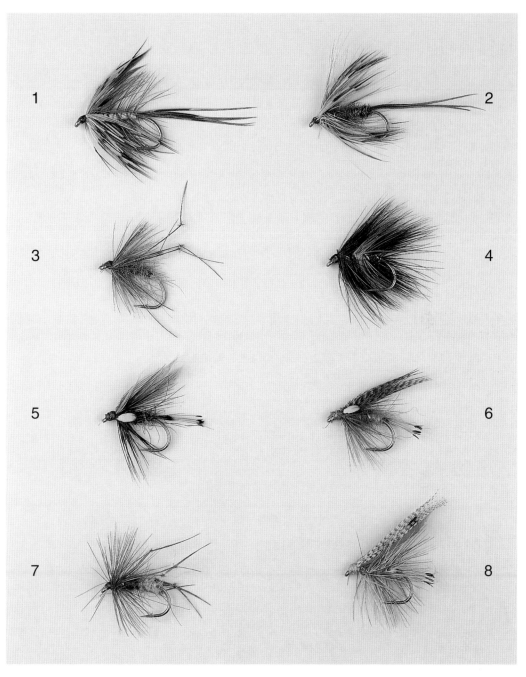

1 Olive Mayfly   2 Claret Mayfly   3 Green Hopper   4 All Hackled Bibio
5 Jungle Cock Sooty Olive   6 Fiery Brown   7 Golden and Claret Hopper
8 Reilly's Raymond

3 Green Hopper

COMMENT

The Green Hopper is a fly that has accounted for a great number of fish on lakes all over Ireland for me. The best time to use this fly is when the 'Daddy' and 'Grasshopper' are being dapped in August and September. When fishing it wet it is best on a floating or intermediate line in any position on the cast. When fishing it dry in light winds it is best fished on the point of the cast.

DRESSING

Hook: Size 10–14.
Tying silk: Black.
Butt: Globrite fluorescent green single-strand floss no. 12.
Body: Olive green seal's fur.
Rib: Fine pearl lurex.
Hackle: Chocolate brown and red game cock.
Legs: Four – six cock pheasant tail fibres, knotted once and tied in at the head, 2–3 each side trailing back.
Head: Clear varnish.

4 All Hackled Bibio

COMMENT

An excellent fly to have in your fly box on any lake and one I really rely on for Corrib and Mask. I find it best on the top dropper on a floating line fished across the wave. It's a fly you can fish all season, particularly during the duckfly on a good wave. The All Hackled Bibio is an excellent fly for the World Cup on Lough Mask. Two of the fish I caught to win the World Cup were caught on this Bibio.

DRESSING

Hook: Kamasan B160 size 8–10.
Tying silk: Black.
Body: Three parts: 1) Black cock hackle 2) Hot orange cock hackle 3) Black cock hackle palmered.
Rib: Light silver wire.
Head: Clear varnish.

5 Jungle Cock Sooty Olive

COMMENT

This is not a new fly, in fact there are many variations of it and they are all called Sooty Olives. However it is still one of the most effective flies around for Corrib and Mask all year round. I like to start off the season fishing it on the top dropper and as the season goes on I move it down the cast. It can be fished on any line. It is an excellent fly during the duckfly and the olives.

DRESSING

Hook: Kamasan B160 size 8–12.
Tying silk: Olive.
Tail: Golden pheasant tippet dyed hot orange.
Body: Dark sooty olive seal's fur (nearly black).
Rib: Light oval gold.
Wing: Grey duck quill.
Hackle: Black.
Cheeks: Jungle cock feathers.
Head: Clear varnish.

6 Fiery Brown

COMMENT

This fly is a must on the cast in the spring when fish are feeding on shrimp and also all through the duckfly. I find it works best on the tail or on the third dropper if you fish a four-fly cast, on an intermediate line. It's also well worth using in September on a bright day. I've done well in the Easter Competition on Lough Corrib with this fly.

DRESSING

Hook: Kamasan B160 size 8–10.
Tying silk: Brown.
Tail: Golden pheasant tippet.
Butt: Hot orange seal's fur.
Body: Fiery brown seal's fur.
Rib: Light oval gold.
Wing: Bronze mallard.
Hackle: Fiery brown cock.
Cheeks: Jungle cock feathers.
Head: Clear varnish.

7 Golden and Claret Hopper

COMMENT

This hopper is one of my favourite all-round flies. It is so adaptable, it can be fished on any Irish lake, at any time of the year and in any position on the cast. However I find it most effective during good hatches of olives and later in the season when sedges are hatching. When fishing it wet the legs should be on the underbody of the fly, and when dry the legs should trail back along the body.

DRESSING

Hook: Kamasan size 10–14.
Tying silk: Black.
Body: Rear half golden olive seal's fur, front half dark claret seal's fur.
Rib: Fine pearl lurex.
Legs: Six cock pheasant tail fibres – knotted once and tied in at the head.
Hackle: Claret cock hackle.
Head: Clear varnish.

8 Reilly's Raymond

COMMENT

I tied this fly about ten years ago for Lough Rea where I learned my fishing as a boy. I won many competitions fishing it on the top dropper, on sunny days with a nice wave. Nowadays I find it an excellent fly for spring fishing on Lough Corrib when trout are foraging in the rocks for shrimp. It is best fished on the tail on an intermediate or slow-sinking line.

DRESSING

Hook: Kamasan B160 size 8–10.
Tying silk: Yellow.
Tail: Golden pheasant tippet (dyed orange).
Body: Yellow seal's fur or SLF.
Rib: Light silver wire.
Multi wing: A slip of red dyed swan, a bunch of golden pheasant tippet (dyed hot orange), silver mallard dyed yellow tied on in this order.
Hackle: Golden olive and red cock palmered down the body.
Head: Clear varnish.

Robbie O'Grady

I love the west of Ireland and I have been staying at the little guest house of Robbie and Nan O'Grady for 20 years. Once or twice a year I make the journey to fish with Robbie on the mighty Lough Mask, in my opinion the most testing and exciting water there is.

Robbie has been a professional boatman on Mask for many years. He enters the World Open Fly Fishing Championships held on Mask each August Bank Holiday. Although there are over 600 entrants Robbie has won the event twice, in 1964 and 1976, and he was a close second in 1995 beaten by ½oz – a great record. Robbie has also represented Ireland in an International between the four home countries. Since I have known him he always disappears to his fly tying room to tie a few specials for the day ahead.

1 Whin Bush

COMMENT

This first fly is a tying of a mayfly called the 'Whin Bush'. This is the bush you see on the mountain, green with thorns and yellow of flower. Fished in a mayfly hatch, it can be a very good dropper, excellent on Mask during the mad mayfly main season. The fibres of the hen pheasant hackle open and close to look like a mayfly hatching.

DRESSING

Hook: Size 8.
Tying silk: Yellow.
Body: Cream or beige seal's fur.
Rib: Medium gold oval thread.
Body hackle rear: Yellow cock.
Front hackle: Two breast feathers from hen pheasant dyed yellow.
Head: Clear varnish.

2 Englishman's Purple Sam

COMMENT

This fly was tied by an Englishman called Sam who was fishing with me on Mask in 1976. He was a beginner fly tyer and the fly was made with offcuts from his wife's crochet work. With it he caught five trout on the top dropper on the first day, three on the tail on the second and four on the middle dropper on the third. He gave it to me on leaving and I had the pleasure of catching seven more trout before it finally fell to pieces – a most unlikely but very successful fly.

DRESSING

Hook: Size 10.
Tying silk: Black.
Body: Dark purple thread.
Hackle: Palmered yellow and red mixed.
Head: Built-up big with black tying silk, clear varnished.

1 Whin Bush 2 Englishman's Purple Sam 3 Robbie's Green Peter Variant
4 Dirty White 5 Robbie's Sooty Olive 6 Robbie's Invicta 7 Robbie's Olive
8 Guskelly Olive

3 Robbie's Green Peter Variant

COMMENT

Robbie found this tying of a Green Peter Sedge excellent for big trout on Mask. He had one of over 7lb while his guest had another of 6½lb in the boat the same day. This fly dates back to the 1950s and 60s and it seems to have been forgotten about by today's high flyers. But I can assure you that if you tie a few up and visit Lough Mask in summer you will have some wonderful sport.

DRESSING

Hook: Size 8.
Tying silk: Black.
Body: Moss green seal's fur.
Rib: Oval gold tinsel.
Rear hackle: Dirty yellow cock palmered.
Front hackle: Furnace cock.
Wing: Shoulder feather of shoveller drake. You need an old bird (4yr) to get the right goldish colour.
Head: Deer hair muddler head.

4 Dirty White

COMMENT

This fly was first shown to me by the late Jack Stack from Westport. Jack was a very respected fly fisher – you could call him in today's terms, an expert. He won the World Wet Fly Cup on Mask in the mid-1950s and this was one of his favourite general wet fly patterns. The fly works throughout the season on all western loughs of Ireland – of course I am confident it would work elsewhere.

DRESSING

Hook: Size 8.
Tying silk: Black.
Tail: Natural bronze mallard feather fibres.
Body: Natural seal's fur (not dyed).
Rib: Silver oval tinsel.
Hackle: Black cock.
Wing: Natural bronze mallard.
Head: Clear varnish.

5 Robbie's Sooty Olive

COMMENT

This dates back to the 1960s and it always produced good catches. I obtained the hair from my daughter who was a hairdresser. After the hair has been treated in the picric acid, when you hold it to the light it shines a beautiful greenish-yellow through the brown. Fish this as a tail fly from the month of May onwards; it works well on all Irish loughs. A slow retrieve and long hold is the method.

DRESSING

Hook: Size 10.
Tying silk: Black.
Tail: Bronze mallard feather fibre.
Body: Brunette human hair dyed in picric acid.
Rib: Gold tinsel.
Hackle: Black cock.
Wing: Bronze mallard feather fibre.
Head: Clear varnish.

6 Robbie's Invicta

COMMENT

This is my idea of smartening the Invicta up and it is a cross between the Raymond and the Invicta. I would describe it best as a general pattern to be used at any time of the year. However, its best form really is when the mayfly are about, and remember this can run from that mad week in May with more sparse but important hatches that go on until August. This happens on Mask, Carra and Conn.

DRESSING

Hook: Size 10–8.
Tying silk: Black.
Tail: Golden pheasant topping.
Body: Golden olive seal's fur.
Rib: Heavy gold tinsel.
Hackle: Red (crimson) palmer down body.
Front hackle: Golden olive hen palmer front half of body.
Throat hackle: Blue jay or blue guinea fowl.
Wing: Woodcock or hen pheasant.
Head: Clear varnish.

7 Robbie's Olive

COMMENT

This is my fly for early May when the olives begin to hatch in high numbers. Olives do hatch at other times throughout the season up until September so you will realize it is a very important pattern because it works so well. My best catch with this olive was when I shared the boat with my guest F.L. Vickerman, who owned the famous race horse *Cottage Rake* that won the Cheltenham Gold Cup. Oh yes, our catch! – we had nineteen good trout from Mask in three hours from 3.00pm – 6.00pm.

DRESSING

Hook: Size 10.
Tying silk: Yellow.
Tail: Three fibres of bronze mallard feather.
Body: Dirty dark green seal's fur.
Rib: Bright copper fine wire (from old cycle dynamo).
Hackle: Light-coloured furnace cock.

8 Guskelly Olive

COMMENT

Ballinrobe shoemaker Joe Guskelly was the man who first showed me this excellent river wet fly. I walked the banks of the Robe River many years ago and came across Joe fishing. It was quite windy and the surface was choppy but olives were still hatching. Joe proceeded to catch a number of good browns up to 2lb on his fly and I have had faith in it myself from that day to this. Works on rivers all over Mayo and Galway when olives are about.

DRESSING

Hook: Size 12.
Tying silk: Black.
Tail: Furnace hackle fibres.
Body: Dyed yellow rabbit fur dubbed finely.
Head hackle: Blue grey dun and furnace mixed.
Head: Clear varnish.

Laurence Gibb

Laurence has been fly fishing for 30 years since he was 10 years old. He owns his own boat, a 19ft Lunny with a 9.9 outboard. His local waters are loughs Melvin and Erne. He also fishes loughs Carra, Mask and Corrib quite often and Loughs Arrow and Sheelin get a few visits during the season.

His achievements at competition level are as follows: top rod two years in a row fishing the Diawa Winter Trophy championships (over nine matches; top rod in the Melvin Open and second overall; top rod in the B & H Northern Ireland heats on two occasions and a second and third fishing the Kinloch Festivals and he has been in the prizes on numerous occasions.

At club level he has been top rod for the last nine years and he ties all the club team's flies. 'I do love fly tying and give quite a lot away to friends and acquaintances.'

1 Rainbow Bumble

COMMENT

I fish this fly on our stocked waters for rainbows. You can change the fritz to any colour but I've found the claret to be the most successful. The two most successful methods are on the top dropper pulled through the waves or fished slow above a booby on a fast sinker. Bob Church says 'I feel this bob fly of Laurence's would work at any big wild reservoir or lough. It would have the ability to get trout to rise up on high winds and big waves during high summer.

DRESSING

Hook: Size 8.
Tying silk: Black.
Butt: Globrite no. 2.
Body: Claret micro fritz.
Body hackle: One yellow & one claret cock saddle hackle.
Head hackle: Blue guinea fowl.
Head: Clear varnish.

2 Steve Ellis's Melvin Bumble

COMMENT

Steve is my fishing pal who tied this fly for Lough Melvin. The first time he used this fly it took him into the prizes of the Melvin Open. We have both had great success all over Ireland with this fly, when the fish are up in the water. Early in the season when the duckfly are on, tie the fly in smaller sizes 14 and 16 – this seems to do the trick. Bob Church says: 'I really do rate this set of Irish flies from Laurence. I shall be tying this one for myself on Lough Mask for the World Fly Fishing Championships in 1998.'

DRESSING

Hook: Size 8.
Tying silk: Brown.
Tail: Golden pheasant tail.
Body: Medium olive seal's fur or substitute.
Rib: Pearl.
Body hackle: Medium olive cock.
Head hackle: Blue jay over claret cock.
Head: Clear varnish.

1 Rainbow Bumble   **2** Steve Ellis's Melvin Bumble   **3** The Orphan Perch Fry
4 Bob's Always Last   **5** The Stewart Charles Bumble   **6** The Rubber Band Daddy
7 The Colin Wilson Mayfly   **8** The Telephone Fly

3 The Orphan Perch Fry

COMMENT

I named this fly the Orphan because you have to fish it on its own. Fished in and around weed beds and when the fish are on perch fry it comes into its own. The fly has also the habit of picking out the better fish. Worked slow or in a figure of eight just hang on for the smash takes. Bob Church says: 'Laurence's perch fry pattern is so different from any we would use on the reservoirs here. The Irish have a lovely fussy style of fly tying, I am hooked every time.'

DRESSING

Hook: Size 10–8.
Tying silk: Black.
Tail: Red pheasant crest.
Body: Brown floss.
Rib: Silver wire.
Shoulder hackle: Lime-green cock tied back over body.
Wing: Bronze mallard.
Head hackle: Blue guinea fowl.
Head: Clear varnish.

4 Bob's Always Last

COMMENT

This fly had no name until recently. It is the one fly in my box that if nothing were moving and the fishing were slow I would put on and, as if by magic, it would produce a fish, but only the one. So it was always last to be fished. Bob Church is an A.L. person (always last). People are always hanging around waiting for him, I found out the hard way! So now my fly has a name as the two of them are always last but both can produce the goods at the end of the day.

DRESSING

Hook: Size 10–8.
Tying Silk: Black.
Tail: Globrite no. 2
Tag: Fluorescent pink.
Body: Claret seal's fur or substitute.
Rib: Gold tinsel.
Wing: Bronze mallard.
Head hackle: Blue cock.
Cheeks: Jungle cock.
Head: Clear varnish.

5 The Stewart Charles Bumble

COMMENT

My cousin Heather lives in England and I hadn't seen her for years until a family reunion was arranged. We sat and chatted about fly fishing for some time. Anyway a few months later she gave birth to a baby boy, Stewart Charles. I tied this fly for her first-born and sent it to her in a box. I have caught fish all over the country with it and it has even had a few salmon out of the River Moy. Rainbows love it when they're on the daphnia; pulled through the wave seems to have the best results.

DRESSING

Hook: Size 8.
Tying silk: Black.
Tail: Golden pheasant crest.
Rib: Silver wire or copper wire.
Body hackle: White cock grizzle palmered.
Head hackle: Red guinea fowl then green guinea fowl and blue guinea fowl tied one over the top of the other.
Head: Clear varnish.

6 The Rubber Band Daddy

COMMENT

I first came across this fly on Lough Arrow where it won a competition. It's not so much the fly but the way it is fished which is unusual. You put it on the tail and strip like mad. This makes the rubber band vibrate which somehow attracts the fish. From the beginning of August this is always a good pattern to fish with confidence on any of the big western Irish loughs. Similar Daddy patterns produced browns of over 3½lb from both Carra and Mask for Bob Church.

DRESSING

Hook: Size 10 grub hook.
Tying silk: Black.
Body: Brown rubber band cut and tied in as a detached body.
Legs: 6 knotted pheasant tail fibres.
Wings: Grey badger hackle point tied back over the body.
Head hackle: Red game saddle.
Head: Black varnish.

7 The Colin Wilson Mayfly

COMMENT

Colin, a good friend of mine, has been fishing Corrib for many years. He created this fly by trial and error over this period. It has taken trout in all the major loughs in Ireland through the season and I wouldn't be without one during the mayfly. Remember that the mayfly stays on many loughs right through to September. Bob Church says: 'Whenever he fishes on Carra or Mask in August he always has a mayfly on his cast. On two days in 1996 he caught twelve fine browns to 3lb from Carra, all to the olive mayfly.'

DRESSING

Hook: Size 10.
Tying silk: Black.
Tail: 3 or 4 strands of pheasant tail fibres.
Body: Natural raffia.
Rib: 6lb brown maxima nylon.
Body hackle: White grizzle cock palmered.
Head hackle: One light olive and one dark olive mixed.
Head: Black varnish.

8 The Telephone Fly

COMMENT

A friend rang me one evening from a bar, and said 'I have a fly here which is catching bags of trout', and he gave me the tying over the phone (he had been drinking quite a lot). A week later when I ran into him I gave him half a dozen of the tyings. He said thanks, but that it looked nothing like the original. A few weeks later while he was fishing Lough Carra things were a bit slow, so he put up this fly to try it. Ten fish later he was back in the bar on the phone to me. 'Tie up more of them flies', he said. I asked what fly was that, 'You know, the telephone flies.'

DRESSING

Hook: Size 8.
Tying silk: Black.
Tail: Golden pheasant crest head.
Butt: Red Globrite no. 2 floss.
Body: Golden olive seal's fur or substitute.
Rib: Gold tinsel.
Body hackle: One red game and one claret cock palmered.
Over wing: Bronze mallard.
Head hackle: Blue guinea fowl over red game cock.
Head: Black varnish.

John Ielden

When John joined his local East Midlands Fly Fishing Club and became interested in match fishing the most popular method at the time was loch style with wet flies. Since then he has had his share of success winning several big events including: the Midlands Federation Final, the Masterline, the Orvis Pairs, the Airflo Pairs and five Internationals, and he was a member of the 1997 team.

'Although wet flies are not as widely used these days they can still be very effective. If at the start of a match I'm not sure where the fish are or what they are feeding on I'll usually put on a team of wets to search the water. Sometimes they will work from the off, but if they don't they will usually give some indication of where the shoals are by inducing pulls or follows.'

'Most of the patterns I'll be describing you will no doubt be aware of, but may not use. We all have our own favourites we rely on on match day and I think that is the most important thing – to be fully confident in a few reliable patterns.'

1 Orange Wickham

COMMENT

The Orange Wickham has caught a lot of trout for me. After tying some wingless Wickhams, one day I decided to tie some variations with a packet of hackles, recently purchased, that were a very unusual pale orange colour. I tied in a collar hackle of the orange to a Wickham and added a golden pheasant crest tail. On my next boat outing at Grafham I tried the new fly on the middle dropper, drifting down the wind lanes; it worked very well as it has on many occasions since. A good pattern for bright days, fished on the top or middle dropper.

DRESSING

Hook: Drennan Wet Fly Supreme size 10–12.
Tying silk: Black.
Tail: Golden pheasant crest.
Body: Flat gold tinsel.
Hackles: Soft ginger palmer, orange collar.
Head: Black varnish.

2 Mini Nailer

COMMENT

The Nailer lure was a very effective pattern in the early 1980s so, with competitions in mind, I mixed the materials to suit a smaller hook. The Mini Nailer uses the same colours but is tied slimmer, using bronze mallard for a wing in place of brown turkey. I always fish this on the point with palmers on the droppers. It is most effective during bright conditions with a decent wave when rainbows are still in the top layers. Dressed sparsely a quick retrieve is not always best, slow steady pulls can often be more effective.

DRESSING

Hook: Kamasan B175 size 10–12.
Tying silk: Black.
Tail: Red cock hackle fibres (bright red).
Body: Flat gold tinsel.
Wing: Bronze mallard.
Hackle: Soft red game mixed with bright red.
Head: Black varnish.

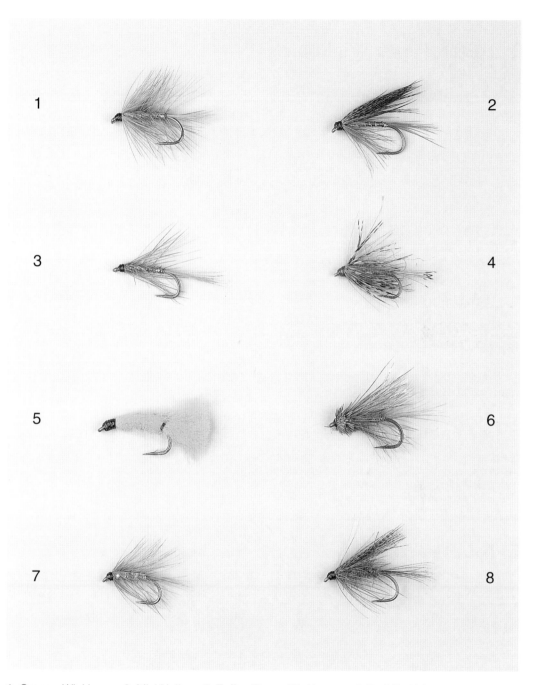

1 Orange Wickham   2 Mini Nailer   3 Toffee Paper Wickhams   4 Red Partridge
5 B.L. Peach Doll   6 Green Muddler   7 Pearl Wickham   8 Harry Tom

3 Toffee Paper Wickhams

COMMENT

Rutland Water is where this fly has worked best for me, mainly in the early season fished slowly on an intermediate or floating line. One memorable day at Rutland I was fishing the Masterline match. Not much happened until the afternoon when the wind dropped and the trout started to rise. At first I tried nymphs on a floater and I had few offers but it was obviously not right. I looked in my box and saw the Toffee Paper Wickhams; I picked a very sparse number 12 and tied it on the point – it was incredibly effective.

DRESSING

Hook: Size 10–14.
Tying silk: Black.
Tail: Ginger cock fibres.
Body: Metallic green tinsel.
Hackle: Sparse ginger palmer.
Head: Black varnish.

4 Red Partridge

COMMENT

This fly is a creation from when I first started fly tying back in the early 1980s. Like everyone else in competition fishing I was looking for a pattern to keep one step ahead and once in a while you come up with one that works. My first success with it came when I was fishing a club match on Grafham; it was perfect wet fly conditions and the more disturbance the flies made the more the trout responded. Although it is a good 'pulling' fly it can also be effective retrieved with a steady figure of eight.

DRESSING

Hook: Lightweight size 12 (Kamasan B400).
Tying silk: Black or red.
Tail: Golden pheasant tippets.
Body rear: Flat gold.
Thorax: Red seal's fur.
Hackle: Partridge.
Head: Black or red varnish.

5 B.L. Peach Doll

COMMENT

Most of you reading this are aware of this fly's origins when Brian Leadbetter met an angler at Grafham taking a regular limit while others were struggling; he was fishing a Peach Doll. The trout were feeding on migrating snails but would go out of their way to take the Doll. Brian took full advantage of this new pattern especially on the match scene. Brian's pattern was a slightly different colour from mine but often when we shared a boat both patterns were equally effective. It has always worked best on a floater.

DRESSING

Hook: Kamasan B175 size 10.
Tying silk: Black.
Tail: Peach wool.
Body: Peach wool.
Head: Black varnish.

6 Green Muddler

This fly is tied on the Toffee Paper Wickham theme. I fish it on the top dropper, usually on overcast days in a decent wave. A good team in these conditions would be a Silver Invicta on the point, a Hare's Ear in the middle and the Green Muddler on the top dropper. One B & H match on Rutland when fish were playing hard to get, I took a decent bag on this fly, but also lost the biggest rainbow I have ever hooked, after it took the fly right in front of the boat and then took off on a long run only to part company as a loop in my line jammed in the butt ring!

Hook: Drennan Wet Fly Supreme or Kamasan B175 size 10–12.
Tying silk: Black.
Tail: Ginger cock.
Body: Metallic green tinsel.
Wing: Few strands of pearl crystal.
Hackle: Ginger cock or red game palmered.
Head: Black or dark brown deer hair clipped short.

7 Pearl Wickham

I usually fish this fly on the middle dropper especially when pin fry are about. My most memorable day with this pattern was on Rutland Water. Andy Linwood and myself arranged to fish the Orvis Pairs. I started to drift away from the crowd near the three trees and luckily I stopped right on the fish; using an intermediate line I took nine fish, sometimes without moving the fly at all. The trout were on pin fry and takes on the Pearl Wickham were very confident. Our combined bags were enough to win the match.

Hook: Drennan Wet Fly Supreme size 10–14.
Tying silk: Black.
Tail: Ginger cock.
Body: Pearl.
Hackle: Ginger.
Head: Black varnish.

8 Harry Tom

This fly has been around a long time, but it is surprising how many anglers have never used it. I first tied some in the mid-1980s after hearing good reports about it – this pattern is a slight variation. I always fish it on point on a floating line once the water has warmed up and trout are feeding near the surface. I feel most confident fishing it during cloudy conditions with either palmers or nymphs on the droppers. I think its appeal is that it's so natural looking that it may be taken for any number of items on the trout's menu right through the season.

Hook: Kamasan B175 size 10.
Tying silk: Black.
Tail: Red game.
Body: Hare's ear fur.
Wing: Bronze mallard.
Hackle: Red game.
Head: Black varnish.

Brian Thomas

Brian is a well-known competition fly fisherman and appears regularly at all big events. He has been an International angler eight times, winning the Grafham Trophy twice, on Lough Conn and Bewl Water, captaining England at Bewl in 1987. He has fished four World Championships in Spain, Luxembourg, Tasmania and Finland. He won the World Championship with England in Tasmania in 1988, and the European Grand Slam Team event in 1991.

To get good wet fly fishing the wild lakes and loughs of Ireland and lochs of Scotland are the places to go. Fishing the 'bob' is one of the most exciting methods, with the likes of Soldier Palmers or Bumbles being to me the *real* trout fishing. Good presentation is a must to catch wild fish. Looking through fly boxes you very often find more variants than originals.

The great joy of fly fishing is searching for more killing patterns and no sooner do you find one than you meet someone with yet another. That is why we have boxes and boxes of them. Here are a few more!

1 Soldier Palmer Variant

COMMENT

This is a variant of the famous fly. I first tied it in the late 1970s when the 'in' method was fishing wets. Grafham was the Mecca of this from the middle of May to the end of the season and I have often said to my fishing companions that we never took it off, because at some time or other of the day this fly would work. I once fished a National in early September and with two hours to go I had three rainbows and finished with twelve all to the Soldier. Today it still has its moments; let's hope this *real* fishing will make a welcome return.

DRESSING

Hook: Mustad 7780 size 10–12.
Tying silk: Black.
Tail: Red wool.
Body: Red wool.
Hackle: Honey soft cock.
Rib: Fine copper wire.
Head: Clear varnish.

2 Golden Olive Bumble

COMMENT

The Golden Olive Bumble is another attractive variant of the Irish version adapted for Scottish lochs, a little darker than its Irish counterpart. With its head hackle of grouse or woodcock it gives this pattern a more natural look and the globrite tail adds an eye-catching look. Fishing this bumble on a good wave on a cloudy overcast day you can expect some action. A good fly for the free-rising browns.

DRESSING

Hook: Kamasan B170 size 10–12.
Tying silk: Black.
Tail: Globrite fluorescent yarn no. 8, amber.
Body: Golden olive seal's fur or substitute.
Rib: Medium oval gold.
Body hackle: Golden olive and medium green olive cock palmered.
Head hackle: Woodcock or light grouse.

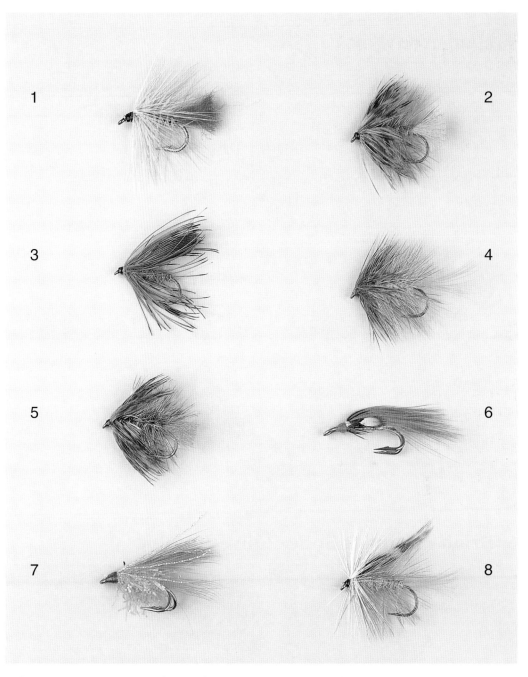

1 Soldier Palmer Variant   2 Golden Olive Bumble   3 Haul-A-Gwynt Variant
4 Orkney Bumble   5 Brian Thomas's Sooty Olive Bumble   6 Orange Jungle Cock
7 Orange Fritz   8 White Hackled Invicta

3 Haul-A-Gwynt Variant

COMMENT

The Haul-A-Gwynt is a very imitative fly with its pheasant neck feathers giving a real insect look. This variant is very successful during the summer as the sedges and dun flies are hatching. I normally fish it on the point and have found it very good for browns. My introduction to this fly was on Orkney where I first fished the original with a black body and found it a fly to have confidence in. Again my variant beats the original for me, so try them both.

DRESSING

Hook: Kamasan B170 or Partridge L2A size 10–12.
Tying silk: Brown Spartan 6/0 prewaxed.
Body: Bright green seal's fur or substitute.
Rib: Gold or silver fine wire.
Wing: Grey duck quill slips.
Hackle: Cock pheasant neck feathers with black tips.
Head: Clear varnish.

4 Orkney Bumble

COMMENT

A very attractive bob fly along the lines of the great bumbles. It was introduced to me by Eric Dyson who found it in an article by Terry Ruawe and Dick Steuart. I have tried it on both browns and rainbows and found it interesting to both. It needs to have a good chop on the water to present it right with its bright mix of orange, gold and yellow. Teamed up with, for example, a Gold Butcher and a Dunkeld you could end up with a good basket of trout as long as water conditions are right.

DRESSING

Hook: Size 10.
Tying silk: Orange Danvilles.
Tail: Golden pheasant crest.
Body: Yellow seal's fur.
Rib: Medium gold oval.
Body hackles: Red & yellow cock hackles palmered.
Head hackle: Guinea fowl dyed blue.

5 Brian Thomas's Sooty Olive Bumble

COMMENT

Another bumble variant to add to the wet fly angler's box, with a mixture of subtle hackles and eye-catching orange tag. A lot of hatching natural flies have a wing-case of orange so fishing this bumble in the surface film is a very imitative design. Fished on the bob it brings up fish, and used with selective point and dropper flies, can be a deadly method. The Sooty types of fly are in my opinion underused, as most flies we see hatching on a day's wet fly fishing are of a drab nature; here we have a touch of both.

DRESSING

Hook: Kamasan B400 or B170.
Tying silk: Brown.
Tail: Fluorescent Globrite yarn no. 6.
Rib: Medium oval gold.
Palmered hackles: Dark green olive and well-marked grizzle wound together (cock).
Head hackle: Grouse long in fibre.
Head: Clear varnish.

6 Orange Jungle Cock

COMMENT

A fly for early season when fishing in competition. When there is a good liberal stock of rainbows, with the waters getting fished heavily, you need something a little different. This fly has worked very well for me for the last two seasons. I fish it on the point with a combination of Vivas and Pinks and when things get hard go down to two flies, or even a single, especially at the end of the day when the fish have seen too many teams. Fished on the sinking line the takes usually come to the lift.

DRESSING

Hook: Double size 10–12.
Tying silk: Fluorescent red.
Body: Pearl lurex.
Wing: Orange marabou, topping pearlescent.
Cheeks: Jungle cock.
Head: Clear varnish.

7 Orange Fritz

COMMENT

I first tied this fly in 1996 when the rainbows of Rutland and Grafham began to feed on the ever-increasing blooms of daphnia. With the fish going deep, a combination of fast-sinking or Hi-Di lines and orange flies could take fish. Fishing orange flies for daphnia feeders has always been known, but the addition of translucent fritz has given that added sparkle. I fish it as a point fly on a two-fly cast, the dropper being a Cat's Whisker – this combination has been very successful for me.

DRESSING

Hook: Kamasan B160 size 6–8 and Double size 10.
Tying silk: Red.
Tail: Hot orange feather fibres.
Body: Lureflash translucent fritz.
Wing: Hot orange marabou or feather fibres, a few strands pearl lurex.
Head: Clear varnish.

8 White Hackled Invicta

COMMENT

This fly I first used when fishing an Orkney competition where everyone fishes a team of three flies. I managed five fish, four of which came to this fly on water where there was a good hatch of sedges. It is a very good variant that I use whenever sedges are evident. When I first tied a creamy/white hackle on my Soldier Palmer it seemed to be more attractive to the fish – quite a coincidence. Fished as a point fly with a team of bumbles or palmered flies you could not be fishing in a more traditional loch style.

DRESSING

Hook: Kamasan B170 or Partridge L2A size 8–12.
Tying silk: Brown or yellow.
Tail: Golden pheasant crest.
Body: Yellow seal's fur or substitute.
Rib: Medium gold oval.
Body hackle: Red/brown cock.
Wing: Hen pheasant quill (slips).
Head hackle: Longish white hen tied in front of wing.
Head: Clear varnish.

Tony Bevan

During his first attempt in the Welsh trials in 1974, Tony qualified for the Welsh team gaining his first cap in Ireland in the spring of 1975. Tony has since represented Wales on sixteen occasions, having the honour to captain the side on two occasions and the good fortune to win the Brown Bowl Trophy on Chew Valley in 1985. He has been captain of the Llanilar Angling Association team in the Benson & Hedges Final on ten occasions.

One of his greatest moments was winning the Benson & Hedges Final at Loch Leven in 1987 and the team has also featured in the prizes on a number of occasions.

Probably the most pleasing individual win was top rod at the Benson & Hedges Final at Rutland Water over the two days in 1992. Tony's most profitable win was undoubtedly the Hanningfield Masters in the spring of 1996 where he went away £1,000 richer. He has also won prizes in the Bob Church/*Angling Times* Classic and in the European Bank Match at Clywedog. He also captained the Llanilar Wychwood 1995/96 Welsh Final.

1 Olive Muddler

COMMENT

This fly started life many years ago, as a Green Peter with a muddler head, with excellent results. It has since been modified by dispensing with the wing, which has improved results. It is a fly that works on all waters, but is particularly effective on the more fertile lakes and reservoirs. It is best fished on a floating line or an intermediate, in the top dropper position, and the higher in the water the better it works. As a wet fly I would probably rate the Olive Muddler in the top five in my fly box.

DRESSING

Hook: Kamasan B405 size 12–14.
Tying silk: Olive.
Tail: Light speckled hen.
Body: Light olive seal's fur.
Rib: Gold wire.
Hackle: Light red game.
Head: Natural deer hair.

2 George's Maclaren

COMMENT

This fly is very near conventional, based on the Kate Maclaren. It was tied and given to me by Llanilar A.A. team member George Barron. I have fished it on Brenig with excellent results, but the place I found the fish going crazy for this fly was on Lake Vyrnwy. George tells me that it also works well for browns in Scotland and Ireland and is usually his most favoured top dropper. It is usually fished on a floating or intermediate line, with the action taking place as the fly breaks through the surface whilst brought to the bob.

DRESSING

Hook: Kamasan B175 size 12–14.
Tying silk: Black.
Butt: Fluorescent green Globrite no. 12.
Tail: Golden pheasant crest.
Body: Black seal's fur.
Rib: Silver wire.
Body hackle: Black hen palmered.
Head hackle: Very light red game hackle from the shoulder of a hen cape.

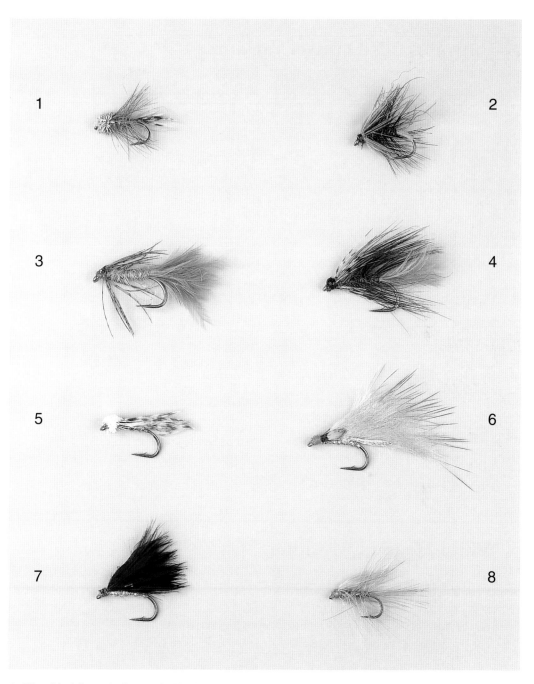

1 Olive Muddler **2** George's Maclaren **3** Tony Bevan's Damsel Variant
4 Willi's Damsel Variant **5** White Headed Muddler **6** Silver Minky Variant
7 Black Flash **8** Honey Wickham's

3 Tony Bevan's Damsel Variant

COMMENT

There are probably more variations of the damsel fly than any other pattern. My best day was in a boat up the top of the North Arm at Rutland Water near the weed beds, in shallow water, where a limit of top-quality rainbows were taken using a floating line with a slow and varied figure-of-eight retrieve. I gave this fly to one of my friends, international angler Emyr Lewis, who fished Rutland in June, when he landed a number of rainbows and a brown of over 7lb. During the same afternoon he hooked into another large brown, that took the fly.

DRESSING

Hook: Kamasan B175 size 10–12.
Tying silk: Olive.
Tail: Olive marabou.
Body: Olive lite brite.
Hackle: Partridge dyed olive.
Thorax cover: Spectra flash.
Head: Clear varnish.

4 Willi's Damsel Variant

COMMENT

Yet again another type of damsel pattern, this one was created by David Williams (Dai Willi) of the Llanilar A.A. team. Dai gave me one of these flies in the spring of 1995 and I must say it has taken its fair share of fish. This is the fly that Dai used to win the Bob Church/*Angling Times* Classic match at Rutland in 1995 taking seven fish in a very difficult day, five of which went to his damsel, whilst his boat partner only managed one fish. It is best fished on an intermediate line with a medium to slow retrieve, and fished on the point.

DRESSING

Hook: Kamasan B175 size 10.
Tying silk: Black.
Tail: Olive marabou.
Body: Sooty olive seal's fur.
Rib: Gold wire.
Hackle: Dark dun cock palmered.
Head hackle: Grey partridge.
Head: Clear varnish.

5 White Headed Muddler

COMMENT

This fly was first tied back in 1982 to International size. I have used it on all types of lines with various success, but without doubt it works best for me on a fast sink line, fished fast during difficult conditions. During an International match on Chew Valley in 1985, the White Headed Muddler was on my top dropper. The fishing was very difficult, in rough conditions. I lost a few fish, but managed to land five browns, four of which came to it. The fly has worked well for me on waters that contain coarse fish fry.

DRESSING

Hook: Kamasan B175 or B405 size 10–12.
Tying silk: Buff.
Tail: Slip of oak turkey.
Body: Silver lurex.
Rib: Silver wire.
Underwing: Grey squirrel.
Overwing: Oak turkey.
Head: White deer hair, clipped short.

6 Silver Minky Variant

COMMENT

The Minky is a fly that has been around for some time. It's a pattern that I have played around with for many years, and have come to the conclusion that this is the final pattern for me. It's a fly I like to use if the Cat's Whisker type flies are the order of the day, particularly if there is heavy angling pressure on the water. It is obviously a good fry pattern and has saved many a day for me. It can be fished on any line, but my favourite is an intermediate to Wet Cel II, with the fly fished on the point and retrieves varying from a figure-of-eight to a fast pull.

DRESSING

Hook: Kamasan B175 or B405 size 10–12.
Tying silk: Buff.
Body: Silver holographic tinsel.
Rib: Silver wire.
Wing: Silver mink body fur (matuka style).
Cheeks: Jungle cock.
Head: Fluorescent Globrite no. 5 and clear varnish.

7 Black Flash

COMMENT

The Black Flash is probably one of the simplest but most successful competition flies I use during the early part of the season, particularly if the 'going' pattern is in the Viva family. Stock fish, after seeing too many large Viva-type flies pulled through, tend to follow but not take. After this heavy angling pressure it's worth trying the Black Flash. It works well on all waters, but in particular I have found it to be successful at Llysyfran, Brenig and also Rutland. I find it works best fished fairly slow on a sinking line.

DRESSING

Hook: Kamasan B175 size 10–14.
Tying silk: Black.
Body: Pearl.
Rib: Silver wire.
Wing: Black marabou (not too heavy).
Cheeks: Silver holographic, one each side, tied short (optional).
Head: Clear varnish.

8 Honey Wickham's

COMMENT

A variation of the Wickham's that was first given to me by a Scottish friend, Willie Patrick, whilst fishing at Chew Valley some years ago. This fly is particularly effective in late afternoon and early evening during a hatch of longhorn sedges. It first started life with a whitish wing, but I modified it a little by using a hen pheasant wing from the Bohemian strain that is a honey colour. It fishes best on a floating line on the top dropper when fishing a team of flies. I have fished it successfully on bright days at Rutland Water on a sinking line.

DRESSING

Hook: Kamasan B160 size 12–14.
Tying silk: Buff.
Tail: Honey cock fibres.
Body: Gold or pearl.
Rib: Silver wire.
Wing: Bohemian hen pheasant wing.
Hackle: Honey cock palmered.
Head: Clear varnish.

Carol Neal

Carol started fly fishing in 1990 and quickly found success with the best, including the top men. She qualified for the England Ladies team and has represented them five times. She was Ladies' National Champion in 1994, when it was held at Draycote Water, with a total of twelve fish for 22lb 8oz.

She now represents Team Fenwick for the Hardy's Championship. Carol captained the England Ladies' team in 1996 when it was held in Scotland on Loch Fitty.

She was a member of a team of four in a two-day competition on Ireland's Lough Corrib. She won top bag and biggest fish with the team finishing in second place. Her best was a wild brown of over 6lb during this competition.

Channel Four featured a programme named 'Hooked' of which Carol was the 'star'.

She has fished for salmon in a few different places – namely, Ireland, Sweden, England and the Outer Hebrides, her best catches yet being a 32lb and a 25lb salmon from the River Mörrum in Sweden.

1 Abortion Variant

COMMENT

After watching Draycote local Steve Cufflin, pulling out fish on his Terry Tandem, I set about tying a competition-size version. It looked like Christmas with tinsel everywhere when Dave, my colour-blind husband, offered his assistance – instead of a silver fly coming out of the vice a green body materialized. I said it looked like an abortion! Over the last three seasons I have lost count of the fish it has taken on Midlands reservoirs, from the beginning to the end of the season. It has worked well on all lines especially the Hi-Di.

DRESSING

Hook: Kamasan B270 Double size 10–12.
Tying silk: Black.
Tail: Silver & gold anglian flash.
Body: Olive micro fritz.
Wing: Silver & gold anglian flash.
Head: Black thread varnished.

2 Red Head Montana

COMMENT

The Montana is well known and found in most people's fly boxes. This really is a simplified version that catches me a lot of fish, so I couldn't leave it out. Everyone knows what a wide range of aquatic life this is taken for, so it's only the way of tying that's different. I always seemed to get lumpy bodies, especially where the black and green chenilles and hackles were tied off, so I tied the black as normal, then the green, but put the hackle in front giving it a red head, and that helps. For me it works better than the original.

DRESSING

Hook: Size 10–12
Tying silk: Red.
Tail: Black feather fibres.
Body: Black and green micro chenille.
Hackle: Black or natural coch-y-bonddu.
Head: Red varnished clear.

1 Abortion Variant 2 Red Head Montana 3 Draycote Special 4 Toy Boy
5 Black-Keld 6 Eiger Fly 7 Solar Panel 8 Poxy Peach

3 Draycote Special

COMMENT

The well-known flies Butcher and Bloody Butcher have always caught good numbers of fish and are included in my trusted few. Like a lot of people, tying wings is not one of my strong points, so when my stocks needed replenishing I tried marabou. I used jungle cock for the eye, with a red tail and a red and blue beard. The resulting fly worked well in small sizes as a wet. The first time I fished the fly on Draycote I had in excess of twenty fish. It has served me well ever since and it seems to work well on the floater in a wind.

DRESSING

Hook: Size 10–12.
Tying silk: Black.
Tail: Red feather fibres.
Body: Silver tinsel.
Wing: Black marabou.
Beard hackle: Red feather fibres and blue jay optional.
Cheeks: Jungle cock.
Head: Black varnish.

4 Toy Boy

COMMENT

Every water has them, the wonderful characters that make fishing so special. They are the people who spend a lot of their time helping others with casting, fly tying and their knowledge of the water. John Hanlon, originally from Ireland, has fished Draycote, which is his local water, for many years. He fishes often with his son and grandson, three generations in one family with a love for fishing. I've only known John for about three years but the Toy Boy sort of adopted me. This is a fly of his that will work for me everywhere.

DRESSING

Hook: Size 10–12.
Tying silk: Cream.
Body: Gold tinsel.
Body hackle: Red game palmered.
Wing: Starling.
Hackle: Hot orange.
Head: Clear varnish.

5 Black–Keld

COMMENT

It is a very unusual day, when fishing, if someone has not given you a fly that is catching. Although I fish competitions and thoroughly enjoy them, my love is for fishing, walking along the bank and chatting. This wet fly came into my possession on such a day. While fishing Carrowmore in the west of Ireland, it looked the part so it went for a swim; brown trout liked it, sea trout liked it, salmon loved it and broke it off. The ones that followed were tied from memory and when conditions are right for wet flies this fly is on my cast.

DRESSING

Hook: Size 10–12.
Tying silk: Black.
Tail: Golden pheasant tippets.
Body: Black seal's fur.
Wing: Dark bronze mallard.
Beard hackle: Orange and blue jay.
Cheeks: Jungle cock.
Head: Clear varnish.

6 Eiger Fly

COMMENT

While sitting stroking my dog, I collected a handful of undercoat, so of course a hook went into the vice and the Eiger Fly was born. Weeks later fishing the RAF Challenge at Rutland I was struggling for a point fly and decided to try the Eiger Fly. To my astonishment it worked and I caught six of my total twelve fish on this fly to finish equal first with Jeremy Herrmann. Eiger Flies now have a permanent place in my box. Hare's ear fur is an excellent substitute for the undercoat if you don't have a dog called Eiger.

DRESSING

Hook: Size 10–12.
Tying silk: Black.
Tail: Claret hackle feather fibres.
Body: Dark hare's ear fur.
Rib: Pearl lurex.
Hackle: Orange dyed badger.
Head: Clear varnish.

7 Solar Panel

COMMENT

While fishing Rainbow Corner at Draycote with Peter Sawrie one evening he landed a superb overwintered rainbow. I asked the usual question 'What was that on?' He showed me the fly and then gave me one to try. I soon tied it on my cast and that session we both caught over our limits of eight each. A simple fly to tie but you must tease out the olive so it looks really rough. Pete cracked a joke about his bald head, he reckons it's a solar panel for a sex machine. Makes a good name for a good fly.

DRESSING

Hook: Sizes 10–12.
Tying silk: Cream.
Tail: Four or five pheasant tail fibres.
Body: Hare's ear fur.
Rib: Fine pearl lurex.
Thorax: Olive seal's fur, two turns picked out to look very rough.
Head: Clear varnish.

8 Poxy Peach

COMMENT

When early season bank fishing, I can not physically cast out and pull back big leaded flies all day. Consequently I tend to use lighter and smaller lures. I use three designs of lures in many colours, these are Jeanette Taylor's Tinheads (no one should be without them), gold heads and epoxy-headed flies. The peach has worked well for me but I have spent nearly as much time cleaning up epoxy blobs from the vice and table as fishing. Epoxy is a very messy, temperamental substance but well worth the effort.

DRESSING

Hook: Size 10.
Tying silk: Orange.
Tail: Peach marabou.
Body: Peach marabou.
Rib: Fine silver.
Hackle: Light grey hackle.
Head: Build up with silk then cover with epoxy.

Mike Forbes

Mike Forbes is a Scottish farmer, who in recent years has created a second business in Kingennie Fishery, a modern rainbow trout put and take water. Mike has always been a keen loch trout fly fisherman and salmon angler. In 1991 he became Scottish National Fly Fishing Champion and so his successful international fly fishing career began.

Mike represented Scotland in 1992 and again in 1993 when he was made captain of his country. In 1994 he won the Phoenix Salver in the Irish International. Then in 1995 he was a member of the Scottish team that won the gold medal in the Chew Valley International when England were hosts.

Throughout his fly fishing years Mike finds time from his busy life to tie up a few flies. He tends to lean towards tradition, but is slowly coming round to some of the new, more outrageous flashy patterns.

1 Yellow Tag Greenwell

COMMENT

This fly is an excellent variation of the old favourite that my grandfather used religiously on most outings. It works especially well for browns but can also be deadly for rainbows. Fish it very slow on a neutral density line, especially at dusk. Waters like Monikie, Loch Leven and Rescobie are places where this is the case. This fly was the idea of my young farm manager Neil Anderson.

DRESSING

Hook: Kamasan B175 size 14–12.
Tying silk: Yellow gossamer.
Tail: Globrite yellow floss.
Body: Yellow silk (waxed).
Rib: Gold wire.
Wing: Starling or grey mallard feather.
Hackle: Greenwell cock.
Cheeks: Jungle cock.
Head: Fluorescent yellow silk and clear varnish.

2 Lintrathen Muddler

COMMENT

Lintrathen is the nearest thing to a lowland/hill loch you can get, with free-rising brown trout in a most picturesque setting. This fly I developed to help catch fish in August and September when fish were looking for terrestrials blown onto the water. Once again, like all muddlers, this fly fishes best on a dropper and the gold band in the middle (should be bare with no palmer) acts as great focus point. I am sure the fish take it for a sedge or hatching buzzer. This fly also works well on Loch Lee and Loch Affric and would work on most hill lochs.

DRESSING

Hook: Kamasan B175 size 12.
Tying silk: Black.
Body: Front half, brown seal's fur; middle, band of gold tinsel; back half, brown seal's fur.
Rib: Gold wire.
Hackle: Ginger cock hackle palmered over seal's fur and not over gold band (should look detached).
Head: Dark natural deer hair clipped to a tight ball.

1 Yellow Tag Greenwell **2** Lintrathen Muddler **3** Mike's Bibio Muddler
4 Epoxy Tinhead **5** Menteith Mini Booby **6** Deceiving Muddler
7 Ger's Soldier Palmer **8** Claret Bumble

3 Mike's Bibio Muddler

COMMENT

I developed this fly for the International on Lough Melvin 1992. The fly covers a multitude of sins from attractor to deceiver. It was developed for the middle dropper as we had nothing else that would work at the time. It proved so successful for myself and some of the team members that it has been used regularly on Loch Leven, Lintrathen and the Orkneys as a brown trout fly. It works best dibbled behind an attractor. This fly helped me to become runner-up in the Scottish team on Lough Melvin.

DRESSING

Hook: Kamasan B175 size 10–12.
Tying silk: Black.
Body: Black seal's fur with red seal's fur belt in middle.
Rib: Silver wire.
Hackle: Black cock palmered.
Head: Black deer hair clipped rough and straggly.

4 Epoxy Tinhead

COMMENT

This fly has proven to be one of the most killing lures apart from the Cat's Whisker variants. It originated from the fly fishing internationalist Dave Wood from Edinburgh. He ties his with chain bead eyes on a long shank. However it is tied it has killed countless rainbow and brown trout on Loch Leven and many other lochs. Best fished on a Hi-Di line by itself or on the point of a cast. The movement in the tail coupled with the epoxy overbody makes it irresistible to the big boys.

DRESSING

Hook: Drennan with tinhead size 8–10.
Tying silk: Black.
Tail: Pink marabou twice the length of body with pearl tinsel strands tied through it.
Body: Pink silk built up then overwrapped with epoxy to give translucent look.
Head: Yellow and black painted eyes.

5 Menteith Mini Booby

COMMENT

This is a booby with which I have had a lot of success upon one water in particular, the Lake of Menteith. It is a mini version that is therefore legal in international competitions. Fished with a fast figure-of-eight retrieve upon a Di-7 line, rainbows find it irresistible. The fast sink line drags the booby down to the bottom, then it floats up vertically on its short nylon leader. Approximately 2–4ft of 5lb breaking strain nylon is about right. This another Neil Anderson pattern.

DRESSING

Hook: Scorpion Competition Heavyweight size 10.
Tying silk: Black.
Tail: White antron floss, trimmed.
Body: Orange fritz, trimmed.
Wing: White marabou with a few strands of pink twinkle.
Eyes: White plastazote trimmed into shape.

6 Deceiving Muddler

COMMENT

As you will now be aware I have the greatest faith in mini muddler patterns. I am able to seemingly draw fish up from nowhere as I dibble this fly through the waves. It works well not only on all the larger Scottish waters but also on the big English reservoirs. The secret is in finding out the speed of retrieve needed on the day – the method could be slow, or as on some days, very, very fast.

DRESSING

Hook: Scorpion Competition Heavyweight size 12.
Body: Split into three segments: rear third claret self dubbing; mid third gold tinsel; front third claret self dubbing.
Body hackle: Ginger cock hackle palmered and ribbed with gold wire.
Head: Standard mini muddler head, tied with the finer roe deer hair.

7 Ger's Soldier Palmer

COMMENT

Gerry Bannister is my regular fishing partner and has a lot of confidence in this traditional fly. Fished on a top dropper on a floating line it is hard to beat for both browns and rainbows. I know this is nothing new, but I feel we have neglected some of our best killing wet fly patterns these last few years. I am informed by some of my English friends that this fly was always their first top dropper choice, but that was twenty years ago. Here in Scotland it is still one of the best for wild browns.

DRESSING

Hook: Kamasan B175 size 12.
Tying silk: Black.
Tail: Fluorescent red wool, left long (important).
Body: Wool as above.
Body hackle: Ginger cock palmered with a gold wire rib.
Head: Clear varnish.

8 Claret Bumble

COMMENT

Again another traditional pattern, but one that is hard to beat for browns and rainbows. Originally an Irish lough pattern for just wild browns, but it has now proved to be a good peaty water rainbow fly. Rainbows are slowly becoming more and more popular in Scotland even with some of the old traditionalists. Again use as a top dropper, and dibble and tease the fly back through the waves. Sometimes trout will follow it, then turn down and take the middle dropper instead.

DRESSING

Hook: Kamasan B175 size 12.
Tying silk: Black.
Tail: Golden pheasant tippet.
Body: Claret self dubbing.
Body hackle: Claret cock hackle tied sparsely, with gold rib.
Throat hackle: Blue jay prominent.

Brian Peterson

Brian has been at the forefront of competitive Scottish fly fishing for over twenty years. He has won virtually every honour there is. Just look at his record – it is mind-boggling!

International medals – ten including two gold; Brown Bowl winner being overall top rod in an International. Phoenix Salver twice which is top Scottish rod, European Team Champions in a team with Brian Leadbetter and Brian Thomas. *Daily Record* Champion of Champions, Mustad European Open Champion, captor of the heaviest fish in a Benson & Hedges International Final, Mustad Gold Hook winner, top rod in a Benson & Hedges Final on the second day. He has been Greenock & District Angling Club Champion thirteen times, Cardwell Gamefishers Club Champion twice and Renfrewshire Fly Only Champion.

He has also found time to be the Men's Scottish team manager for six years and the Ladies' team manager for five years.

1 Chocolate Palmer

COMMENT

I got this pattern from Scottish International Archie McClymont when we were fishing Lough Owel in Ireland. It helped me gain top rod for the officials match on the day. Since then it has produced the goods on waters throughout the country. It fishes well just under the surface using a floating line, and does well for wild brown trout as well as rainbow trout. I like to dibble it along the surface and keep it in the water until the last possible moment, having had fish take when lifting off; it also works well when buzzers can be seen hatching.

DRESSING

Hook: Wychwood Wet Fly Medium size 12–14.
Tying silk: Brown.
Body: Brown tying silk.
Hackle: Three palmered dark ginger cock.
Head: Clear varnish.

2 Welsh Lady

COMMENT

This is a pattern that was given to me by Welsh Lady International Wynora Thomas when I was boatman to her on Loch Fitty during an International match. This fly accounted for the largest part of her Top Welsh Rod catch. It fishes well on the bob position of the cast and seems to do well when fished extremely slowly, almost static, on an intermediate line; it also pays to hang it for a while. I put this down to its similarity to the Peter Ross. Any time of the season seems to do, with June being particularly good.

DRESSING

Hook: Partridge Captain Hamilton size 10–12.
Tying silk: Black.
Tail: Golden pheasant tippets over red wool.
Body: Rear silver lurex, front black seal's fur.
Rib: Silver wire.
Wing: Teal flank.
Head: Clear varnish.

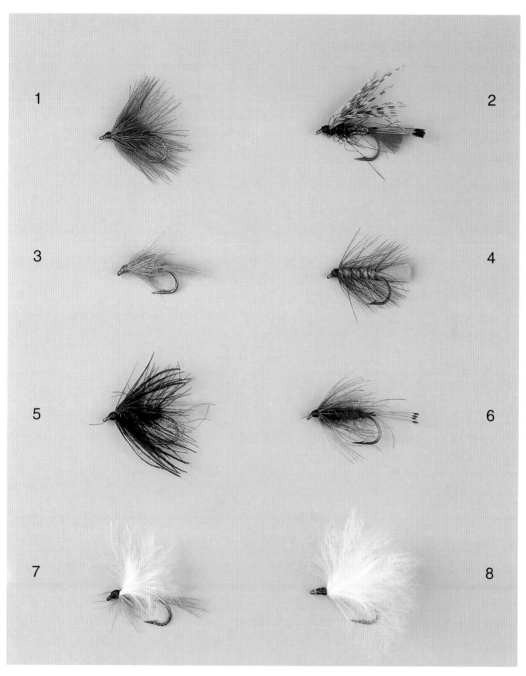

1 Chocolate Palmer   **2** Welsh Lady   **3** Hare's Ear Shrimper   **4** Draycote Drone
5 Peterson's Pennel   **6** Chew Claret   **7** Marabou Kingfisher   **8** Bruce's Bug

3 Hare's Ear Shrimper

COMMENT

Devised by my good friend David Heseltine from Bridgnorth. David and I have fished together for many years and during those years we have concocted a fair few variations together, this one being no exception. It works well on most waters with Draycote trout being particularly partial to it. Fished on the top it appears to be best retrieved with a figure of eight. If you are tying these, make sure that you use very lightly coloured hare's fur, as it is very important for the success of this pattern.

DRESSING

Hook: Kamasan B175 size 12–14.
Tying silk: Brown.
Tail: Buff hare fibres.
Body: Buff hare's fur.
Rib: Fine oval gold.
Hackle: Honey cock.
Head: Clear varnish.

4 Draycote Drone

COMMENT

This is one of my own and it has turned out to be a cracker on several occasions especially at Draycote and Rutland. When fishing at Rutland in the Benson & Hedges for the West Midlands this fly proved the winner on the day. Fished on an intermediate line with a very slow steady retrieve is the best method with this fly. It is a pattern that works well on any position so it is worth remembering that when you are looking for a middle fly some day. The summer months appear to be the best but I have caught fish on it during May and September.

DRESSING

Hook: Drennan Buzzer size 10.
Tying silk: Black.
Tail: Orange floss.
Body: Orange floss.
Rib: Fine gold wire.
Hackle: Palmered furnace cock.
Head: Clear varnish.

5 Peterson's Pennel

COMMENT

The name for this fly was the idea of Orkney angler Stan Headley. I had created the pattern for an International match on the lovely Lough Melvin in Ireland. On practice days this fly fished its head off catching sonaghan brown trout as though they were going out of fashion. Since than I have had some pretty good catches on waters nearer home. On our Scottish lochs May has proved the best month and then again in September. I usually use a floating or an intermediate line, with a slow steady retrieve coming out tops.

DRESSING

Hook: Kamasan B175 size 10–14.
Tying silk: Black.
Tail: Yellow goose.
Butt: Silver lurex.
Body: Black wool or floss.
Rib: Silver wire.
Body hackle: Palmered black cock.
Head hackle: Peacock blue.
Head: Clear varnish.

6 Chew Claret

COMMENT

I created this pattern for fishing on Chew Valley Lake in an International match. It went a long way to helping me to win the coveted Brown Bowl Trophy that is awarded to the angler with the heaviest bag of fish overall. I used the colours favoured at the time and it did the trick. I still do this today, tie a special fly for that special occasion, and it still works. The bigger size fishes better on an intermediate line and the smaller on a floater, both using a slow steady retrieve and hanging for a while near the boat.

DRESSING

Hook: Drennan Wet Fly Supreme size 10–12.
Tying silk: Black.
Tail: Golden pheasant tippets.
Body: Rear, claret seal's fur; front, black seal's fur.
Rib: Oval gold wire.
Hackle: Sparse furnace cock.

7 Marabou Kingfisher

COMMENT

This is one from my good friend Stuart Billam. This pattern has produced the goods for me on Rutland and on many other waters throughout the country. It has been successful used with any line but my favourite is with an intermediate when the fish are moving freely upwind. If you cast the Kingfisher a few yards ahead of these moving fish, nine times out of ten, interest is shown. I put this down to the colouring of this fly along with the mobility of the marabou wing; it can be used on any position on the cast with much success.

DRESSING

Hook: Kamasan B175 size 10–14.
Tying silk: Black.
Tail: Blue cock fibres.
Body: Gold lurex.
Rib: Gold wire.
Hackle: Orange hen.
Wing: White marabou.
Head: Clear varnish.

8 Bruce's Bug

COMMENT

This pattern is my variation of Wychwood partner Bruce Vaughan's bug pattern. This fly has been proved a great hit in the past up until the end of August terrific during June when conditions got difficult; however in September it was of no use at all. I think it was the warmer water that caused it to be so popular with the trout. Who knows – maybe it resembled something that was hatching under the surface. It has caught on various waters over the years with Rutland Water, Grafham Water, Draycote and Blithfield being really prolific.

DRESSING

Hook: Drennan Wet Fly Supreme size 12.
Tying silk: Black.
Tail: DFM lime-green wool or floss.
Body: Fluorescent peach floss.
Wing: White marabou.
Head: Clear varnish.

Richard Philp

I have known Richard for quite a few years as we bump into each other regularly at the Home Countries International competitions. As an organizer he has no equal: he arranged the Commonwealth Championships in Scotland in 1994 which was a tremendous success for all the visiting countries.

Richard was the youngest ever competitor in a Scottish National final. He was 12 years old and it took place on the mighty Loch Leven. Richard has two Scottish caps at International level. He is also a past winner of the coveted Loch Leven Open Championship. He was a member of the successful St Serfs A.C. team that came close to winning the Benson & Hedges final in 1992. Currently Richard is chairman of the competition section of the Scottish Anglers National Association.

The wet fly variants here are mainly designed for Loch Leven but also do well on a variety of lochs. A few date back to the brown-trout-only days of Leven, but with some minor variations are doing well with today's resident rainbows.

1 Dunkeld Variant

COMMENT

This fly does exceptionally well for both fry feeders and daphnia feeding trout. Both browns and rainbows are attracted to it. This particular fly accounted for a 4lb Leven brownie. It is especially good fished on a sinking line fairly deep and brought up on the hang. When fishing like this, remember to pause for several seconds before lifting off.

DRESSING

Hook: Size 10.
Tying silk: Hot orange.
Tail: Fluorescent yellow floss.
Body: Yellow fritz.
Wing: Bronze mallard with jungle cock cheeks.
Hackle: Hot orange marabou (throat hackle).
Head: Clear varnish.

2 Yellow Tailed Greenwell

COMMENT

This pattern has to be one of my favourites, particularly effective during evening rises when large buzzers are hatching. Fish it on either a floater or an intermediate line just before dusk. This accounted for my best Leven rainbow weighing 7lb 6oz in 1996. The rainbows in Leven during high summer are just like fresh run grilse and provide some of the best sport available in this country. For those who haven't visited Loch Leven, day bookings with ghillie are available.

DRESSING

Hook: Size 12–14 double.
Tying silk: Primrose yellow.
Tail: Fluorescent yellow floss.
Body: Primrose tying silk.
Rib: Fine pearl tinsel.
Hackle: Badger.
Wing: Grey duck with jungle cock cheeks.
Head: Black varnish.

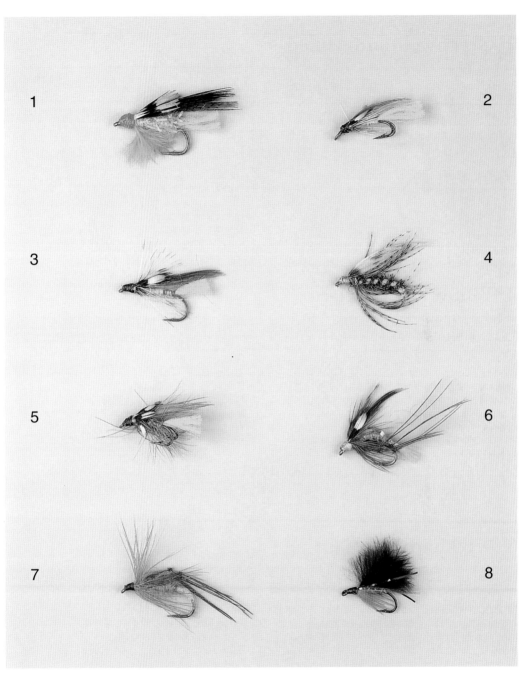

1 Dunkeld Variant **2** Yellow Tailed Greenwell **3** Greenwell and Mixed
4 Yellow Owl Variant **5** Wickham's Variant **6** Grouse and Green Buzzer
7 Green Butt Hopper **8** Mini Prairie Dog

3 Greenwell and Mixed

COMMENT

A fly for summer evenings: June, July and August. Most effective fished very slowly on a floating line. Use as the bob fly and dibble well on the surface. One evening I recall that this fly accounted for eleven super brownies to 3½lb. This is a good all-round general pattern.

DRESSING

Hook: Size 12.
Tying silk: Yellow.
Tail: Fluorescent yellow floss.
Body: Rear half, red floss; front half, yellow floss.
Rib: Yellow tying silk.
Wing: Grey duck.
Hackle: Badger hen.
Eyes: Jungle cock.
Head: Clear varnish.

4 Yellow Owl Variant

COMMENT

A take-off of a real old-fashioned Leven fly, probably as old as Leven itself – the Yellow Owl, designed by anglers of yore to imitate the large chironomid midges that hatch in great profusion in the evenings around July and August. Can be fished on the bob or tail – some anglers fish four of these at a time; I always found it safer to fish just one.

DRESSING

Hook: Size 10.
Tying silk: Yellow.
Body: Peacock herl.
Rib: Fluorescent green floss.
Hackle: Grey partridge.
Wing: Hen pheasant.
Head: Black varnish.

5 Wickham's Variant

COMMENT

A great all-round fly fished mainly on the tail, as being a double it helps to take the cast fractionally further down in the water. Fishes equally well subsurface or well sunk. Many large grown-on rainbows have a bit of a preference for it fished very slowly. A great summer fly for when the sedges are about.

DRESSING

Hook: Size 14 double.
Tying silk: Black.
Tail: Fluorescent yellow floss.
Body: Gold tinsel.
Rib: Gold wire.
Hackle: Palmered red game.
Wing: Grey duck with jungle cock cheeks.
Head: Clear varnish.

6 Grouse and Green Buzzer

COMMENT

A fly for late July and August best fished on the bob on an intermediate line, pulled through the surface film in the evening with a light ripple and left to hang in the surface before slowly trailing it towards the boat. Watch out for savage takes at the last minute. Yet another Leven special.

DRESSING

Hook: Size 12 buzzer curved.
Tying silk: Yellow.
Tail: Fluorescent yellow floss.
Body: Insect green seal's fur.
Rib: Pearl lurex.
Wing: Grouse with jungle cock cheeks.
Hackle: Olive cock hackle.
Head: Clear varnish.

7 Green Butt Hopper

COMMENT

This extremely successful fly was brought down to Loch Leven from the Orkney team who do so well on my home water. Definitely not fished as a dry, but more of a pulling wet fly on an intermediate line. It is now very popular with local anglers during August and September.

DRESSING

Hook: Size 10.
Tying silk: Black.
Tag: Pearl lurex.
Body: Hot orange seal's fur with fluorescent green butt.
Rib: Fine pearl tinsel.
Hackle: Hot orange.
Head: Clear varnish.

8 Mini Prairie Dog

COMMENT

A tremendous taker of trout all season. Fished deep or near the surface and normally pulled quite quickly, particularly when the trout are on the perch fry that abound in Loch Leven. Equally effective in larger sizes.

DRESSING

Hook: Size 14.
Tying silk: Black.
Tail: Golden pheasant topping.
Body: Silver tinsel.
Rib: Fine silver wire.
Hackle: Hot orange cock hackle.
Wing: Black marabou with blue flashabou strips up each side.
Head: Clear varnish.

Bob Church

Wet fly fishing is a superb, satisfying, skilful method to fish and I personally get great pleasure from using it on the Irish loughs. Until a few years ago the method could also be guaranteed for catching lots of trout on any day during the season on the big English reservoirs. Sadly this is now not the case and only occasionally do wet flies work in the subsurface of the reservoirs as I write.

Many theories have been given as to the reason for this: some say less natural fly life, others blame algae growths, then there are the daphnia feeders that would naturally stay deep on a bright day. Trout stay deep as a safer means of keeping away from the dreadful cormorants – surely a cull must take place soon. I feel that two-thirds to three-quarters of many reservoirs' stocks are being eaten or maimed by cormorants each year. When their numbers are thinned I would expect our once lovely wet fly fishing to return. My selection here is for my beloved west of Ireland loughs.

1 Mask Peter

COMMENT

Veteran English International fly fisher Peter Thomas always used to take a holiday so as to fish in the World Wet Fly Championships in early August. Peter used to get impressive results in this event and was twice top overseas rod and heat winner. Peter had his own successful version of the famed Irish pattern, the Green Peter, and this was the fly he did so well with. Peter passed on the dressing to me a few years ago – the fly shown is one of Peter's actual dressings. Fish on the point or top dropper.

DRESSING

Hook: Partridge Captain Hamilton size 8–10.
Tying silk: Brown or olive.
Tail: Optional brown or olive cock hackles.
Body: Medium to dark green seal's fur mix.
Rib: Gold oval medium tinsel.
Body hackle: Olive cock.
Wing: Turkey slip or dark hen pheasant.
Front hackle: Two turns olive cock.
Head: Clear varnish.

2 Little Claret Sedge (Mask)

COMMENT

During our visit to Mask in 1996, Kevin Garn and I tied up all sorts of new flies. Early August is a time on the lough when sedges are quite prominent and, although some of the big murroughs are about, in the main there are lots of small dark sedges everywhere. In practice Kevin observed this and said he would tie a few up to try out on our eliminator day. We both tried the small sedges and Kevin won the 150 entry heat with a 3½lb brown and I finished fourth with a 2lb 5oz fish. Both were caught on the size 14 version of this fly of Kevin's.

DRESSING

Hook: Size 12–14.
Tying silk: Black.
Body: Dark claret seal's fur.
Rib: Fine oval gold thread.
Wing: Dark grouse.
Hackle: Coch-y-bonddu cock.
Head: Clear varnish.

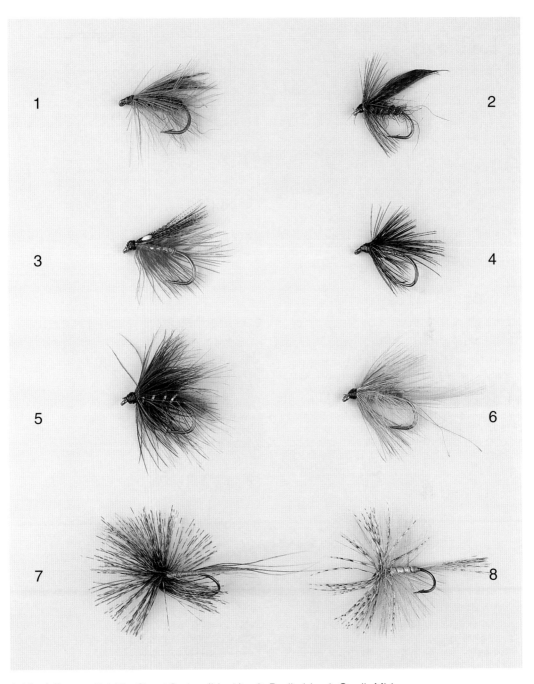

1 Mask Peter **2** Little Claret Sedge (Mask) **3** Redkeld **4** Corrib Midge
5 Geordie Fly **6** Raymond Variant **7** B.C. Mask Mayfly **8** B.C. Carra Delicate Mayfly

3 Redkeld

COMMENT

I am not sure how I came across this fly, but it was shortly before going on a trip to Ireland's Lough Melvin. Using it as a point fly and fishing it through the surface quite quickly on a floating line I had great success. The subspecies of brown trout known as sonaghan is a shoal fish and usually feeds by swimming upwind over deep water picking out daphnia and various surface fly. On the right type of day with cloud and wind they are bold takers – this fly proved that. Since then I have found the Redkeld to work in many other situations.

DRESSING

Hook: Size 10–12.
Tying silk: Black.
Tail: Golden pheasant crest fibres.
Body: Silver tinsel.
Body hackle: Bright red cock.
Wing: Natural bronze mallard.
Cheeks: Jungle cock.
Head: Clear varnish.

4 Corrib Midge

COMMENT

The first time I fished Lough Corrib at duckfly time (March) my party and I had good sport on a plain Black Spider pattern with a silver body. In the years that followed I never forgot this, and more recently found the above variant an even better pattern. It can be fished on the point or top dropper in conjunction with actual black nymph patterns. This is a specialist early season Corrib fly.

DRESSING

Hook: Size 10–12.
Tying silk: Black.
Body: Silver tinsel.
Rib: Fine silver wire.
Wing: Natural bronze mallard.
Hackle: Black cock.
Head: Clear varnish.

5 Geordie Fly

COMMENT

Similar to a Zulu apart from the hackle this is a terrific all-round Mask fly. It originates from Geordie anglers who stay with Robbie O'Grady every year and all fish on Mask. It is a versatile fly that has done well for me both as a pulled fly or ginked up and bobbed slowly on the top dropper. It seems to attract the better quality trout and is regularly on my cast when fishing Mask.

DRESSING

Hook: Size 8–12.
Tying silk: Black.
Tail: Red wool.
Body: Black seal's fur.
Rib: Medium silver oval tinsel.
Body hackle: Long-fibred coch-y-bonddu.
Head: Clear varnish.

6 Raymond Variant

COMMENT

I had been fishing the west of Ireland for about fifteen years before I got round to trying this Raymond which is a very popular pattern. It is mainly a summer fly that does well during and after the mayfly and continues through the sedge period to September. There are many variants and in more recent years Murt Folan of Galway has helped to repopularize the pattern with his impressive catches. Works on all Irish Western and Midland loughs.

DRESSING

Hook: Size 10.
Tying silk: Black.
Tail: Golden pheasant crest.
Body: Rear, ⅛ inch bright red seal's fur; rest, olive seal's fur.
Rib: Medium gold oval thread.
Body hackle: Dull yellow cock.
Head hackle: Two turns light ginger cock.
Wing: Six fibres of blue jay.
Head: Clear varnish.

7 B.C. Mask Mayfly

COMMENT

Having studied the Lough Mask fishing for over 20 years I am beginning to know a little bit about it! After the main mayfly week when everything comes alive, there are still other mayfly hatches through well into August. I have caught good trout of 3½lb on mayfly during this late period and this is a good pattern to try in a high wave. The extra hackles mean this fly skitters through the waves perfectly and lifts fish up in waters up to 12ft in depth.

DRESSING

Hook: Size 10.
Tying silk: Black.
Tail: Few fibres pheasant tail cock.
Body: Yellowish/buff silk floss.
Hackle: One natural black cock, two speckled cock of Leon (sub grizzle), three cock of Leon dyed yellow. Two turns each in the order given.
Head: Clear varnish.

8 B.C. Carra Delicate Mayfly

COMMENT

As many regular west of Ireland visitors will know Lough Carra is small by Mask and Corrib standards but it is still over 3,000 acres. High in bottom limestone content, its silts calcify everything; it looks more like a coral reef than an Irish lough. This high calcium content means an abundance of healthy fly life and in turn a good head of perfect fish. I do very well on Carra and usually average six to ten fish a day – in good conditions. They fall to this delicate mayfly pattern that accounted for twelve fish in 1996 and perhaps got 25 others to rise. This is a very good pattern for Ireland.

DRESSING

Hook: Size 12.
Tying silk: Claret.
Tail: Light-coloured fibres from natural cock of Leon.
Body: Butt ¹/₁₆inch red rest creamy white floss.
Head hackle: Light grey speckled cock of Leon or grizzle cock sub.
Head: Clear varnish.

Index

Index